CREATING
A
CULTURE
OF
COMPETENCE

CREATING A CULTURE OF COMPETENCE

MICHAEL ZWELL, Ph.D.

JOHN WILEY & SONS, INC.

New York • Chichester • Weinheim • Brisbane • Singapore • Toronto

Published by John Wiley & Sons, Inc.

Published simultaneously in Canada.

Library of Congress Cataloging-in-Publication Data:

Zwell, Michael.
    Creating a culture of competence/Michael Zwell.
      p. cm.
   Includes bibliographical references and indexes.
    ISBN 0-471-35074-5 (cloth: alk. paper)
    1. Management   2. Performance standards.   3. Competencies   4. Interpersonal relations.   I. Title.
    HD31 .Z88   2000
    658—dc21   99-059524

Contents

Acknowledgments

This book is the result of the contribution of too many people to mention, the managers and employees of all the companies through whom I have learned about how organizations and people work. I would be negligent, however, if I did not mention those who played a key role in the development of our competency methodology.

I deeply appreciate all the employees, past and present, of Zwell International and Metamorphics. They have been willing guinea pigs for every experiment and every instrument I have wrought upon them, and their support has allowed this work to build. We have learned many lessons together about managing organizations and people.

In particular, Jen Rosen and Naomi Wilson, employees of Metamorphics, have tirelessly contributed to the development of the concepts and applications presented in this book. They, along with other Metamorphics employees—Linda Burridge, Cory Jones, Allison Hegedus, Catherine Munier, and Christina Fradelos—also spent many hours editing and improving the book. The employees of Zwell International—especially Leslie Nair, Mike Grant, John Francis, and Corey Haas—all contributed to the experiences in executive search that led to this book. Paul Cholak contributed extensively in terms of both content and formulation. Other readers of the book included Jesse Elliott, Leo Zwell, David Jewell, Jim Duke, and Raissa Trend.

A number of clients encouraged me to apply myself fully to help them and their organizations, and their support was critical to the development of this material. These clients include Monica Rottman, Larry Harkness, and especially Tom O'Donoghue from American National Can. Other key clients have been Tom Gregory, Bill Morro, and Michael Allen.

I am grateful for the patience of my wife, Knoxie, and my children, Daniel and Rachel, who tolerated my disappearance in front of a keyboard for too many evenings and weekends.

Finally, I owe this book to Bob Wright, president of the School for Exceptional Living, who has coached and mentored me over the past 10 years. Bob coached me into my vision for Zwell International and Metamorphics, and has helped me learn countless lessons about the fundamentals of people and organizations that apply to every concept and application in this book. I dedicate this book to the common vision that I share with Bob: that of a business world in which people are fully supported to learn, grow, and work together for the benefit of their customers, the employees, themselves, the shareholders, and all humanity.

Introduction

This book is about performance and satisfaction. It is about helping organizations and people succeed in accomplishing their desires. It is about building a *culture of competence*, an organizational system that encourages, motivates, and develops people to work cooperatively to accomplish the organization's purposes and objectives in accordance with its values. This is also a book about improving organizational performance and achieving superior business results.

- Research conducted by John Kotter and James Heskett[1] found that over a 12-year period, companies with high-performance cultures outperformed their more average peers by:
  - *Four times* in revenue growth.
  - *Eight times* in employment growth.
  - *Eleven times* in stock price growth.
  - *Seven hundred and fifty times* in net income growth.

- A difference of one standard deviation in the performance of salespeople resulted in a **120% increase in revenue**.[2] In a study of a group of 44 companies in the Southeast, superior salespeople sold an average of $6.7 million, while average salespeople sold an average of $3 million. The average total compensation for those superior salespeople was only **$20,000 more** than that of the average salespeople.

[1]Kotter, J. P. & Heskett, J. L. *Corporate Culture and Performance*. New York: The Free Press, 1992, 15.
[2]Adapted from Hunter, J. E., Schmidt, F. L., & Judiesch, M. K. "Individual Differences in Output Variability as a Function of Job Complexity." *Journal of Applied Psychology, 75* (1990): 28–42.

- Among 222 public companies analyzed, those with high-performance work practices (advanced employee feedback systems, improved selection techniques, quality programs, etc.) had an **increased public market value of between $35,000 and $80,000 per employee** (one standard deviation).[3]

High-performance cultures are not created by magic, though it may seem so without an understanding of how they are created. Why did GE flourish and Westinghouse get broken up and sold off? Why did Boeing thrive and McDonnell Douglas get acquired? Why does the San Francisco 49ers football team have winning seasons year after year and the Chicago Bears do not?

How to lead organizations to peak performance is a question that every business leader should be trying to answer. In particular:

- Is there anything that really predicts performance?
- Why are so many smart people such mediocre performers?
- Why do managers and employees complain rather than fix the problem?
- Why do managers hire the wrong people so often?
- Why don't managers make their lives easier by developing their subordinates?
- Why are so many managers afraid of talking honestly and directly to their subordinates?
- If they want more money and better careers, why don't more employees take responsibility for improving themselves?

At first glance these inquiries seem like the pesky questions young children ask: "Why is the sky blue?" "Why is an apple bigger than a plum?" After patience has worn thin, parents finally answer in exasperation, *"It just is!"*

But suppose these questions can be answered. Suppose . . .

- You knew what predicts performance?
- People improved their performance and really worked at their full capacity?
- Managers and employees fixed problems instead of complaining about them?

---

[3]Spencer, L. & Morrow, C. *The Economic Value of Competencies: Measuring the ROI*. Speech presented at the Third International Conference on Using Competency-Based Tools and Applications to Drive Organizational Performance, Chicago, Illinois, September 1996.

- Managers selected and hired people who were strongest in the behaviors, traits, and qualities that determine successful performance?
- Managers really cared about developing their subordinates?
- Managers talked honestly and directly to their subordinates?
- Employees took responsibility for improving themselves?
- Managers sought and used feedback to understand their strengths and weaknesses?

This book is intended to explain the why's and how-to's related to creating organizations in which managers and employees fit these descriptions.

My own career began in academia, culminating with a Ph.D. in anthropology from Yale University and a stint teaching at Rutgers University. After a few years of consulting, I became an executive recruiter, initially filling searches for computer and office equipment salespeople. Nineteen years later, I fill searches for CEOs and other senior management positions. I have managed my own search firm called Zwell International since 1982.

In the first 10 years of my search career I practiced executive search like every other recruiter, treating it like a matchmaking function. My goal was to find candidates whom the client would like and want to hire (and vice versa)—to get a match. I had no idea what made a successful performer, and was primarily concerned with completing a hire—the basis on which recruiters are paid. By the late 1980s I realized that there were huge gaps in my process and the process of the other recruiters that I knew. The selection process that most companies used did not do a very good job of hiring superior performers.

In 1990 I was encouraged by Bob Wright, president of the School for Exceptional Living, to bring the best of social science to the executive search field. I began researching and developing assessment tools for analyzing corporate culture, personality, job fit, chemistry, and competency. I discovered that there was important and relevant research that applied to the processes of selection and hiring that was not being used by anyone I knew in executive search. With the permission of my clients I developed and tested one instrument after another, seeking ways to help them identify the characteristics of individuals, teams, and organizations that determine success.

When I developed a process for applying the concept of behavioral competencies to executive search, the response among my clients was phenomenal. Behavioral competencies, the traits and characteristics that differentiate superior from average performers, have been shown to be significantly more predictive of performance than aptitude, skills, or experience. Zwell International not only used competencies to assess candidates in the search process, we also trained our clients to use them to evaluate candidates. In addition to giving us enthusiastic feedback, our clients started using the process for *all* their hiring. I developed a systematic process for installing company-wide competency-based selection systems. A competency-based performance management system followed, based on an obvious premise: If competencies are the best predictors of performance we know, they should be used throughout the employment life cycle—for hiring, appraisal, development, succession planning, high-potential tracking, training, and career planning. They should also be a key determinant of strategies and tactics for corporate culture development, organizational change, and corporate reengineering.

In 1998 I started a new company, Metamorphics, to develop CompetencySuite™, an integrated set of Internet applications to make competency-based HR practices simple and easy to use and administer. Metamorphics has translated the competency-based paper-and-pencil tools we developed into computer-based tools that can be delivered over the Internet. Eighty to 90 percent of the senior human resources executives for large companies know the value of competencies; their key question is how they can make them work. That is the purpose of CompetencySuite.

Although I have quoted third-party research and used some examples from companies where I had no direct role, the vast majority of this book is based on my personal experience and/or research activity. Wherever I have used the words "Zwell," "Zwell International," "Metamorphics," "I," "we," or "our," I am referring to my personal experience and involvement.

Creating a Culture of Competence is divided into two parts. Chapters 1 through 5 focus on understanding the relationship among the three cornerstones of high-performance organizations: culture, competency, and leadership. The corporate culture of an organization determines the rules and norms that shape employee behavior. Employee competence determines the impact employees have on organizational performance. And leadership shapes both corporate culture and employee competence. These chapters explain how culture, competencies, and leadership interact to determine organizational success.

Chapters 6 through 14 provide the how-to section of the book, detailing a step-by-step, pragmatic approach to creating that culture of competence. This section includes chapters on using vision and competencies for cultural transformation, creating competency models, and using competencies for selection and performance management.

Competency-based practices can work. Over an eight-year period Zwell International transformed from a typical transactional search firm comprised of traditional, self-centered recruiters to one in which its employees are committed to serving its clients, performing excellent work, and increasing their competence. In four years, revenue per employee more than doubled. Competency-based selection, performance management, and cultural change were the tools we used to implement the transformation.

Creating a Culture of Competence

This book is about creating an organization in which employees are learning and growing, working together, and doing their best. It does not discuss specific structures to improve particular organizational areas or functions, such as quality circles, *kaizen*, self-directed work teams, and so on. Instead it concentrates on the development and implementation of processes that enhance competency in the organization: the use of vision to provide organizational and individual motivation and direction, the hiring and selection process by which people are brought into the organization and promoted, and the process of competency development. It is our view that managers and employees strong in the critical competencies and in the right culture will have little trouble determining the particular structures and systems needed to maximize organizational success.

It is the job of leadership to analyze the current state of the organization and its environment, envision the ideal state, and define a set of pathways to move the organization toward the ideal. It is a worthy journey for any leader to undertake, and one of the most satisfying. For at the end of the day, there is little more worthwhile than helping people improve themselves, work together to satisfy the needs of others, and at the same time greatly improve organizational performance.

What Makes an Organization Successful? The Role of Culture and Competence

The question of how to help their organizations succeed is one that senior executives ponder over daily.

Every organization has characteristics and features that drive managers crazy and keep them awake at night. If managers allowed themselves to complain out loud, here are some of the things they would say:

- Why aren't our employees more motivated?
- Why do they keep making the same mistakes?
- Why don't they think about how they can do their work better?
- Why aren't we closing more sales?
- Why doesn't someone else come up with ideas to solve problems?
- Why don't people do what they say they're going to do?
- Why don't they work harder?
- Why am I doing my work and their work, too?
- Why don't our managers work together to accomplish goals instead of protecting their turf?

If the readers of this book were to fulfill my vision for them, they would change their organization, managers, and employees in ways that would diminish the causes that give rise to these questions. They would feel more satisfied with themselves and their organization, as employees initiate the actions that reflect their vision.

A VISION OF ORGANIZATIONAL POSSIBILITY

The vision I hold of organizations is that they are dynamic, vital, nourishing places to work in which people set and achieve challenging goals and take responsibility for their own success. Employees go out of their way to satisfy their internal and external customers, act to improve quality, and learn and grow to become more satisfied and effective team members and employees. Employees engage in conflict constructively to reach sound decisions, and communicate openly and directly throughout the organization. They take initiative and seize opportunities for themselves and the organization, and act on their own to solve problems. They pride themselves on their innovation and their creative approaches to product and business development. They anticipate the consequences of different options and alternatives, and make decisions based on their analysis. In this visionary organization, employees are encouraged and supported to work at their highest potential, and succeed at doing so.

Managers in this organization lead by example. They display the aforementioned characteristics to an even greater degree than other employees. They are excellent motivators and developers of people, giving their subordinates constructive feedback and coaching to help them improve their performance. They help employees align themselves with organizational initiatives and objectives, and build organizational commitment through creative and continually changing methods.

Senior executives are strategic thinkers and visionary leaders who understand industry trends and develop long-term strategic plans based on the organization's strengths, weaknesses, and competitive position. They communicate a vision for the organization and the individuals in it that inspires employees to stretch themselves and work together to achieve the vision. They view the development of leaders as one of their most important job functions, and look for opportunities to expand managers' responsibilities and opportunities.

Finally, all employees, from the chief executive officer (CEO) down to the most unskilled workers, are committed to continually learn and improve themselves. They are known for their honesty, integrity, and personal credibility. People can be counted on to do what they say they will do. They admit and take responsibility for their mistakes, and put themselves at personal risk to take stands based on their deeply held values.

As a consequence of the commitment, behaviors, and traits manifested by all its employees, the organization is recognized as the industry leader and universally respected for its integrity, values, and business success. Its retention rate is the highest in its industry, and it attracts quality candidates more easily than any of its competitors. It is known as a place where people work hard and morale is high.

THE THREE COMPETENCY CORNERSTONES SUPPORTING ORGANIZATIONAL SUCCESS

There are three cornerstones that form the foundation for organizational success:

1. The competence of its leadership.
2. The competence of its employees.
3. The degree to which the corporate culture fosters and maximizes competence.

By strengthening these cornerstones, organizations can improve almost every aspect of their functioning and come closer to achieving the vision described. To understand how these cornerstones interrelate, let us begin with the concept of culture.

Culture is defined as the way of life of a people that is transferred from generation to generation. In business, corporate culture is the way of life of an organization that is passed on through successive "generations" of employees. Culture includes who we are, what we believe, what we do, and how we do it. Most people are not aware or conscious of their culture: Culture is to people as water is to fish. Unless we have been exposed to different cultures, we are largely unconscious of our own. We maintain a set of beliefs, act in certain ways, and follow rules and customs, assuming that this way of life is the natural order of things.

When I speak on the subject of corporate culture, I sometimes begin with the following scenario:

Imagine that you are driving on a highway in the desert. It is completely flat, devoid of vegetation, and absent of any sign of civilization. You approach an intersection with another road, and you can see that there is no car in any direction for at least three miles. There is a traffic light at that intersection, and the light is red. Do you stop at the light?

Typically, one-third of the audience say they will keep driving, one-third say they will slow down and then keep driving, and one-third say they will stop. I then ask the people who said they would stop, "Why?" They answer, "Well, because it's the law." In other words, they follow the rules because they are the rules. They do not think about whether they fit the circumstance in which they find themselves. Every day people unconsciously perform hundreds of small acts in customized ways that form the fabric of their cultures.

Another story that illustrates the concept of culture is the custom in the United States of men opening doors for women. If you ask men why they do it, the response is generally that it is the courteous or "right" thing to do. If you then ask them what the right or proper thing to do is in the case of revolving doors, you get a more uncertain and confused answer. Should they allow women to go first, because that's the right thing to do at doorways? Or should they go first in order to push the revolving door, thereby making it easier for the woman?

The anxiety men experience in this situation results from the conflict between two cultural rules: On the one hand, men should let women go first. On the other hand, men should do the hard work and make it easier for women. Notice how the word "should" appears in each of these examples. The concept of correct behavior, the behavior we *should* be doing, shows the process by which the culture conveys its norms and rules to people. Almost all cultural norms and rules operate on a subconscious level. Once they have been learned, we never consciously think about them unless they're broken. The invisible walls of culture become apparent only when someone bangs into them.

These examples seem innocuous and irrelevant to business. But what if that red light is a bureaucratic procedure in your company that prevents people from being innovative or satisfying customer needs? And what if that revolving door is a new information system that your employees are not comfortable with and that breaks some unconscious tradition in the organization that is no longer relevant to the current environment? Resistance to change resulting from an adherence to unconscious cultural rules is a problem facing all organizations.

Corporate culture defines the rules of the game. It says, "This is how we do things. This is what we believe. This is how we interact with each other. These are our attitudes toward work." The rules of corporate culture set the limits of organizational capabilities and effectiveness. One manufacturing client recently related to me a story about an individual who took over the job of operations manager at one of the plants. He was in the job for two years, and during that time made some significant changes in procedures that improved productivity and efficiency in the plant. Because of this success, he received a promotion to a position in another plant. However, six months after he left his initial post, the operations area he had improved had abandoned all his procedures and reverted to the prior practices. The result, of course, was decreased productivity and efficiency. This story illustrates how cultures work: They tend to reject new and different behaviors and operate to maintain the traditional behaviors that people know and are comfortable with.

Changing Culture Today Is a Necessity, Not a Luxury

Improving corporate culture (though they may call it something else) is a top priority of almost every major corporation. The values and behaviors associated with organization improvement—becoming more customer-oriented, becoming more efficient, cutting costs, becoming more team-oriented, thinking globally—are all aspects of corporate culture.

The demands of today's marketplace mandate these kinds of cultural changes. Global competition has put a downward pressure on pricing that has never been seen before. It used to be that in a tight labor market, companies would raise wages to attract workers, and would then raise prices to cover the increased wages. Today, with markets full of products from other countries with lower labor costs, companies can no longer afford to raise prices based on internal margin and profit concerns. Customers will simply go elsewhere. Because of these factors, for example, the large car and truck companies can actually demand that their suppliers *reduce* the cost of their products by 5 or 10 percent. To maintain competitiveness and profitability, companies have no choice but to increase their productivity. They need to get more results from their resources, more revenue per employee. This requires a change in corporate culture.

People are not machines, and treating them as such seldom works very well. We cannot just say to our subordinates, "Increase your productivity by 15 percent this year," and expect it to occur. It usually isn't that easy. People have emotional needs, desires, and feelings. They want to feel cared about and they have their own motivations. They will not help you succeed in achieving the organization's objectives or your personal objectives unless their own wants and needs are satisfied in the process.

Another factor causing corporate culture to change is the transformation of the employment contract. Thirty years ago, the employment contract was an exchange of loyalty for security. Employees agreed to give their loyalty and labor, and employers agreed to continue employment un-less there were drastic reasons for not doing so. While there was (in the United States) no formal employment for life in the implied contract, there was a clear understanding that employees need not worry about los-ing their jobs so long as they showed up most of the time and put in a "de-cent day's work for a decent day's pay." Employment with the same organization for 20 or 30 years was commonplace.

Several events and factors have caused this contract to change. The re-cessions and reengineerings of the 1970s and 1980s changed people's fun-damental beliefs about what they could and should expect from their employers. From the employer perspective, and employee showing up for work and doing a "decent" job was no longer sufficient. The economic pressures of the marketplace have forced employers to become more cost-conscious. The need continually to do it better and cheaper has deem-phasized the concepts of loyalty and security. The attitude of many younger workers today—"What's in it for me?"—is a direct result of the economic factors that have caused the decline of loyalty and security in the workplace.

The new employment contract is based on the exchange of reward for performance. Employers say to employees, "The better you perform, the more you will be rewarded. Depending on your position, your reward will include salary, bonus, stock options, and career opportunities." Employ-ment is more tenuous now than it was 30 years ago. It is more likely that employees will be required to leave their jobs if they (or the company) are not performing up to standards. On the positive side, those who perform well will more likely reap the benefits of their performance.

A natural consequence of this transition to a performance-oriented work environment is that those organizations that create a culture that fosters and rewards employee performance will be more successful at achieving their objectives than those that don't. From this perspective, a successful culture has several specific characteristics:

1. *A successful culture fosters employee development and encourages employ-ees to maximally impact the organization.* The culture has programs and processes to help employees take more initiative, set more challenging goals, be more innovative, become better leaders and managers, and in gen-eral take more responsibility for the success of their work unit as well as for the organization as a whole.

2. *The culture provides an avenue for highly competent employees to exercise their talents and impact the organization.* If an employee comes up with a good

idea to improve production, it will be implemented, and the employee will be recognized for the contribution.

3. *The culture creates a work environment in which employees are engaged, challenged, and motivated.* Leaders take responsibility for hiring and developing managers who motivate their subordinates. They structure jobs and teams in ways that keep employees stimulated and help them improve their skills and abilities. Work is a source of pride for employees.

4. *The culture's systems of compensation and recognition reward employees for their performance and their contribution to the organization's success.* Compensation may be financial, but it may include other rewards that for many people are at least as important. These rewards include recognition and acknowledgment of their contributions; leadership opportunities; training and development that improve competence; and work opportunities that are challenging, stimulating, and important to the organization. If employees significantly impact the organization and are not rewarded for that impact, expect them to go to other organizations where they will feel more appreciated.

The Current Situation

Few organizations come close to maximizing success and productivity. First, most managers are weak strategic thinkers. They tend to be strong at performing tasks and solving problems—they probably wouldn't have become managers if they weren't good in these areas. However, the ability to step back, see the big picture, put together a strategy, and turn it into a workable plan is something that eludes many managers. They tend to be much better at putting out fires than analyzing the fundamental causes for the fires starting in the first place.

Second, managers are typically poor motivators. To get people to work at their best, managers need to understand what drives them, what they care about, and what is important to them. Employees need to be communicated to in ways that address their motivations, concerns, and needs, and managers need to create a work environment in which those drives and needs are met through performing the job. Since few managers have models from their personal experience of people providing or creating such an environment, most have acquired little skill or experience creating a motivating environment for their subordinates.

Third, most managers are poor developers of people. In a recent study performed by Metamorphics of 300 organizations, developing others was found to be the weakest leadership competency. Most managers have few examples to use to help them develop others. Lessons from childhood and prior work experiences tend to teach motivational and developmental philosophies that are less than optimal.

Developing people requires a complex set of skills. It requires getting to know them, understanding their strengths and weaknesses, developing rapport and a relationship with them, and finding out what motivates them. It requires developing a plan for strengthening weaknesses, utilizing strengths, and providing the right kind of support to help them change their behavior. It is a daunting task, but it is a task demanded by the workplace today.

Finally, most managers do not have a sufficiently broad vision of their job as manager. Many are not even aware that there are things they should be doing that they are not. For example, one key function for many managers is developing the leadership ability of their subordinates. Yet if you ask most managers about the purposes of their jobs, this would not be mentioned. (It is not a surprise that most organizations do not reward managers for developing the leadership ability of their subordinates.)

Most employees have developed beliefs and behaviors that are at odds with those necessary to function in the ideal corporate culture. From the earliest experiences at home and at school, they developed relationships with authority figures that often stray far from the collaborative, free-flowing interaction required to maximize innovation and productivity. The attitude represented by the statement "It's not my problem" expresses the basic orientation of many employees. They would like to do a good job, but do not feel ownership of or act in accordance with the larger mission, vision, or goals of the organization.

Many people don't have the competencies and skills to reach or maintain the high level of performance that organizations need today. Competencies like results orientation, initiative, teamwork, innovation, and conceptual thinking are weakly represented in the general workforce. The development of these critical competencies has usually not been fostered by the American educational system, the home, or prior work experiences.

Finally, work cultures themselves are often not conducive to bringing out the best in people. The customs, rules, norms, and systems seldom fully promote the behavior needed to maximize motivation, learning, efficiency, and productivity. I do not know of any organizations that have in place all of the programs and processes necessary to train leaders, develop employees, resolve conflicts productively, and continually improve processes and systems.

On the positive side, the inherent nature of human beings is probably the most powerful force to help us overcome these deficiencies. In general, people have an innate desire to exercise their creative intelligence and natural abilities. They usually want to learn and grow, be engaged, be challenged, solve problems, and be successful. They have hopes, dreams, passions, and wants. They have a desire to be affirmed, to be recognized, and to be appreciated. They want to be in relationships with other people, to work together and interact in ways that provide mutual satisfaction. These characteristics are common to people of every culture.

The aim of cultural transformation is to create integrated structures, processes, and systems that harness the basic human nature of employees. Organizations can become the vehicles through which employees exercise their drives, motivations, talents, and needs, as they work together to achieve the corporate mission.

Creating a Strategy for Changing Your Culture

A senior human resources (HR) executive for a large insurance company told me about efforts to change its culture and the way its employees worked. The company brought in a new CEO who was committed to making the organization more results-oriented, more nimble, more responsive to the market, and more aggressive. Toward that end he immediately launched some initiatives, one of which was to establish a performance management system to evaluate and reward behaviors that were aligned with his vision. Another was to spread the message throughout the organization that no job was secure unless the employee secured that job with strong performance.

Eighteen months later, the senior management team was trying to understand why the performance management system failed to generate the desired change. It became evident in our discussion that management had not clearly thought through the strategy for changing employee behavior, beliefs, and perceptions. In other words, they had not thought through the strategy for changing their culture. The pursuit of cultural transformation is in many ways like a revolutionary war. Entrenched forces dig in their heels to resist change and keep things the way they have always been. Every culture has its loyalists, people who enjoy benefits in the current culture that they will lose unless they change as the culture changes. Change agents also have allies, people who can be enlisted to support change efforts, who are unhappy with the way things are currently and are excited by the possibility of improvement.

As you attempt to transform your culture you will have battles and skirmishes. You will win some battles and lose others. You will need to choose your battles carefully. The challenge is daunting, but as worthy an endeavor as any you will pursue. If you successfully change your corporate culture, you will create a work environment that supports people to maximize themselves and their contribution to the company. As a result, employees will have more challenging, stimulating lives, the company will be more successful, its customers will be better satisfied, and you will have more reason to be proud of your leadership. What follow are the elements of a culture change strategy.

The Elements of a Culture Change Strategy

1. *A clear vision of your desired culture.* In the preceding pages I outlined some of the key elements of a successful culture. By articulating in some detail what your desired culture looks like, you will provide the foundation for your strategy. You will need to communicate this vision over and over again, and use it as a source of inspiration and motivation as you transform the culture.

2. *A statement of organizational mission.* This is the "Why?"—the reason for an organization's existence and the source of the need for cultural change. The combination of vision and mission provides the reason the culture needs to change and is key to communicating to employees, shareholders, and customers.

3. *A set of values and principles that underlie and support the desired culture.* A calling to higher purpose inspires us. By grounding your vision and mission in a set of inspiring values and principles, you will make it easier to align the organization with your objectives. You will also have a foundation from which to challenge old assumptions and beliefs and replace them with agreements based on these values.

4. *A language and associated conceptual framework that helps change the way people think and act.* The words people use reflect attitudes, beliefs, and behavior. Building a common vocabulary that embodies the vision, mission, and values to which you aspire will help people begin to think and act in accordance with the vision.

5. *An in-depth analysis of your current culture to identify the elements of support and those that will sabotage change efforts.* Analyze your systems of hiring and promotion, compensation, production, communication, technology, management style, decision making, and so on, to determine how they function to support or resist your desired culture.

6. *A set of goals to bring about the change in beliefs, behaviors, and systems needed to create your desired culture.* These provide the organizational direction and context in which specific initiatives will be developed and implemented.

7. *A plan with initiatives, tactics, action steps, and time lines, whose purpose is to create a detailed pathway to lead you from your current culture to your desired culture.* This plan will include specific objectives and action steps with clearly defined, measurable results to be achieved by specific times. This is the battle plan to which you and the organization can be held accountable.

8. *Systems to measure, monitor, and improve progress toward the achievement of the culture.* These include procedures to regularly measure how each initiative is progressing and processes for making prompt adjustments to keep the cultural change effort on track.

The Role of Leadership

There is probably no domain in which the role of leadership is more important than that of cultural transformation. The scope of the project should not be underestimated. As we are reminded every New Year's Eve, it is difficult for even one person to change entrenched habits. Our neural pathways have been programmed to create a sense of comfort that is associated with performing a sequence of behaviors that have become routine. These behaviors have been continually reinforced by reward and punishment, often in the form of others' approval or disapproval. Once behaviors have become routine, they feel as comfortable as an old shoe.

Try sleeping on the opposite side of the bed from the side where you usually sleep. Even a behavior change as minimal as this produces feelings of discomfort that are relieved only when you return to your usual habits. Imagine a more significant behavioral change, such as taking initiative when you haven't before, or coming up with new ways of doing some of the things that you have done the same way every day for years. Or, imagine giving subordinates direct, honest feedback about their behavior when you have never done it before. Multiply this by the number of employees in your organization and you see the magnitude of the effort you face trying to change an entire culture.

Leaders of corporate cultural transformation need a full range of leadership skills. Ideally they will be visionaries. They will be able to articulate a vision of the ideal culture, one that inspires others not only to want the new culture, but to commit themselves to its achievement. They will model the behavior that exemplifies the vision, and show people by example what they want to create. They will be excellent communicators, conveying the mission, vision, values, and plans throughout the organization. They will be mentors and coaches who help people see their potential, identify barriers to improvement, and create plans to change their behavior. They will provide ongoing encouragement and support as the culture change progresses. Finally, they will see that progress is measured, monitored, and maintained.

In my experience, there is nothing more rewarding or challenging than changing corporate culture. The real legacy of leaders is not in their short-term successes or failures but rather in the quality of the cultures they create. Managers and leaders who develop a culture of competence and help people become their best can truly take pride in their accomplishment.

The Use of Behavioral Competencies to Drive Cultural Transformation

A strategic plan is only as good as its components. One of the most critical elements in the plan to change corporate culture is the conceptual framework that contextualizes the change. The concept of behavioral competencies provides such a framework, and can serve as the core of a system and practice that can help you create the culture you want.

Competencies can be defined as the enduring traits and characteristics that determine performance. Examples of competencies are initiative, influence, teamwork, innovation, and strategic thinking. The competency methodology grew out of research whose goal was to determine the traits and characteristics that differentiate superior performers. For example, influence and results orientation are two of the competencies that most differentiate superior salespeople from average salespeople.

You may notice that these individual competencies include the same terms and concepts that describe a culture of competence. This should not be surprising, because the same traits that determine superior individual performance are the traits that describe the key features of a successful culture. The power of the competency concept derives from how easily it translates organizational mission, vision, and values into concrete behaviors and actions that employees can understand and perform. The use and repetition of the language of competency—"results orientation," "innovation," "teamwork," and "service orientation," for example—will help move the culture toward the vision.

Competencies can provide the foundation for an assessment process for use in selection, appraisal, and development that orients the entire organization to the behaviors most essential to a culture of competence. To the extent that one can accurately measure proficiency in a competency, it will be possible to bring people into the organization who will manifest the behaviors needed in the desired culture. By using competencies as the basis for appraisal, one can communicate to the entire organization the kinds of behavior one wants and needs in the organization. By using them in the development process, you can create concrete pathways that enable employees to change their behavior in ways that are consistent with your vision of your desired culture.

This book provides both the theoretical foundation and a practical guide to creating the culture of competence that you need to succeed in today's world. The widely stated dictum that our employees are our greatest asset is true. This book is about maximizing the value and contribution of that asset, so that its potential value can be realized for the benefit of all of the organization's stakeholders. To create a culture of competence, you need to develop your human assets so that they are working together as effectively as possible to achieve the corporate mission.

A management philosophy and practice will succeed to the extent that it is in sync with human nature. If it does not inspire and motivate people to become the best they can be, it will be of limited benefit. A culture of competence is one in which employees work for their own learning, growth, development, and personal satisfaction. It is one in which employees strive to do their best for themselves, for their team, for the organization, and for the customers. They do so because it is the thing that most satisfies them. This book is about creating that culture of competence.

Creating Your Own Culture of Competence: Chapter 1—Exercises

EXERCISE 1—WHY WOULD WE CHANGE?

Ask yourself or others in the organization:

- What keeps your leaders awake at night when it comes to the organization and its people?
- What complaints do you or others have about how people achieve goals or work together?
- What about the current business environment would drive the need to change the culture?
- How would you describe the ideal culture for your organization?

EXERCISE 2—IS IT WORTH THE EFFORT? WHAT IS THE CURRENT STATE OF THE CULTURE?

If you are looking to change your culture, here are some qualities you can assess in your current state. It can be the first step in determining if such an undertaking would be worth the effort.

QUALITIES   YES/NO

The Culture

1. Our culture fosters employee development.
2. The culture makes it easy for employees to contribute their skills and talents to the business.
3. Employees are engaged, challenged, and motivated by the environment.
4. There are recognition and compensation systems in place that reward employees for their performance and contributions.

Managers

5. Managers are able to develop a business strategy around the business and translate it into a workable plan.
6. Managers understand the diverse needs and concerns of employees.
7. Managers help create development plans based on the strengths and weaknesses of their employees.
8. Managers take action to develop the leadership capabilities of employees at all levels.

Employees

9. Employees have the needed behaviors and skills to help achieve long-term business success.
10. Employees clearly understand the role and contributions they make to the business.
11. There is a high level of partnership among employees across the organization.
12. Employees as a rule avoid blame and excuses, and focus instead on solving problems, serving the customer, and improving the quality of their work.

2

The Building Blocks of Culture: Behavioral Competencies

While it is possible to modify behavior without conscious cooperation, it is much easier if people are *motivated* to change behavior. This is especially true with respect to changing organizational culture, which requires hundreds or thousands of people changing how they do things each day. To change the culture you need to engage people's hearts and minds in the endeavor, to tie their personal desires to the journey toward a culture of competence.

In a revolutionary war, the fight on the battlefield is actually less important than the fight for the support of the people. Whichever side wins the people's trust and allegiance will eventually gain control of the government, despite whatever short-term losses may occur. In the fight to create a new culture, we also need to convince the people that they are best served by winning that war. The competency paradigm provides a conceptual framework, a language, and a set of tools to enable people to want to change and help them accomplish the change.

The History and Background of Competencies

It is a part of the natural human condition to want to control the future, to turn the unknown into the known, and to attempt to reduce the uncertainty that we constantly face. The Egyptians created a god of locusts, for example, to help them cope with the uncertainty of a two-week period in the autumn when a deluge of the insects could destroy their entire crop. The same urge to reduce uncertainty has fueled the search for the causes and predictors of behavior in the workplace. How can we tell how well people will perform on the job before rather than after we hire them?

The question of what predicts performance has been the subject of scientific inquiry for the past two hundred years. Scientists and pseudoscientists have proposed a wide range of factors that determine behavior and performance. These factors have included size and shape of the head, brain weight, skin color, ethnicity, social class, birth order, handwriting, religion, intelligence quotient (IQ), cultural heritage, astrology, heredity, gender, and so on. Additional factors that have been used to attempt to predict performance in the workplace are technical skills, years of experience, education, certification, and personality traits.

It is against this background that the study of competencies began in the early 1970s. In 1973 David McClelland published an article demonstrating that behavioral traits and characteristics are much more effective than aptitude tests in determining who is and is not successful in job performance.[1] Superior performers did things such as exercise good judgment, notice problems and take action to address them, and set challenging goals—behaviors relatively independent of aptitude, skill proficiency, and experience level.

The research that began with this article has resulted in hundreds of job studies that all attempt to answer one basic question: What is it that differentiates strong performers from average performers? If we know what these differentiators are and can measure them, they can be used to hire better employees, assess and appraise employees, and help them improve their performance.

These differentiating characteristics have come to be called competencies. The most useful definition of the term that I have heard is that competencies are enduring traits or characteristics that help determine job performance.

In the business world today, there is some confusion over the definition of a competency. The biggest confusion is between competencies and skills. Skills generally refer to the mastery of techniques and knowledge that apply to a specific area or profession. Sales skills include prospecting, handling objections, and closing. Drafting skills include measuring and drawing. Managerial skills include writing and forecasting. Some companies use the

---

[1]McClelland, D. C. Testing for competence rather than Intelligence. American Psychologist, 28: 1–14, 1973.

word "competency" to mean skills. This causes them big headaches for two reasons. First, there are so many skills in every position in an organization that management of a skills database is a time-consuming and difficult activity. The bigger problem is that the focus on skills distracts people from the use and assessment of competencies, which play a much bigger role in determining performance.

For instance, among chief financial officers, some have a better grasp and knowledge of the financial structure of organizations than do others. Being able to understand a balance sheet involves what I would call skills and knowledge. Zwell International has conducted many searches for CFOs, and we know that superior CFOs do not necessarily understand balance sheets or other aspects of finance better than average CFOs. More importantly, what they possess is the ability to partner with CEOs, to understand business issues, and to impact and influence the organization using their financial acumen as a tool. They are able to help reduce costs in manufacturing operations by working with the manufacturing personnel to come up with better ways to do things. In short, it is competencies, not knowledge or skills, that differentiate superior performers.

In some of the largest accounting and manufacturing firms, senior managers and top professionals have spent hundreds of hours attempting to develop lists of skills important to different positions. While such a list may be of some value for training and development, I have never seen a situation in which the benefit provided by a comprehensive skill list came close to covering the cost of the resources expended to gather it. More importantly, focusing on knowledge and skills misses the point. Having the greatest knowledge and skill on the planet won't make any difference if people have no desire and no drive to use that skill and knowledge.

It is not that skills are unimportant. A threshold level of skill is necessary to do a job. If you are hiring an electrical engineer to work at a nuclear power plant, you need someone who knows electrical engineering. Assuming that technical ability determines successful performance, however, is a costly mistake. People with basic skills who are strong in the important competencies for a position will, because they're strong in those competencies, acquire whatever knowledge and skills they need to become a superior performer in that job. If people strong in initiative do not know the answer to a problem, they'll use their initiative to find it. If people strong in service orientation do not know the answer to a customer's problem, they'll find someone who does. Keeping the focus on competencies is keeping your eye on the ball. It is paying attention to what matters, paying attention to the things that actually determine the difference between strong and weak performance.

There is nothing magical about competencies. The competency paradigm is simply one way to break behavior down into its component parts. Like any paradigm, it is useful to the degree that it helps explain reality as we know it, and helps us influence and predict the reality of the future. Competencies are a useful concept to the extent that they can help explain why some people perform better than others, to the extent that they help people improve their performance, and to the extent that they help people make decisions that will enable them to accomplish their objectives. When used effectively, the competency paradigm is a tonic for managers trying to improve their organization in these areas.

One of the benefits of competencies is that the concepts are easy for most people to understand. People have a common understanding of what we mean when we say influence, or initiative, or teamwork. Not only are the terms easily understood, they also generally have positive connotations. If you ask most people if they would like to be results oriented, they will say yes. If you ask them if they would like to be innovative, they'll say yes. If you ask them if they would like to be good team players, they'll say yes. So in the battle to win the hearts and minds of employees and to create a culture of competence, the language of competencies provides a means for translating the concept of a high-performance culture into terms that people can embrace.

Categories of Competence

Every consulting firm has its own set of names for particular competencies and its own way of classifying them. In my opinion the important question is not whether a competency is the most important or is defined correctly, but rather how competencies can be utilized to help the organization accomplish its objectives. The concept of competencies is simply a good way to break down behavior into its component parts. The exact taxonomy of competencies is less important than the use to which those components are put. One rail transportation firm spent $1 million putting together a competency model for its information technology group. A telecommunications giant paid $500,000 to have a consulting firm develop a competency model for a single sales position. In my opinion, these kinds of dollars are better spent making sure that the organization gets the maximum value from whatever competency framework is developed. Ultimately, the value of competencies is determined not by their intellectual rigor so much as by their effect on the organization through their implementation.

That being said, at Metamorphics, we group competencies into several categories, each of which reflects a different aspect of behavior at work. These categories are listed in Table 2.1.

These categories are to some degree developmental, in that people tend to progress up through the categories as they advance in their careers. When they first join the workforce, people usually begin their careers as individual contributors. Their jobs are to perform tasks and accomplish objectives through their labor. At the individual contributor stage, where many people stay for their entire careers, the competencies in the categories of task achievement, relationship, and personal attribute all contribute to career success. When people take on the responsibility of supervising people and managing projects, managerial and leadership competencies become more important: Success on the job is determined more by how well subordinates do than by direct individual contribution.

The success of an organization depends on how strong or weak managers and employees are in the competencies critical to job success. One of the most important jobs of executive management is to ensure that the entire workforce is as strong as possible in the competencies that most affect organizational performance and the bottom line, and to continually increase that strength.

The following sections provide an overview of Metamorphics' competency categories and illustrate what a competency library can look like. Each competency is discussed and contextualized in terms of its contribution to successful job performance. Each of the competencies is broken down into key behaviors, smaller units of behavior that, when demonstrated, result in proficiency in the competency. In order to provide some examples of how the competency is demonstrated, each competency description is followed by a sample of key behaviors.

Table 2.1   Metamorphics competency categories.

Task achievement	Competencies associated with performing a job well.
Relationship	Competencies that relate to communicating with and working well with others and satisfying their needs.
Personal attribute	Competencies intrinsic to an individual and that relate to how people think, feel, learn, and develop.
Managerial	Competencies that specifically relate to managing, supervising, and developing people.
Leadership	Competencies that relate to leading an organization and people to achieve an organization's purpose, vision, and objectives.

Task Achievement Competencies

Task achievement competencies relate to what we work toward, the way we work toward it, and, in general, how we work. Are people highly motivated and driven toward accomplishing something? Do they affect the company? Are they adaptable to changing circumstances? Are they concerned with quality? Are they able to get things done in an organization? These are the kinds of capabilities that make somebody an effective worker and an effective achiever. If you want to build a culture of competence, a core of your organization needs to be people whom you can count on to get the job done well and on time.

Task achievement competencies include results orientation, managing performance, influence, initiative, production efficiency, flexibility, innovation, concern for quality, continuous improvement, and technical expertise.

RESULTS ORIENTATION

Results orientation includes setting, striving to achieve, and achieving challenging goals. In study after study, results orientation proves to be one of the competencies that most differentiates superior performers. Strong performers, when they talk about what they do, over and over describe the goals they set in one situation after another:

> Manager: I knew that our waste was too high—it was over 15 percent—so I decided to try to bring it down to 12 percent by the end of the year. *To do that I needed the support of the plant manager, so I set up a meeting with him the next day.*
>
> Q: Did you have a plan for the meeting?
>
> Manager: When I went into the meeting, I knew that I needed to get his agreement to commit some resources to the effort. I needed him to commit some of the operations manager's time to analyzing our process flow. *By the end of the meeting we had a preliminary game plan laid out, and we were underway.*

Managers strong in results orientation naturally think in terms of what they can accomplish in a meeting, a day, a week, and so on. For the results oriented, accomplishing a task is a finite process that has appropriate limits on completion time and on the magnitude of the task itself.

At a 1997 competency conference, Michael Lombardo[2] reported on a

[2]Lombardo, Michael. Presentation at the Fourth Annual International Conference on Using Competency-Based Tools and Applications to Drive Organizational Performance, Boston, Massachusetts, September 1997.

study that showed that people who regularly set goals accomplished more, even if they forget exactly what the goals were. It seems that the act of setting goals focuses our minds on our pursuit, regardless of whether we stay conscious of the goals.

People weak in results orientation tend to go into situations without a clear idea of what they want from the situation. As a result, they are less likely to complete tasks on time, to use resources effectively, or to gain satisfaction from accomplishment.

Sample Key Behaviors for Results Orientation

- Sets achievable goals.
- Strives to achieve goals.
- Develops standards against which to measure behavior and performance.

MANAGING PERFORMANCE

This is the competency by which people plan their strategy and tactics, monitor and measure their performance, and address performance problems. This competency often overlaps with results orientation, but we distinguish it because many people set challenging goals but are weak at monitoring and measuring their own and subordinates' performance.

In our experience with clients, this competency is the one that most often evokes employee resistance. For many employees, the idea of measuring performance conjures up the vision of a punitive parent or teacher who will punish them for their transgressions. I was recently talking to a salesperson whom I was considering hiring who said, "Experienced salespeople care only about results. There is no reason to count phone calls and meetings. No experienced salesperson worth their salt wastes time measuring activity."

Sound familiar? Yet the best salespeople I know can tell you exactly what their numbers are regarding both results and activity. I have watched successful salespeople double their production by focusing on improving their "blocking and tackling"—increasing the number of times they dial the phone and the number of sales meetings they have every week.

Setting challenging goals without effective monitoring and tracking will work for only a small percentage of people. They will be like New Year's resolutions: I will lose 20 pounds, exercise every day, be kind to my wife, my children, my dog, and my subordinates every day, and so on.

Let's take the example of weight loss. It is much easier to lose weight when you regularly weigh yourself and keep track of what you eat. It works even better if you weigh yourself every Friday and send an e-mail with your weight to five friends. Keeping track of progress and reinforcing behavior change are critical to achieving challenging goals.

As a manager, managing performance includes keeping track of the projects you manage as well as of the people you supervise. The cost of not addressing performance problems promptly is staggering for any business. The damage will be lessened to the degree that managers are strong in managing performance.

Sample Key Behaviors for Managing Performance

- Pays attention to the quality and quantity of performance.
- Sets clear, well-defined desired outcomes for work activity and tracks progress.
- Seeks performance feedback from others.

INFLUENCE

Influence vies with results orientation as the competency most differentiating superior performers, but it is one that managers unfamiliar with competencies are less likely to identify on their own. For many sales positions, it is twice as great a differentiator as the next most differentiating competency, results orientation.[3]

Influence is the competency that demonstrates the importance of the competency paradigm itself. It doesn't matter how much you know or how good your judgment is if you can't influence others to change the course of events based on your knowledge and judgment. It is through influence that people impact the world.

A common group process exercise instructs a team to get from one place to another, with the group task being to prioritize a list of items from most essential to least essential to the journey. Participants prioritize the list individually, then do it as a group. What usually happens is that the common group list is better than the average individual list, but there are one or two relatively shy people who score higher than the group. Their weakness in influence prevented the group from benefiting from their knowledge and experience.

Zwell International has performed many executive searches for analysts for investment management firms. When they describe the characteristics

---

[3]Spencer, L. M. & Spencer, S. M. *Competence at Work*. New York: John Wiley & Sons, 1993.

they desire in an analyst, they don't talk about the ability to analyze companies; instead, they want analysts *who are good influencers*, who can present persuasive arguments with personal presence , and who will have credibility within the firm and the larger investment community. Being right is less important than being credible.

There are few positions in which influence doesn't differentiate superior performers. As professionals move ahead in their careers, influence becomes more and more important, as the ability to impact the organization becomes the key to promotion and advancement.

Sample Key Behaviors for Influence

- Develops and presents persuasive arguments to address the concerns, wants, and needs of others.
- Elicits and responds effectively to objections.

At a more advanced level, influence is manifested by the following traits:

- Identifies key decision makers and the people who influence them.
- Anticipates reactions and objections and plans how to overcome them.

INITIATIVE

If the fairy godmother of managers offered them one wish that would change the character of their employees, initiative is the competency that would be the most popular choice. One of the biggest emotional burdens on managers is the feeling that the responsibility rests solely on their shoulders, that they have to do it or it won't get done. The entry into the English language of the word "proactive" is evidence of the driving need to have employees *on their own* do the things that will make themselves and the business successful.

When I am selling Metamorphics' services, I often begin with this vision:

"Imagine if every employee in your company did two things every Friday in addition to their current job. First, they thought of one problem in their department and decided to take one action during the following week to help fix it. Second, they sent an e-mail to their manager simply stating what they did this week to help fix a problem, what area they were going to address next week, and what action they planned to take. What do you think the effect would be on your company?"

Almost every executive responds that it would make a tremendous difference in almost every aspect of the company's functioning. Imagine if employees demonstrated that kind of initiative every day. This is why initiative consistently appears in studies as one of the top competencies differentiating superior performers.

Sample Key Behaviors for Initiative

- Takes action without being asked or required to do so.
- Initiates individual or group projects and takes complete responsibility for their success.

PRODUCTION EFFICIENCY

Production efficiency is the competency through which work gets performed quickly, at a high standard of quality, and with minimal use of resources. We identified this competency as critical for a law firm that wanted to capture and measure the set of behaviors that caused one associate to be more efficient than another. Associates high in production efficiency were considered to be the "go to" associates. Whenever partners needed to get a legal document done quickly and accurately, they would go to these associates. People strong in this competency have the intention and commitment to complete projects with swiftness and accuracy, and they have the ability to organize and break down projects in ways that speed their accomplishment.

Sample Key Behaviors for Production Efficiency

- Performs tasks efficiently.
- Breaks down projects into component tasks.
- Assigns and utilizes resources effectively even when scarce.

FLEXIBILITY

People who adapt and respond quickly and effectively to changing circumstances are strong in the competency of flexibility. With the increasing rate of change in the business world today, it is essential that we all be able to turn on a dime, to change strategy and tactics as needed. People strong in flexibility are open and responsive to new ideas, perspectives, strategies, and positions. At their highest level of flexibility proficiency, people are able to respond immediately to changing situations by coming up with innovative, creative ideas and actions, and are able to reconsider even the most strongly held ideas.

In today's complex world, how managers respond in ambiguous and complex situations can have literally hundreds of millions of dollars of consequence to large corporations. In one situation, for example, the new CEO of a U.S. company that manufactures electronic components was meeting with the CEO of its main customer, a company in Germany to whom it sold almost all its product. In the meeting the German CEO became more and more frustrated with a position taken by the American CEO, who refused to reconsider his viewpoint. The German CEO finally said, "That's it. We will do no more business with your company." And when the current contracts ran out, they didn't. The CEO of the American company was soon terminated, but the damage was done. The company eventually found new markets for its products, but the financial damage was considerable. There are costs to not being flexible and not responding well in ambiguous situations.

Sample Key Behaviors for Flexibility

- Promptly switches strategies or tactics if the current ones are not working.
- Operates well in situations when the consequences of decisions and actions are unclear.

INNOVATION

Innovation is the competency through which people originate new ideas, methods, solutions, and products. In many industries strong innovation is necessary for an organization to be an industry leader or even to remain competitive. For an organization to stay on the cutting edge, its employees not only must be strong in innovation, but also must be able to create organizational structures and processes that foster innovation in others.

Innovation involves an orientation toward creativity and invention. How can we do it better? What might be a different approach to accomplish the task or solve the problem? It is also associated with conceptual thinking, the competency that involves noticing patterns in disparate phenomena and arenas and putting ideas together in new and different ways.

Sample Key Behaviors for Innovation

- Supports and implements new methods and processes.
- Proactively seeks to test, validate, modify, and improve new ideas or methods to make them as effective as possible.

CONCERN FOR QUALITY

Concern for quality ensures that the output of all work is accurate and meets or exceeds internal standards and the needs of both internal and external customers. It is not unusual to observe a wide variation in concern for quality within a job category in an organization, particularly at lower levels. Some people care more about the quality of their work than others. Concern for quality can be affected by personality factors, upbringing, training, and values. At its highest level, concern for quality involves influencing large parts of the organization to adopt processes, policies, and procedures to ensure the highest standards of quality.

Sample Key Behaviors for Concern for Quality

- Carefully prepares materials, approaches, and resources.
- Monitors accuracy and quality of others' work and takes action to correct mistakes.

CONTINUOUS IMPROVEMENT

Employees high in continuous improvement habitually ask the question, "How can we (and I) do things better?" Individuals committed to continuous improvement typically demonstrate a high degree of initiative and concern for quality. They orient toward excellence and naturally look for ways to make job tasks or processes more efficient and easier. They usually need no prompting to begin talking about operational problems or issues, and enjoy the creative process of brainstorming and coming up with new ideas. Continuous improvement is a critical competency for most organizations today, given the competitive business environment and the need to obtain any possible competitive advantage.

Sample Key Behaviors for Continuous Improvement

- Regularly analyzes systems, processes, and performance trends to identify opportunities for improvement.
- Provides others with tools and approaches to solve problems and improve processes.

TECHNICAL EXPERTISE

Technical expertise is the competency through which people exercise their technical skills and knowledge. There is some debate about whether technical expertise should be considered a competency, because technical skills and knowledge are less predictive of overall performance than more behavioral competencies, and tend to distract people away from the other competencies. (People are considerably more comfortable talking about and assessing technical skill and knowledge than competencies such as integrity and truth or concern for quality, for example.) Nevertheless, without sufficient technical expertise, no amount of behavioral competence will allow someone to perform a job requiring that expertise.

Sample Key Behaviors for Technical Expertise

- Has and uses knowledge of basic techniques and concepts.
- Develops technical solutions requiring modifying existing methods and sometimes creating new methods and techniques.

These are the competencies critical to performing tasks and accomplishing individual objectives. To be superior individual contributors, people need to be strong in many if not all of these task achievement competencies. They are the individual building blocks of a successful company. In most organizations, however, proficiency in task achievement competencies alone is not sufficient to ensure individual and organizational success.

Relationship Competencies

Since organizations are groups of people working synergistically to produce a collective result that is greater than the sum of its parts, the competencies associated with relationship are also critical to individual and organizational success. The competencies in this category relate to traits and characteristics involving relationships and interactions between self and others. While there are some individuals whose brilliance compensates for their weak interpersonal skills and relationship competencies, for the rest of us mortals the ability to relate positively and constructively with our bosses, our coworkers, our subordinates, and our customers is an essential aspect of job success.

TEAMWORK

Teamwork is the relationship competency most commonly written and talked about in management circles these days, almost to the point of being a fad. Be that as it may, the ability to function effectively as a part of a group

of people working together *is* a defining characteristic of a superior performer in many positions. While everyone agrees that being a team player is
crucial, most people have not explored what it really means to be one.
Teamwork is more than playing your role and holding up your end of the
stick, so to speak. Excellent team players elevate the performance of other
team members through a multitude of behaviors and styles.

Teams are complex entities, and there are many different ways that people can contribute to team success. Some team members are excellent orga-
nizers and can break down and assign tasks to other team members that
result in quick and effective task completion. Other team members are tireless workers who can carry the team with their effort. Others are strong in
group process and facilitation, and help the team coordinate and cooperate
to work together well. Others contribute by motivating and encouraging
team members with their energy and enthusiasm. Others contribute by being truth tellers, naming problems and issues that otherwise would have
gone unsaid and eventually disrupted group functioning. Ideally a team
would have members strong in each of the areas important for project completion, so that the team's work wouldn't be slowed or stalled by a gap in
team skills.

Sample Key Behaviors for Teamwork

- Fulfills commitments to other team members.
- Provides others with feedback to help them be better team members.

SERVICE ORIENTATION

Service orientation is the competency upon which all business is based.
Satisfying customer needs is the ultimate requirement for all organizations.
If customers do not feel well served and they believe that they might be better served elsewhere, the organization will eventually die. The commitment
to serve and satisfy the needs of others is key to this competency. This applies not only to external customers but to all relationships. We serve our
bosses; we serve our internal customers; we serve our subordinates. I believe
it is the job of managers to serve their subordinates and help them have the
most satisfying, successful work lives possible.

At its most basic level, service orientation involves providing services either explicitly or implicitly contracted in a relationship. An implied contract between all employees, for example, is that they will treat each other
with respect. Another implied contract is that each of us will do what we
say we will do—that we will follow through on our commitments. Service

orientation involves responding to customers' complaints, solving their problems, and responding to their requests in ways that make them feel that their needs are being met.

At a more advanced level, service orientation includes eliciting feedback from customers to identify their needs and monitor their satisfaction. It includes a dedication to their satisfaction that implies putting in whatever time and effort is necessary to obtain that satisfaction. If that means staying up all night to meet a deadline, you stay up all night. Whatever it takes.

At the highest level, service orientation includes a commitment to the long-term best interests of others. Sometimes that may seem counter to the organization's short-term interests. If a competitor can satisfy a customer's needs better than you can, what do you do? At the highest level of service orientation, you may recommend that the customer go to your competitor. If you believe that your customer does not need one of your products or services, you say so. This level of service orientation requires a high level of trust in oneself and one's organization, and a belief that if you do your best to serve to your highest capacity, you will ultimately be treated well in return.

Sample Key Behaviors for Service Orientation

- Responds to customer requests in a timely, professional manner.
- Elicits feedback from customers to monitor their satisfaction.

INTERPERSONAL AWARENESS

Interpersonal awareness is the competency that involves eliciting, noticing, interpreting, and anticipating the concerns and feelings of others. It is one of the competencies that Daniel Goleman emphasizes as a critical component of emotional intelligence.[4] Almost all leaders need to respond to the concerns and feelings of the people they lead and the people they serve. Every worker, to be effective, must be able to respond to the needs of managers, coworkers, subordinates, and of course customers. These include the need to be heard and understood, to be affirmed, to be appreciated, and to be accepted. Even if people are not fully aware of their needs, it is critical that others be sensitive to their feelings and concerns.

A key component of interpersonal awareness is the ability to listen effectively. Listening accomplishes a number of important functions:

---

[4]Goleman, Daniel. *Working with Emotional Intelligence*. New York: Bantam Books, 1998.

- It gives people the opportunity to develop their thoughts and ideas and to express their concerns and feelings. Many people actually think more clearly when they have someone listening to them.
- It gives listeners the opportunity to understand others' thoughts and feelings. Often people are so wrapped up in their own issues and thoughts that they don't bother to find out what is really going on with the other person. Listening counteracts this tendency.
- When people feel that they are being listened to, they also tend to feel accepted and affirmed.

Many managers feel the urge to solve others' problems rather than simply to listen to what they have to say. While problem solving is often the appropriate response to someone talking about a problem, many times people just need a safe forum in which to express themselves and feel heard. When managers instinctively act to solve the problems brought to them by subordinates, the subordinates learn that it is easier to have a superior solve their problems than to solve them on their own. It is usually better for managers first to listen to their subordinates and then ask them for their own solutions. Managers can then coach subordinates as they forge their own way through whatever the difficulty is and make suggestions that will help employees feel as though they rather than their superiors were responsible for the solution.

Empathy is another key component of interpersonal awareness. Empathy is the communication of caring about and understanding what another is feeling. It can be expressed with a caring facial expression, a touch on the shoulder, or words.

Sample Key Behaviors for Interpersonal Awareness

- Listens attentively to people's ideas or concerns.
- Approaches others about sensitive issues in nonthreatening ways.

ORGANIZATIONAL SAVVY

Using organizational savvy, people understand and utilize organizational dynamics in order to achieve objectives. It is a key component of the ability to influence and impact organizations, both one's own and others. Organizations are complex entities; they have formal organization charts, formal lines of authority, formal decision-making processes, and all the rules and policies that are meant to guide decisions, distribute power, and determine how things get done. The reality of how organizations function, however, is usually far different from the formal system. If you don't know who the real influencers are, you are unlikely to achieve the goals you want. In some organizations, one of the key people influencing the CEO is the CEO's administrative assistant. In some organizations, the head of human resources is a key strategic partner of the CEO. If you do not know who has the ear of the decision maker, your ability to make things happen is greatly diminished.

The competency of organizational savvy has at its core the desire to understand how decisions are really made and how power is really distributed in an organization. It includes understanding the alliances and relationships among groups of people within the organization. What is the relationship between sales and manufacturing? Who is in and who is out? If you are seen as an ally to one person, who else will distrust you because of that alliance?

Organizational savvy is not critical for an entry-level position, or for many individual contributor (nonmanagement) positions. As one moves up the organizational structure, however, organizational savvy becomes more critical. And for individual contributor positions such as sales, organizational savvy is important when you need to influence a complex organization in order to achieve your objective.

Sample Key Behaviors for Organizational Savvy

- Keeps current on formal and informal communication channels and reporting relationships.
- Develops strategies to gain commitments to projects and strategies based on knowledge of the organization's culture.

RELATIONSHIP BUILDING

The ability to build relationships is an important competency for both individual contributors and managerial positions. At most jobs, success involves obtaining the cooperation of others. When people can develop caring, trusting relationships, they are likely to succeed in the people aspects of their jobs. For jobs involving customer or other external contact, relationship building is critical to success. Managers can better motivate, coach, and challenge employees when they have strong relationships. Employees will have more satisfying and more successful careers when they experience with other employees mutual feelings of cooperation, of wanting to help each other, and of being able to count on each other to provide help.

Sample Key Behaviors for Relationship Building

- Develops rapport easily with a variety of people.
- Modifies communication style to fit the personality and culture of others.

CONFLICT RESOLUTION

The ability to resolve conflicts is a must for anyone in a leadership position and is important in most individual contributor positions as well. A common way in which managers resolve conflicts is by ordering their subordinates to do it "my way." This approach to resolving disagreements tends to discourage employees and create resistance and resentment that eventually sabotages performance. The battle to win the hearts and minds of employees will not be won by ordering them to do it "my way." At its highest level, the purpose of conflict resolution is to resolve issues and disagreements in a way that all parties feel satisfied and affirmed, and that brings out the best thinking of all parties to create the most effective and elegant solutions to problems. Conflict resolution is a complex competency that involves a number of key behaviors.

Sample Key Behaviors for Conflict Resolution

- Expresses disagreements in a way that does not attack or disparage.
- Knows when to compromise and when to take a stand.

ATTENTION TO COMMUNICATION

Attention to communication is the competency by which people keep others informed of important information, whether daily activity, crises, or progress on long-term projects. The underlying assumption is that people can make more intelligent decisions, will feel more a part of the organization, and be more motivated and empowered if they have more information about the business. One of the best examples of this is "open-book" management, popularized by Jack Stack in *The Great Game of Business*,[5] a practice in which employees have open access to the company's financial information, including income statements and balance sheet. At Stack's company, Springfield Remanufacturing Corp., workers on the plant floor learn how to read income statements and balance

[5]Stack, Jack. *The Great Game of Business*. New York: Doubleday, 1992.

sheets and use the information to improve productivity in all areas of the company.

People tend to be more motivated when they know why they are doing what they are doing. If you ask someone to perform a mundane task without explaining the importance of the task, that person will be unhappy doing it and make less of an effort to do a good job. At its highest level, attention to communication reflects the philosophical position that information flow increases synergy and efficiency: I can't help you if I don't know you have a problem. People who are strong in attention to communication not only keep others informed, but also think about maximizing the efficacy of the means of communication. Different channels are used to ensure that the message gets across to various recipients with diverse needs.

Sample Key Behaviors for Attention to Communication

- Organizes and expresses ideas clearly.
- Creatively identifies and utilizes effective communication methods and channels.

CROSS-CULTURAL SENSITIVITY

More organizations today are recognizing the need to take advantage of the diversity of our workforce. It is logical that those organizations that can attract and develop talent from the widest possible employee pool will have a competitive advantage in their fields. Given the fact that we live in a society with deeply ingrained cultural traditions of racism, sexism, and stereotypes about a wide variety of ethnic groups, cross-cultural sensitivity is an extremely important competency for managers to master.

Sample Key Behaviors for Cross-Cultural Sensitivity

- Develops a knowledge and understanding of different cultures and backgrounds.
- Modifies communication and behavior based on an understanding of cultural differences.

Personal Attribute Competencies

Competencies in this category are intrinsic to the individual, and reflect the traits and characteristics that relate to what individuals believe, how they think, how and what they feel, and how they learn and develop. While these competencies affect people's ability to achieve tasks and their relationships with others, they are especially related to their sense of self-identity.

INTEGRITY AND TRUTH

Integrity and truth is the competency that reflects how we feel about ourselves, how well we accept ourselves, and the degree to which we know we are okay no matter how well we do or how well we are accepted by others. In the workplace the integrity and truth competency is demonstrated by a number of behaviors that result in cooperative activity and a high level of achievement.

People with high integrity and truth tend to admit mistakes and take responsibility for their actions. Because their self-worth is not dependent on doing everything right, they are much more at ease with making mistakes. Not only are they less defensive, they blame others less and make fewer excuses. They are also free to take more risks to try new things and to say what they really think, because they are always acceptable to themselves even if they are disagreed with or even disliked by others.

One of the surest signs of low integrity and truth is defensiveness. We all know employees who always point the finger at someone else when there is a problem—it is never their fault. "The copier was broken." "Accounting didn't get me the financial figures on time." "You didn't tell me that I was supposed to do that." The responsibility always rests with others.

Sample Key Behaviors for Integrity and Truth

- Follows through on commitments and agreements.
- Admits mistakes in spite of the potential for negative consequences.

SELF-DEVELOPMENT

Self-development is the competency by which people demonstrate a desire to continually grow, learn, and develop. This competency is intrinsic to all human beings. Humans have the ability to process information, learn, and create new, unpatterned responses to the environment to a degree not found in other life forms on our planet. The desire to learn and grow is an innate trait in all human beings.

People strong in self-development accurately assess their current skills as well as those they need for increased success on the job. They also take the initiative to identify what skills they will need in future positions and do what is needed to acquire those skills. They assess themselves accurately on the competencies important for their current and future positions, and invest considerable time and resources to improve those competencies. Those strong in self-development consistently seek out opportunities that will foster growth and development. They put themselves in challenging situations in which they are not 100 percent assured of success and that demand the rapid acquisition of new capabilities. They crave the steep learning curves that require self-development.

People strong in self-development elicit feedback from others regarding their strengths, weaknesses, skills, and competencies. Rather than being defensive, they seek out and are grateful for any feedback that might help them improve. They habitually ask themselves the questions, "How can I do it better? What could I have done differently?" and look for opportunities to apply their skills and knowledge. Finally, leaders manifest self-development by creating an environment that rewards and recognizes people who stretch themselves, learn to make mistakes, and demonstrate a desire to continually learn and grow.

Sample Key Behaviors for Self-Development

- Identifies personal skill areas to be developed.
- Seeks feedback on personal strengths and weaknesses.

DECISIVENESS

Decisiveness is the act of making decisions in a timely manner. At its highest level, decisions are made even under conditions of high stress when the stakes are high and the circumstances ambiguous. Some of the best examples of decisiveness occur when crisis managers take over management of troubled companies. Such companies are often rapidly losing money, about to be thrust into bankruptcy by their creditors, losing employees, and so on. The strength of good crisis managers is that they can go into a rapidly deteriorating, highly complex, enormously stressful situation; quickly assess it; and rapidly make decisions that alleviate and even take advantage of the crisis.

When managers are weak in decisiveness, opportunities are lost, poor decisions are often made, and employees become unmotivated as a result of inaction. The mistakes of the generals who led the Northern armies in the Civil War provided excellent examples of a lack of decisiveness, causing

President Abraham Lincoln to wonder in despair whether he could ever find a decent military leader.

The competency of decisiveness, however, is not simply the ability to make decisions quickly. Sometimes it is better to wait and postpone decisions. During periods of rapid change and when there is insufficient information to form an accurate picture of the situation and the potential consequences of different options, it may be important to delay decisions in order to keep options open. People strong in decisiveness are able to assess when it is time to decide, and then do so.

Decisiveness also involves the ability to take charge of a group when it needs to act. Groups are often mired in prolonged discussions that cause opportunities to be missed and valuable time wasted. People do not need to be a designated leader to move a group to action. Anyone in the group can decide that the group is going to act, and use tools of communication, persuasion, and group process to help make it happen. This level of decisiveness requires courage as well as strong influence capability.

Sample Key Behaviors for Decisiveness

- Makes decisions in a timely manner when the options and consequences are clear.
- Takes charge of a group when it is necessary to facilitate either action or a decision.

DECISION QUALITY

While decisiveness determines the appropriateness of the timing of decisions, decision quality determines the soundness of decisions. Decision making involves a series of processes:

- Perceiving a choice point containing at least two options.
- Gathering information and analyzing the situation, including facts, feelings, theories, opinions, risks, and opportunities.
- Determining objectives.
- Determining options, including creating "out-of-the-box" alternatives.
- Assessing both the short- and long-range consequences and implications of each option, taking into account all the relevant kinds of consequences to the organization, to people, to the client organization, to the environment, and so on.

- Evaluating the risks and potential rewards from each option, based on the assessment of potential consequences.
- Making the decision based on the preceding steps and the underlying principles, values, and standards to which the decision maker is committed.

Weakness in any of these steps can interfere with sound decision making. Often the biggest problem is not perceiving that there is a decision to be made, that there is a choice other than continuing to go on the same path at the same speed as yesterday and the day before. Companies often fail to examine the implications of *not* changing their policies and processes. One of the classic examples of the twentieth century was the refusal of Detroit's Big Three automobile makers to listen to W. Edwards Deming's approach to manufacturing after World War II. He found a receptive audience in Japan, and while the Ford Motor Company, General Motors, and Chrysler Corporation kept their competitive sights on each other, Japanese carmakers were learning to make better cars.

At its highest level, decision quality includes the ability to make decisions based on higher principles, purpose, and values. Choosing to do the right thing, when the consequences are personally painful, is an act of courage that transcends personal feelings and requires a deep commitment to something bigger than personal self-interest and comfort. Courage is as important in making the right decision as knowing what to do.

Sample Key Behaviors for Decision Quality

- Bases decisions on an analysis of short-range consequences or implications of options, including people's reactions and potential problems.
- Gathers sufficient information to identify gaps and variances before making a decision.
- Foresees the long-range consequences or implications of different options.

STRESS MANAGEMENT

Stress management is the ability to deal with emotions in ways that keep oneself and others in good physical and emotional shape and that support the accomplishment of business objectives. It involves containing one's feelings when appropriate, expressing them when appropriate, and helping others do the same. People strong in stress management can interact with courtesy and restraint in difficult situations, and can also choose to use emotional expression to communicate and help get things done.

Stress management does *not* mean remaining unemotional or calm all the time. There are times, for example, when getting angry is an effective tool to control disruptive behavior. Someone who cannot express anger may be as weak in stress management as someone who expresses anger too often.

Stress management is actually a complex process that involves a number of elements:

1. *The ability to be aware of one's emotional state, to know whether one feels happy, sad, scared, angry, embarrassed, or hurt.* Many people are not in touch with how they are feeling. Being aware of your emotional state and how you are feeling can help you deal with situations in an appropriate way.

2. *The ability to express and release emotions in ways that relieve stress and cause no damage to relationships, productivity, or oneself.* Effective and healthy means of relieving stress include laughing, crying, pounding a body bag at a gym, talking through issues and problems, and similar means of expression.

3. *The ability to utilize perspective and humor to reduce stress.* Laughter is one of the most effective and socially acceptable means of reducing tension and stress. It is a skill to use humor to help oneself and others relax and regain a feeling of serenity.

4. *The ability to utilize listening and empathy to help relieve the stress of others.* Often the act of listening empathetically to others is sufficient to reduce their emotional stress level. This skill is underutilized in the business world. Most managers immediately focus on fixing problems rather than allowing people to talk and work through the problems themselves.

5. *The ability instantly to change one's emotional state in response to the needs of the moment.* When you are leading an organization in crisis, your ability to exhibit the appropriate emotional response can affect the stress level of the entire organization.

6. *The ability to track one's emotional response back to its root causes.* Often we project our distress from one situation onto another. If a manager is upset about the revenue figures for the last quarter, he or she may yell at the administrative assistant for misfiling a document. By keeping in mind the original source of distress, one can more easily deal with subsequent situations in a way that everyone can find more productive.

7. *The ability to use emotional expression to communicate a message.* As mentioned earlier, there are times when it is appropriate to express joy, to release anger, and even to cry. Doing so inappropriately can cause difficulties, but having access to emotional expression is useful.

Sample Key Behaviors for Stress Management

- Remains calm under pressure.
- Expresses emotions in ways that relieve stress without damaging relationships or productivity.

ANALYTICAL THINKING

Analytical thinking is the competency that involves the use of logical, systematic reasoning to understand, analyze, and resolve problems. Analytical thinking is a key competency in most professional positions, because the ability to analyze and solve problems is tied to this competency. People strong in analytical thinking can break down phenomena into their component parts and consider each part in detail. They are able to identify and evaluate many possible causes for a problem, and develop and execute a plan to find the actual cause. They notice discrepancies, gaps, and inconsistencies in available information.

At a high level of proficiency in analytical thinking, people successfully diagnose the causes of complex problems, and identify the root causes of the problems. They accurately assess the costs, benefits, and risks associated with different options, and use the information to assist in decision making.

Sample Key Behaviors for Analytical Thinking

- Breaks down concepts, issues, and problems into their component parts.
- Analyzes the costs, benefits, risks, and chances for success in a decision.

CONCEPTUAL THINKING

Conceptual thinking involves the use of concepts and abstractions to find similarities and to put ideas together in ways that increase understanding, solve problems, result in innovation, and otherwise benefit the organization. It is the competency most critical to innovation and invention. New ideas and products typically involve taking ideas and concepts from one arena and using them in another. This ability to compare and contrast data and come up with new patterns is an essential element of human intelligence.

Strong conceptual thinkers are able to grasp key concepts and central underlying issues quickly. They can then use their experience or knowledge from other situations with similar dynamics to create effective approaches and solutions. They may also effectively utilize values and principles to guide policy and decisions, since they are adept at going from the general to the particular.

Sample Key Behaviors for Conceptual Thinking

- Identifies the central or underlying issues in a situation.
- Creates and uses examples or analogies to help others understand concepts.

Managerial Competencies

Often when a sales management position becomes available, a company takes its best salesperson and promotes him or her to sales manager. It is also common that outstanding salespeople then become mediocre (or worse) managers. They often hate performing the necessary administrative tasks. Many would rather be out selling than spending their time working with other salespeople to help them succeed. The job of coaching others to do a job is very different from doing the job oneself. Most of the successful managers in baseball were not the star players of the game but rather competent journeymen who had long careers and learned about how to develop people and manage them. There are competencies relevant to managerial success that hardly affect the success of individual contributors.

Managerial competencies are those that determine whether someone will be an excellent manager. This competency category includes three key managerial functions: managing projects, supervising people, and developing people in order to increase their near- and long-term contribution to the organization.

A number of competencies from the previous three categories are also important managerial competencies. These include attention to communication, influence, decisiveness, decision quality, and integrity and truth. In addition to these, the following competencies make up the managerial set.

BUILDING TEAMWORK

The competency of building teamwork is a complex competency that involves building work units that are cooperative and that function at high levels. It involves putting people together and helping them bond into an effective working unit, and helping them deal with the issues that cause dissension and disruption. Strong team builders understand the developmental phases a team goes through—"forming, norming, storming, and performing"—and helps teams move to performing as easily and quickly as possible. They also understand group dynamics and use that understanding to help groups function and to develop strong team leaders.

Sample Key Behaviors for Building Teamwork

- Establishes direction for projects and assignments for team members.
- Helps remove organizational barriers and identifies resources to assist the team.

MOTIVATING OTHERS

Motivating others is the competency through which managers enhance others' commitment to their work. To motivate subordinates, managers need somehow to activate employees' own natural motivation: Subordinates need to want to do it *for themselves*. There are many different key behaviors that contribute to motivating others.

Sample Key Behaviors for Motivating Others

- Promptly recognizes and tackles morale problems.
- Uses a variety of approaches to energize and inspire others.

EMPOWERING OTHERS

Through empowering others, managers help others grow in responsibility and competence. Managers strong in empowering others will leverage themselves better than those weak in the competency, as their subordinates take on more responsibility and free the managers to perform their most value-added functions. When managers are weak at this competency, they tend to become bottlenecks in the company. Decisions cannot be made without their approval, and work slows down because employees line up waiting to see them and get approval for all kinds of minor things. These managers will feel overworked, overwhelmed, and burdened, complaining about their workload but not seeing how they are creating their own problems.

Sample Key Behaviors for Empowering Others

- Allows others to make mistakes and take risks to learn and grow.
- Delegates responsibility to others based on their ability and potential.

DEVELOPING OTHERS

This competency is essential to creating a learning organization that supports employees to become their best. As mentioned earlier, our research shows this competency to be the weakest leadership competency. This is confirmed by research performed by Michael Lombardo in a study of 700 managers.[6]

Weakness in developing others is understandable. Few people have had firsthand experience being coached and developed well. How many of us had teachers who could really pinpoint problem areas so that we learned more effectively? How many of us had managers who committed time and resources to help us improve our skills and abilities? Few if any organizations develop and track action plans to develop competencies as they do for other business objectives. Few companies explicitly include developing others in determining compensation and/or advancement.

When I ask candidates for senior-level searches for examples of times when they developed subordinates, I receive some typical responses. In the first response, they tell of promoting people to opportunities that helped move their careers forward: "I had a controller who was a really good finance guy, and I gave him an operating position in one of our plants. He is now head of our most profitable division and is doing a great job." In the other common response, managers declare that their approach to employee development is to tell their subordinates what they want accomplished and leave it to them get it done.

Both of these responses belong in the "sink or swim" category of employee development. There are many employees who strive in response to such challenges, but there are many others who do not. There are many things managers can do to develop their subordinates that go be-

---

[6]Lombardo, Michael. Presentation at the Fourth Annual International Conference on Using Competency-Based Tools and Applications to Drive Organizational Performance, Boston, Massachusetts, September 1997.

yond simply providing them with an opportunity or a goal to accomplish. They can give subordinates feedback on their behavior and performance, and help them better understand what is working and what isn't. They can help subordinates analyze situations and offer examples and alternatives that will expand their capabilities. They can encourage them and push them to do things that they might otherwise avoid, helping them learn and grow from experiences that they would otherwise not have had. Perhaps most importantly, they can maintain and communicate high expectations for employees that will help inspire them to perform at their best.

Sample Key Behaviors for Developing Others

- Provides accurate feedback on individual strengths and weaknesses.
- Helps others examine the barriers to their growth and development.

Leadership Competencies

Just as there are managerial competencies that are not as significant for individual contributors, there are also leadership competencies that are particularly important to help people lead others toward a purpose, vision, and mission. The development of leaders is one of the elements of an organizational culture that needs to be strong if that organization wants to be successful over the long term.

Every competency in the managerial category is also important for organizational leaders. The personal attribute competency of conceptual thinking is also usually a necessary component of leadership, because of the importance of seeing the big picture and identifying and focusing attention on the most important issues facing the organization. These, in addition to the following list, make up the leadership competencies.

VISIONARY LEADERSHIP

Visionary leadership is the competency through which leaders create and communicate an inspiring corporate mission, vision, and value system. As we will discuss in Chapter 6, the development of an inspiring corporate philosophy is a powerful tool to help create a culture of competence. Ultimately employees want to be motivated by more than a desire to make money and have a decent place to work. They want to be a part of something bigger than themselves that provides a sense of meaning and purpose to their work and their lives. Leaders strong in visionary leadership can help satisfy that need.

Sample Key Behaviors for Visionary Leadership

- Explains the vision and mission to others within and outside of the company.
- Ensures that the organization's strategic plan and business practices are consistent with its vision and mission.

STRATEGIC THINKING

Strategic thinking is the competency through which leaders use their understanding of their organization, its position in the market, and business trends to create and execute an organizational strategy. Weakness in strategic thinking among the leaders in an organization will result in a short-sighted perspective that will tend to result in long-term difficulties.

One of our clients, for example, was a middle market company that manufactured automobile parts. The company was a family-owned business run by the third generation of family members. The founder of the company had started the business when he left his employer and obtained a contract with a major automobile manufacturer. Fifty years later, 75 percent of the company's revenue still came from that original manufacturer. They were proud of their engineering and manufacturing expertise, and had a solid relationship with their big customer. However, when their customer followed a consulting firm's suggestion to open all parts contracts up to a worldwide bidding process, the company's very existence was jeopardized. If the company's leadership had been stronger in strategic thinking, they would have realized the danger of having so great a concentration of revenue in one customer, and would have taken action to address the danger.

Sample Key Behaviors for Strategic Thinking

- Understands the organization's strengths and weaknesses.
- Utilizes knowledge of industry and market trends to develop and champion long-term strategies.

ENTREPRENEURIAL ORIENTATION

When using the competency of entrepreneurial orientation, leaders seek business opportunities and take well-calculated business risks to grow the organization. In today's environment of global competition, resting on one's laurels is no longer a viable business option. No matter how strong or dominant a company's position is in the market, it cannot afford *not* to seize new business opportunities. Companies like Hewlett Packard and Xerox Corporation have maintained their market position by re-creating themselves with new products in new markets. Such makeovers only occur in companies that have leaders who are strong in entrepreneurial orientation.

Sample Key Behaviors for Entrepreneurial Orientation

- Uses market, product, and industry knowledge to identify new business opportunities.
- Accurately analyzes and evaluates the pros, cons, and business risks associated with new business initiatives.

CHANGE MANAGEMENT

The ability to guide an organization through extensive change and transformation is more important today than ever before because of the rapid rate of change in so many different areas. Managing a change process requires a set of capabilities equivalent to the needs of a military leader to win a war. It is a complex job that requires mobilizing forces to change habits, beliefs, policies, and the feelings of many people, a significant number of whom will feel threatened by the change. A change leader must be a communicator and motivator, an analyst and a visionary, a strategist and a fighter. It is a tall order and a challenging job.

Sample Key Behaviors for Change Management

- Accurately identifies and assesses the current situation, including cultural elements supportive and resistant to change.
- Provides resources, removes barriers, and acts as an advocate for those initiating change.

BUILDING ORGANIZATIONAL COMMITMENT

The ability to build organizational unity and alignment with the organizational mission, vision, and objectives is another important leadership competency. A leader's ability to build loyalty and commitment to the organization affects recruitment, retention, and every aspect of company performance dependent on employee morale, loyalty, and motivation.

Sample Key Behaviors for Building Organizational Commitment

- Expresses and builds concern for the organization's welfare.
- Takes responsibility for building loyalty and commitment throughout the organization.

ESTABLISHING FOCUS

Establishing focus is the competency through which managers ensure that their subordinates are aligned with the business's objectives and that resources are appropriately prioritized and allocated. Communication is a key element of establishing focus, because employees usually perform better and accomplish more when they understand their role and how it relates to the bigger picture. Of course, to help others get and stay focused on the most important business objectives, managers need to stay focused themselves. It is a common complaint of many employees that their manager is not well focused and does not help them focus, either. Establishing focus is critical to ensuring that employees are all pulling in the same direction and making the best use of their time.

Sample Key Behaviors for Establishing Focus

- Helps others understand how their work relates to the business's goals.
- Ensures that resources, time, and attention are allocated in proportion to business priorities.

PURPOSE, PRINCIPLES, AND VALUES

Leaders who live from purpose, principles, and values inspire others to live in accordance with their own principles and values. Operating at the highest levels of this competency, leaders demonstrate a consistency of purpose and direction, with all decisions and actions fully aligned with their personal value system. Employees at any level can operate in accordance with personal principles and values, though it takes courage to consistently take the stands necessary to remain true to them. As a leadership competency, it will ultimately help lead organizations to achieve their highest purposes and missions.

Sample Key Behaviors for Purpose, Principles, and Values

- Encourages others to base their decisions and actions on the organization's purpose, principles, and values.

- Uses purpose, principles, and values to explain personal motivation and decisions to others.

Which Competencies Matter Most?

When I speak at conferences or introduce a company to competencies, I often lead them in a short exercise. I show them Metamorphics' competency library and ask them, "Which competency most differentiates outstanding salespeople from mediocre salespeople?" The most common responses are influence, results orientation, integrity and truth, service orientation, and attention to communication. I then show them the following weighted list of competencies, generated from actual research.[7] The competencies are ranked in order of the frequency with which they differentiate superior performers from average performers.

Weight	*Competency*
10	Influence
5	Results orientation
5	Initiative
3	Interpersonal awareness
3	Service orientation
3	Integrity and truth
2	Relationship building
2	Analytical thinking
2	Conceptual thinking
2	Information gathering
2	Organizational savvy

Once they see this list of competencies, I have their attention. Continuing my speech, I say, "When I first looked at the relative weightings of the competencies, it became clear to me that in my search practice I was not doing enough to assess candidates. I was being swayed by their interviewing presence and the matchmaking aspect of the search business. (Search firms get paid for making matches, and it is easier to focus on how well the candidate and the client will like each other than it is to focus on how effectively the candidate can do the job.) It became clear to me that I should instead

[7]Adapted from Spencer, L. M. & Spencer, S. M. *Competence at Work*. New York: John Wiley & Sons, p. 173, 1993.

focus on assessing the competencies that most determine superior performance. It was also clear to me that I should be using these competencies to hire, appraise, and develop my own employees. Because if they determine performance on the job, I should use them in every phase of employment to see that I am evaluating and developing employees on the basis of what matters most." At this point in the presentation, I have the rapt attention of every manager in the room.

The predominant methodology in the field of competencies is to create competency models for different positions or job functions, each model containing from 7 to 16 competencies. Chapter 9 discusses the different ways to formulate competency models. It suffices to say here that organizations can spend hundreds or millions of dollars developing competency models for their organizations. Our viewpoint is that resources should be expended on the actions that create the most value, and that competency modeling is but a small part of the process.

I am personally driven by a desire to maximize impact. And to maximize impact, we need to help people change the way they think and act in a world in which the demands on both time and money are already significantly greater than the supply. I keep two key principles and questions in mind when I work with organizations to implement competency-based practices: leverage and workability. (See Table 2.2.)

Once a senior HR executive from one of the largest New York banks told me about the training he had received in competency-based candidate assessment several months earlier. He expressed great enthusiasm over the rigor of the interview process and how comprehensive it was. When I questioned him, I learned that it took him three hours to interview a candidate using the process. I then asked him how many times since the training he had used it. "Oh, I haven't used it," he responded. "I don't have time." Workability is what makes or breaks a competency-based HR practice.

From the perspective of workability, it could be argued that an organization would do best if it chose one set of competencies and used them for all

Table 2.2 Principles of leverage and workability.

The leverage principle	How can we get the most done for the least amount of time, effort, and cost?
The workability principle	How can we make the process easy and simple enough so that line managers and individual contributors will actually use it?

its employees. From the body of competency research to date, a basic set of six competencies would differentiate the top quartile of performers from the rest in most positions in an organization:

1. Influence.
2. Results orientation.
3. Initiative.
4. Teamwork.
5. Service orientation.
6. Concern for quality.

If you added to this list two or three more competencies for managers and a few more for executives, you would have the basis of a workable competency model. I am not suggesting that every company use only these competencies to hire, appraise, and develop their people. I *am* suggesting that it is important to remember that the objective is to positively impact the organization as efficiently and effectively as possible. Too many organizations have competency models that are lying in drawers and are not being used to help them hire better people and develop their people to improve organizational performance.

My point of view is simple:

1. Competencies should be used to help organizations create high-performance cultures.
2. To work best, the same competencies should be used for every HR process—selection, performance management, succession planning, and so on.
3. The more HR processes they are used for, the more effectively organizations will create high-performance cultures.
4. Competencies should be used to:
   - Communicate your corporate values and standards.
   - Analyze and improve your corporate culture.
   - Select and hire your workforce.
   - Appraise and develop your workforce.
   - Develop your leaders.
   - Manage your succession planning process.
   - Establish the foundation for a training strategy.
   - Assist the compensation process.

Can Competence Be Improved?

If a competency cannot be improved far enough fast enough, it makes little sense devoting resources to improving it. The improvability of competencies has significant policy implications for organizations, and is central to decisions regarding hiring and development.

The issue is more complex than the "nature versus nurture" debate, which addresses the degree to which behavioral traits are inherited. For the purposes of organizational change and development, the relevant question is not how much a competency is genetically determined, but rather how easy it is to improve the competency. The improvability of a competency is determined by the components that make people proficient at the competency, and how easy it is to change them. Competency proficiency is affected by:

- Beliefs and values.
- Skills.
- Experience.
- Personality characteristics.
- Motivation.
- Emotional issues.
- Intellectual capabilities.

BELIEFS AND VALUES

What people believe about themselves, others, and the world has a big impact on behavior. If people believe that they are not creative or innovative, they will typically not attempt to think about new and different ways of doing things. The belief of many employees that management is "the enemy" will keep them from taking initiative that they otherwise might take. Similarly, if managers believe that they have little impact or influence, they are less likely to expend effort and energy identifying how they can improve things.

Beliefs and values are clearly changeable, though the more deeply held they are and the closer they are to people's sense of identity, the more difficult this will be. The social environment has a big influence on beliefs and values, and corporate culture has a significant impact on this aspect of competencies.

SKILLS

Skills play a role in most competencies. For example, public speaking is a skill that can be learned, practiced, and greatly improved. Writing skills can also be improved with instruction, practice, and feedback. By improving public speaking and writing skills, individuals will probably increase their proficiency in the competency of attention to communication. Skill development specifically related to competencies can impact both the corporate culture and individual competence.

EXPERIENCE

Mastery of many competencies requires experience organizing people, communicating in front of groups, solving problems, and so on. For example, people who have never had contact with a large, complex organization are unlikely to have developed the organizational savvy to understand the dynamics of power and influence in such an environment. People whose jobs require little strategic thinking are less likely to have developed the competency than those who have used strategic thinking for years.

Experience is an element of competence that is necessary but not sufficient for mastery. While a receptionist or machine operator is probably not strong in strategic thinking, in part because of a lack of experience, many CEOs with lots of opportunity to think strategically are still weak in the competency. Nevertheless, experience is another aspect of competency that can (and usually will) change with time and circumstance.

PERSONALITY CHARACTERISTICS

What we call personality includes many factors, many of which are difficult to change. Recent studies have shown, for example, that some infants are more shy and others more assertive almost from birth. Few introverts become extroverts through a change process.

Personality does change, however. In fact, it is changing all the time, as people respond to and interact with the forces around them. Many introverted people become more outgoing and social as they become older and more self-confident. People can become less tense through the use of exercise, meditation, and therapy.

Personality affects proficiency in a number of competencies, including conflict resolution, interpersonal awareness, teamwork, influence, and relationship building. People who are quick to anger are likely to have a more difficult time becoming strong in conflict resolution than those who have an easier time managing their emotional responses.

Personality does not tend to change easily. Just as we were taught not to marry someone with the expectation the person will change, it is not wise to expect people to improve their competence by changing their personalities.

MOTIVATION

Human beings are intentional creatures—what they want has a big effect on what they get. People tend to learn when they want to learn. They tend to have greater influence when they care more about the result. They do a better job of serving customers when they *want* to serve the customer.

Motivation is a factor in competence that can change. Encouragement, appreciation, recognition, and individual attention can all have an effect on motivation. If managers can elicit employees' personal motivations and align them with business needs, they will often find proficiency rising in a number of competencies that impact performance: results orientation, influence, initiative, and so on.

EMOTIONAL ISSUES

Emotional blocks and barriers can limit mastery of competencies. Fear of making mistakes, of being embarrassed, of not being liked, of not belonging all tend to limit motivation and initiative. Feelings about authority figures can affect the ability to communicate and resolve conflicts with managers. People may have a difficult time listening to others if they don't feel listened to themselves. Not having experienced a positive learning environment in school often results in a diminished desire to learn in adulthood.

Overcoming unpleasant experiences will improve proficiency in many competencies. However, it is unreasonable to expect employees to overcome emotional blocks and barriers without assistance, much of which is considered taboo in many work environments. There is plenty of evidence that emotional blocks and barriers can be removed through a variety of therapeutic modalities. However, whether your organization will encourage and support people to work through those barriers is another issue.

INTELLECTUAL CAPABILITIES

The degree to which IQ is inherited is an emotionally charged issue that fortunately we do not need to address. No matter how much intelligence is inherited, there is considerable research that it is not easy to substantially improve. Competencies dependent on cognitive thinking such as conceptual thinking and analytical thinking are unlikely to improve greatly through any intervention an organization might perform. Of course, factors such as experience can increase proficiency in these competencies.

Research has confirmed that certain competencies are more easily changed than others. Table 2.3 illustrates several differences in the improvability of competencies and is based on research provided by Robert W. Eichinger and Michael L. Lombardo,[8] Bradford D. Smart's *Topgrading*,[9] and our own findings.

As we work to change corporate culture and to improve individual and group performance through competency development, three points will become clear:

1. Understanding the components of competencies is important to helping people improve them. By analyzing where the problems reside, resources and attention can be focused on addressing them.
2. Positive expectations produce better results than negative expectations. No matter how difficult it is to improve a competency, employees will improve more when more is expected from them.
3. Drastic change does not happen easily or quickly. None of the elements comprising competencies change overnight, and some of them are difficult to change at all.

Despite the difficulties, there is a significant potential gain resulting from the attempt to improve competency. A small improvement in competency by a large number of employees can have a huge impact on an organization. The fact that competency development is often slow and tedious is not a good reason not to do it. You never know what tiny improvement in competency will result in a new invention, an improved process, or a customer being retained who would otherwise have gone to your competitor.

---

[8]Michael Lombardo. Talk given at the Fourth Annual International Conference on Using Competency-Based Tools and Applications to Drive Organizational Performance, Boston, Massachusetts, September 1997.
[9]Smart, Bradford D. *Topgrading: How Leading Companies Win by Hiring, Coaching, and Keeping the Best People.* Paramus, NJ: Prentice Hall, 1999.

Table 2.3   Improvability of competencies.

Improvability	Competencies
Easier to Improve	Developing others, production efficiency, teamwork, technical expertise, service orientation, managing performance
Somewhat difficult to improve	Results orientation, decision quality, influence, conflict resolution, strategic thinking, analytical thinking, organizational savvy
Difficult to improve	Initiative, innovation, integrity and truth, stress management, flexibility, conceptual thinking

Creating Your Own Culture of Competence: Chapter 2—Exercises

EXERCISE 1—WHAT IS MISSING?

Select a position with a large employee base or one that has a strong impact on the organization's ability to achieve its objectives. Using the competencies highlighted in this chapter, take some time to list in the "Current" column the top six competencies that best describe the position. Under the "Ideal" heading, list those that will be needed for business success in the long term. Where are the gaps? How does the culture support or discourage the use of these barriers?

Position: _____

    Current   *Ideal*

_____   _____

_____   _____

_____   _____

_____   _____

_____   _____

_____   _____

EXERCISE 2—WHERE DO WE BEGIN?

Review the following human resources best practices and check those that would contribute most to your efforts to initiate culture change and close some of the competency gaps between the current and ideal state in Exercise 1.

(✓) *Human Resources Best Practices*

Analyze the corporate culture relative to the requirements of the business and develop a strategy for making changes in order to ensure that everyone's behaviors are aligned with the business needs.

Develop a selection system based on the competencies needed by executives, managers, and employees to help the organization make needed changes in the workforce and minimize the need for training.

Appraise and develop the workforce to build accountability and reinforce the need for changing behavior.

Develop leaders so they are able to model the needed leadership competencies to help employees change their behavior in response to business needs.

Manage the succession planning process so that the organization has leaders in place who are ready to manage and lead the business.

Establish a training strategy linked to the competencies that are critical to high performance.

Review and/or redesign the compensation process so that employees are rewarded for demonstrating the right behaviors.

CHAPTER

3

Using Competencies to Analyze and Change Your Culture

A ny organization that increases the proficiency of its managers and employees in the competencies discussed in the previous chapter will become more successful. The point of this book is that to have an organization whose employees take initiative, strive to achieve challenging goals, focus on satisfying customers, and so on, it is critical to create a culture of competence—a corporate culture in which improvement in behavioral competencies is fostered, encouraged, and rewarded. But in order to create such a culture, it is first necessary to understand what culture is and how it works.

Culture is defined by anthropologists as the way of life of a people that is transmitted from generation to generation. It includes the language, beliefs, values, customs, behaviors, social norms, social structure and status, shared knowledge, economic system, and material characteristics of the group. It is the fabric that binds people together and the edifice that structures their interaction so that they can function together as a society.

The following simple example helps illustrate some dynamics of what can be called culture. When children learn the "proper" way to use a fork, they learn that the "proper" way is the *only* correct way to use a fork. It never occurs to the properly socialized child that there might be other ways to hold a fork, and that in some parts of the world forks are not used at all. Even if they were told about other ways to use a fork, they were also told emphatically, "This is the way *we* use a fork"—in other words, do it the way *we* do it if you want our approval. If children use the silverware differently, they are corrected and sometimes scolded. Their parents point out other children to them, commenting on their "good" or "bad" table manners. Eventually they learn to use a fork the "right" way, and as adults they use a fork that way without a conscious thought. And when they have children of their own, they do the same thing to them.

This small example depicts a number of the key characteristics of culture:

1. *Culture is learned.* When we are born into a particular culture, we immediately begin to learn about it. From our childhood surroundings we learn the language and beliefs that will guide our behavior throughout our lives. We learn the "right" and the "wrong" ways of doing things, and are rewarded and punished to reflect our relative "rightness" or "wrongness." The trouble older immigrants have adapting to a new culture demonstrates how difficult it is to erase ingrained behaviors and acquire a whole new set that belong to the new culture.

2. *Norms and customs are common throughout the culture.* Not every person will behave in accordance with the norms and customs, but members of the society who are fully integrated into the culture will at least know what they are. When you go to a baseball game and the national anthem is played, you know that you should stand up. When you are introduced to people at a business gathering, you know that you should shake their hands.

3. *Culture operates mostly subconsciously.* Only a small fraction of thought processes occur at a conscious level, and most cultural beliefs, customs, and behaviors do not occupy conscious thought. We do not consciously think about how to hold and use a fork every time we use one— we just do it. Similarly, we do not usually consciously question beliefs that we hold.

4. *Cultural traits and characteristics are controlled through many social mechanisms and processes.* Norms, beliefs, customs, and behaviors are learned in many different ways. The socialization process that children undergo serves to teach and reinforce cultural learning. School, religious training, peer pressure, and the media all function to shape values and behavior to ensure that they fall within acceptable boundaries. People who act outside the boundaries of accepted cultural behavior are punished by many mechanisms, including social reprimand, ridicule, ostracism, divorce, termination of employment, and imprisonment, for example.

5. *Cultural elements are passed down from one generation to the next.* People tend to learn how to hold a fork just like their parents, who learned it from their parents, and so on. Cultural continuity is one of the hallmarks of human society.

6. *Customs and patterns of acceptable behavior tend to become associated with moral righteousness and superiority.* People who hold a fork the way I do are good, and people who hold it differently are bad. This righteousness reinforces cultural beliefs and behaviors by identifying alternative beliefs and behaviors with feelings of shame and loathing.

7. *Like other habits, cultural behaviors are comfortable and familiar.* Behaviors and beliefs outside the boundary of cultural norms feel uncomfortable. Anthropologists who go to live in other cultures to study them regularly experience a degree of distress and disorientation unknown to most people who haven't had such an experience. The beliefs that they grew up with and held as sacred and true are frontally assaulted as they live among people who hold diametrically different beliefs. It often takes them months after they return home before they begin to feel and act "normal." The discomfiture with discordant belief systems is another process that discourages cultural diversity and reinforces conforming cultural behavior.

The Culture of an Organization

Corporate culture is defined as the way of life of an organization that is manifested at and transmitted across all organizational levels and to succeeding generations of employees. It includes the set of beliefs, behaviors, values, goals, technologies, and practices that is shared by members of the organization.

Organizations are integrated elements of the larger culture, and as such are shaped by that larger culture. Companies often do not recognize the consequences and difficulties when they try to create a corporate culture with beliefs and customs contradictory to those of the larger cultural context. A CEO recently told me about his manufacturing operation located in China, and about how his employees regularly "took from the till"—that is, they pilfered from the company. Not only that, but they did so without shame or embarrassment. In fact, they considered it part of the conditions of employment. He told me that it is such a common custom in Chinese culture to take a little here and there, that *not* stealing is looked upon with disdain and incredulity. Beware the western business executive who expects to run a plant in China without taking into account Chinese culture.

The dynamics of societal culture apply to corporate culture in being based on past results and being resistant to change:

CHALLENGES OF THE PAST

Corporate culture developed to meet the challenges of the past. Policies, procedures, corporate philosophy, customs, and so on are responses to past situations and past threats. If employees were never late to work, companies would not have lateness policies. If every employee were totally committed to satisfying customers to the fullest extent possible, no company would need to include customer satisfaction in its mission and vision statements. If all manufacturing practices had produced the same results, there would have been no need to standardize manufacturing processes.

The main problem with basing current behavior on the results of the past is that when conditions change more rapidly than the speed of cultural adjustment, the organization's success and even its survival can be in jeopardy. What follows are two examples that illustrate how different cultural elements became unsuitable when circumstances changed. The cultural elements described are an avoidance of conflict and a resistance to new business development.

- *Case 1.* In the late 1970s Continental Illinois was recognized as one of the best banks in the world at which to work. It possessed a brisk growth rate, an enthusiastic workforce that was intelligent and motivated, and a strong entrepreneurial orientation. I know many ex-Continental bankers who still reminisce wistfully about the good old days. A few years later, the bank lost the confidence of the investment community, shareholders lost all their equity, and the Federal Deposit Insurance Corporation essentially took over the bank. A number of disastrous loans had cost the bank billions of dollars, the most notorious of which were made through Penn Square Bank, a small bank located in a shopping center in Oklahoma. What happened? Could Continental Illinois's culture have changed so quickly and drastically that the upheaval could have destroyed such a solid financial institution?

In fact, it wasn't the culture that changed, but the environment. The economy went into a recession, and the cultural practices that worked wonderfully for the bank in a booming economy had disastrous consequences in a weakening economy. A major cause of Continental Illinois's downfall lies in a particular cultural element that valued harmony at the expense of constructive conflict. In the expanding economy of the late 1970s, this collegial environment and the cultural norm limiting internal questioning and challenging encouraged lending activity and increased profitability. However, when times changed and lending risk grew as companies weakened, the cultural norm discouraging conflict resulted in catastrophe. Many Continental bankers knew about the corrupt and unsound lending practices occurring in the oil and gas group, but in the interest of maintaining a harmonious atmosphere, no one raised the issue to senior management (except for one junior officer who wrote a memo that was ignored). What had appeared to be a robust, healthy corporate culture turned out to contain norms and beliefs that destroyed all the shareholder value when circumstances changed.

• *Case 2.* A manufacturing company was formed 35 years ago to supply parts to a Fortune 500 manufacturer of heavy-duty equipment. The company is heavily engineering oriented, and has relied on the quality of the relationship with that single customer for continued success. It serves this customer faithfully, and has used its engineering expertise to help solve customer problems and grow revenue with the customer. This customer accounts for almost 80 percent of the company's revenue. The role of sales in the company has been essentially defined by the attitude: "Take care of our big customer, and it will take care of us."

With such a good customer relationship, it seems reasonable for an organization to continue this scenario indefinitely and to expect it to generate continued success. Of course, things change. Because of financial difficulties, the Fortune 500 manufacturer brought in a major consulting firm to recommend a cost reduction strategy. As a result, the company announced that it was going to open up a worldwide bidding process for every part it needed. Suddenly, the entire existence of the parts supplier was in question. Its survival became dependent on its ability to expand its market beyond its big client fast enough. The lack of appreciation for new business development in the culture went from being the most minor of the company's issues to the key factor determining the organization's survival and ongoing success.

Corporate cultures form and develop in response to the situations organizations face and the internal and external threats they perceive. The cultural traits and characteristics that are created may or may not be adaptive as circumstances change.

RESISTANCE TO CHANGE

Corporate culture is essentially reactive and regressive, and will tend to resist change at every opportunity. This resistance is multifaceted and comes in many forms:

- Corporate policies and procedures.
- Habits, customs, and traditions.
- Beliefs.
- Corporate socialization processes.

Every organization develops sets of rules to guide what individuals and groups do. The formal, defined rules are called policies and procedures, and the informal ones are described as "how we do things here"—customs, norms, and traditions. Corporate policy functions to control behavior and eliminate as much nonconformity as possible. Customs, norms, and traditions play the same role. Behavior outside the formal and informal sets of rules is negatively reinforced by a variety of mechanisms including disciplinary action, lack of promotion, poor work assignments, or social exclusion.

I had a friend a number of years ago who worked in the maintenance department for a municipality. At the end of his first day on the job he was told in no uncertain terms that he had better slow down, because he was making the rest of them look bad. In other words, "Don't break the norm that we work only hard enough to avoid getting into trouble." The threat of becoming a social outcast is usually an effective technique to change people's behavior to conform to the cultural norm.

Here are some other common examples of corporate cultural norms that interfere with maximal functioning:

- Department managers don't criticize each other and prefer to avoid conflict.
- Subordinates follow the dictum "Don't stick your neck out," and avoid speaking their minds.
- People don't take initiative.
- Employees are not given feedback directly and are criticized behind their backs.
- Employees promise only what they need to and deliver as little as they can get away with.

CORPORATE CULTURE CAN WORK FOR YOU AS WELL

Once cultural norms that reflect a culture of competence have been established, they will have the same power and effect as any other norm. Behavior inconsistent with the norms will be discouraged and socially penalized. In a company in which a high degree of initiative is highly valued throughout the culture, employees not demonstrating initiative will receive plenty of nonverbal and often direct verbal encouragement to change their behavior.

Culture and Competence

Corporate culture plays a key role in determining the degree to which employees demonstrate the competencies that determine success. The competencies discussed in the previous chapter—initiative, results orientation, decisiveness, service orientation, teamwork, and so on—are interwoven throughout corporate culture. Continental Illinois had difficulty with conflict resolution. The parts manufacturer has difficulty with strategic thinking and decision quality.

If behavioral competencies are the traits and characteristics that determine individual performance, the corporate culture determines the extent to which competencies manifest themselves throughout the company. The following are some of the ways that corporate culture affects competence:

- *Hiring and selection practices determine which employees are brought into the organization and their degree of proficiency on competencies.* How people are hired is an important cultural process that relates to organizational standards, values, beliefs, reward systems, decision-making processes, and so on. Companies in which managers hire people based on whom they like will usually hire less competent people than those in which hiring is based on competency assessment.

- *Reward systems communicate to employees how the organization values competence.* If employees weak in teamwork receive the same compensation and recognition as those strong in teamwork, employees are unlikely to focus their attention on working well together and helping others succeed.

- *Decision-making practices affect the competencies of empowering others, initiative, and motivating others.* If managers are expected to make all the decisions and their subordinates are expected to follow orders, the subordinates will tend to take less responsibility and less initiative, and be less motivated.

- *Corporate philosophy—mission, vision, and values—relates to all the competencies.* Organizational values are communicated to employees every day in thousands of small ways, and each one of them affects employee behavior. If the plant manager walks down the hall and passes by a piece of crumpled paper on the floor, a message is communicated to employees that quality is not that important. If quality really matters in the culture and managers demonstrate its importance through both their words and their actions, employees will demonstrate more of the key behaviors associated with the competency.

- *Customs and procedures inform employees of how much competence is expected of them.* People want to belong and feel like they are a part of the organization. When new employees join the company, they learn how things are done there, and tend to adjust their behavior to fit in with their peer group. If, for example, it is the custom for employees to set challenging goals for themselves, new employees will be much more likely to do so than in a company in which goals either are not set or are not challenging.

- *Commitment to training and development communicates to employees the importance of the competency of continuous development.* If organizations don't support employees to improve their skills and competencies, employees are less likely to be strong in the competency.

- *Organizational processes that develop leaders directly affect leadership competencies.* These programs, including leadership training, mentorships, and so on, not only help develop better leaders, but also transmit a set of values and beliefs about how leaders ought to act and manage, and how employees should be treated.

These are but a few of the ways that corporate culture affects the level at which employees demonstrate proficiency in different competencies. If competence is examined only from the individual perspective, one of the key factors that causes organizational success or failure will be missed: its corporate culture. Without changing your corporate culture to support competence, trying to improve competence is like swimming against a strong current. You are unlikely to make it.

In order to design and implement a corporate culture change strategy to create a culture of competence, it is important to understand your current corporate culture and how it affects competence.

Competency Culture Analysis—A Case Study

Techno is a middle market manufacturer of instrumentation for the communications industry. (I have changed the name and some of the details to preserve confidentiality.) With approximately 250 employees, the company prides itself on its engineering expertise and its ability to stay on the cutting edge of technology. Its customers, the major communications companies, are both demanding and particular, and continually put forth new requirements for technology, timing, pricing, and service.

Just prior to the cultural assessment, the company announced a major revenue shortfall. The CEO was replaced, and the company began the arduous process of restructuring and rationalizing to put the business on a sound footing. A number of poor business practices had contributed to the company's problems:

- Production deadlines were not met.
- Engineering problems kept plaguing new product development.
- Low sales results were covered up by offering customers big discounts in December if they would accelerate the following year's sales.

CultureScope™, a tool developed by Metamorphics for analyzing and measuring corporate culture using behavioral competencies, was used to analyze Techno's culture in terms of the five competency categories outlined in Chapter 2 (see Table 3.1). The cultural data revealed some of the organizational behaviors that contributed to Techno's problems, and provided the foundation for a strategy to change the corporate culture.

Within the task achievement category, the company is strongest in re-

Table 3.1 Techno's competency strengths and weaknesses.

Competency Category	Strengths	Weaknesses
Task achievement	Results orientation Innovation Initiative	Managing performance Concern for quality
Relationship	Organizational savvy Teamwork Service focus	Attention to communication Conflict resolution Relationship building
Personal attribute	Decisiveness Analytical thinking Conceptual thinking	Stress management Decision quality Integrity and truth
Managerial	Building teamwork	Motivating others Developing others
Leadership	Establishing focus Change management	Visionary leadership Strategic thinking

sults orientation, innovation, and initiative. This is a company dedicated to getting the job done. Employees focus on results, and do what it takes to get them. They are weakest in managing performance and concern for quality, which is reflected in their excessive waste and a high return rate. These problems contribute to the company's delays in getting new products to market and its problems with on-time deliveries.

Within the relationship category, the company is highly proficient in organizational savvy and teamwork, though not nearly as much as in results orientation and innovation, the strongest task achievement competencies. The company does a good job of navigating through its customers' decision-making processes; it understands how decisions are really made and who makes them. Employees are also relatively strong in service orientation. They are dedicated to satisfying customers and follow through on commitments made to them.

On the negative side in the relationship category, there is a relative lack of attention to communication, conflict resolution, and relationship building at Techno. Employees don't feel that they are well informed of new decisions, policies, successes, losses, and so on. They often feel that they are told to do things without also knowing the reason for doing them. This lack of communication causes employees to feel unappreciated and unimportant. It also adversely affects production and customer relations, as problems are not promptly communicated and immediately dealt with.

The weakness in conflict resolution means that employees either avoid conflict altogether or argue and fight irresponsibly. Conflict tends either to fester under the surface and linger longer than necessary or to be dominated by one side, leaving the loser with resentment and hurt feelings. In either case, poor conflict resolution results in poor communication, less effective teamwork, and passive resistance that reduces motivation and productivity. With Techno, poor conflict resolution causes continual problems between the sales and manufacturing departments, creating tension and increasing delays in establishing pricing, product development, and production.

Techno's employees are also weak in the competency of relationship building. Employees in general do not exhibit a high degree of skill in developing warm, lasting relationships. They don't display much personal interest in each other, and tend not to build deep interpersonal loyalty. This has caused efforts to address the problems to be met with less enthusiasm and commitment than would otherwise have been the case.

In the realm of the personal attribute competencies, Techno's strengths lie in decisiveness, analytical thinking, and conceptual thinking. Employees are good at making critical and difficult decisions, and generally do so with good judgment. They are strong at the thinking competencies that, not surprisingly, correlate highly with superior performance in engineering occupations. Their strength in analytical thinking reflects their ability to solve problems. They show excellent proficiency in understanding complex technical issues and breaking problems down into component parts. Techno's high level of product innovation illustrates employees' ability to use conceptual thinking to come up with new ways to serve customer needs.

Techno is weakest at stress management, decision quality, and integrity and truth. Stress management is the overall weakest competency in the culture, which indicates that employees are continually under stress and do not handle it in a satisfying way. They also do not adequately anticipate short- and long-range consequences and results that stem from current circumstances, or from the options and choices they face. They are relatively weak in integrity and truth. Employees tend to be defensive and not to admit mistakes easily. They also tend not to take stands for their values that might involve personal risk. These weaknesses contributed to management's covering up their poor sales performance by stealing from next year's sales and not telling the board.

Among managerial competencies, building teamwork is the strongest and motivating others and developing others are the weakest. Managers are effective at helping people work together to accomplish tasks and projects, but are less effective at getting to know their wants and needs and helping them achieve them.

Among the competencies in the leadership category, Techno is strongest in establishing focus. Managers do a good job of aligning employee jobs with the business priorities, and allocate resources appropriately to get the job done. Employees know what the priorities of the business are, and know how their jobs relate to those priorities.

The second strongest leadership competency is change management. The new management team at Techno is perceived as doing an excellent job of adapting to new market conditions and responding to the organizational challenges. Employees are aware of the strategy for change, understand the need for it, and cooperate with it.

COMPETENCIES AND CULTURE AT TECHNO

What does this competency analysis tell us about Techno and its culture? Like many manufacturing companies, it excels at solving problems and getting things done. Employees have a strong short-term focus, and respond quickly and decisively to crises. The weaknesses in the corporate culture relate to three areas:

1. People skills: developing and motivating others, interpersonal awareness, and conflict resolution.

2. Process skills: concern for quality and managing performance.

3. Planning skills: strategic thinking, visionary leadership, and decision quality.

The weak people skills at Techno cause low employee morale. Employees don't feel that they are important enough to the company to be developed or kept informed about important issues. Employees do not operate at their peak capacity as conflicts fester and apathy ensues with the lack of an inspiring higher vision. While employees are results oriented, their contribution would be much greater if they also felt enthusiastic and highly motivated by a supportive work environment. And if they were being consciously developed, the company would reap the benefits of the improvement in their performance.

The weakness in process skills results in waste, inefficiency, and weaker customer relationships. Employees tend to think about how to fix the immediate problem quickly instead of how to anticipate problems before they occur.

The lack of strong processes relates to the third area of weakness as well—planning skills. Managers have difficulty seeing the big picture and using that vision to plan, act, and lead. They have missed significant business opportunities because they were unable to see what was coming in the market. Techno has focused so much of its resources on short-term needs that it was not prepared to compete as larger companies with more resources entered its market. The culture was able to adapt to minor changes in the business environment, but unless the culture gets stronger in some of the competencies just described, the business will not adequately recover and prosper.

Most of the leaders and managers in the company have been blind to these cultural shortcomings. Most of them have never worked for a company in which employees were developed well or conflict was effectively resolved. Few of them are aware that they lack the skills necessary to create and operate from a vision either for individuals or for the business entity. Most of them cannot define or describe what these skills would be. Their lack of awareness of their weaknesses has kept them from even considering whether they want to take action to improve themselves in these areas.

The simple corporate culture analysis in terms of concrete factors—competencies—brought these issues to the surface. As a result, Techno's leaders decided to take action to improve their culture in the weak areas, because they could foresee the consequences of their shortcomings and the benefits of eliminating them. This was the beginning of a corporate culture transformation.

A Process Outline for Changing Your Corporate Culture Using Competencies

Changing your corporate culture requires all the skills and abilities of a commander in chief attempting to win a war. You need to be an expert on the current situation and the strengths and weaknesses of your employees and your organization. You need to identify your allies and your enemies and *their* strengths and weaknesses. You need to design strategy and tactics based on your long-term and short-term objectives. You need to choose your battles wisely, and know when to cut your losses and when to take a stand. You continually need to rally the troops and remind them of the purpose, principles, and values for which you are fighting.

The following steps define a process by which to change your corporate culture using competencies:

1. Create a vision of your ideal corporate culture.
2. Analyze your corporate culture in terms of competencies.
3. Identify its key strengths and weaknesses.
4. Determine the consequences of your organization's weaknesses.
5. Prioritize which weaknesses to improve.
6. Identify which cultural elements will support change and which will resist.
7. Brainstorm possible pathways—actions and initiatives—that will lead to your ideal culture.
8. Determine your most powerful levers for corporate culture change.
9. Assemble a plan of action: communications strategy, action steps, time lines, and means of measuring progress.

10. Implement the plan.
11. Monitor progress.
12. Modify the plan based on changing circumstances and conditions.

To this point we have described how to analyze corporate culture using competencies through the fifth step in the change process. The sixth step, identifying culture change supporters and resisters, requires a different level of cultural analysis.

Culture Change Supporters and Resisters

Because the natural tendency of a culture is to resist change, in order to plan a cultural change campaign a manager needs to know which elements will support change and which elements will resist it. These elements include policies, beliefs, organizational structures, departments, manufacturing processes, organizational customs and norms, and individual managers and employees.

It is common, for example, for compensation policies to reward behaviors that are inconsistent with the corporate culture managers are trying to create. They may be trying to build a culture that is teamwork oriented, for example, and find that their compensation structure does not reward team-oriented behavior. This is a common problem in the sales areas of many companies. Salespeople are told that they should be team players and help each other succeed, and that they should cooperate fully with other departments in the company. Yet, all their bonus pay is based on their personal sales figures, and any time they spend helping others instead of selling actually means less money in their paychecks. Which communication is more powerful, management rhetoric or the paycheck?

It is important to determine what norms and customs will resist change. If you have a nine-to-five culture, for example, you may find that it is difficult to build a results-oriented frame of mind throughout the company. If everyone leaves the office when the clock strikes 5 P.M., an employee will have to buck the social system to stay late to complete a project on time. If a culture is one in which everyone avoids conflict, it will take much work to turn passive-aggressive interactions into ones in which people thoroughly discuss and resolve issues. Attempts to resolve conflicts openly will be met with silence and "deer in the headlights" stares as if they don't understand what you are talking about. In other words, the attempt to change a passive-aggressive conflict style will be resisted passive-aggressively.

In terms of organizational structure, managers may find that certain departments may be particularly resistant to change. In one insurance company, for example, management wanted their underwriters to play a much more active role in the sales process. Because of their own self-perceived weakness in the competencies of influence and relationship building, the underwriters felt threatened and resistant to the change in their role.

It is important not to minimize the role particular individuals can play in leading the resistance to changing the corporate culture. In one of our client's plants, for example, the operations manager, occupying the second most powerful position in the plant, openly expressed cynicism about the company's desire to change its culture. He had a reputation for disparaging the company's senior management team, and told other employees that all management cared about was getting as much work out of them as possible. It was clear that if the culture of the plant was going to change, its operations manager was going to have to change as well. Because he was one of the best engineers in the company, the company decided to devote resources to help change his attitude. A senior manager began developing a deeper relationship with him, and through this contact the engineer began to change.

Though many elements of a culture can resist change, as illustrated in the preceding examples, many organizations have elements of culture that will support it as well. A company that prides itself on innovation, for example, will be more likely to embrace change than a company that sticks to tradition. A company that prides itself on being on the leading edge of its industry will be more open to change if it is necessary to remaining the industry leader.

To generalize from this example, when change is perceived as supporting key values of the organization, it will be easier to obtain support for it. If employees are committed to high quality, a change process designed to increase quality will probably be supported by many of the employees. If serving customers has primary importance, change resulting in better service will likely obtain significant support.

This chapter presented the first stages of a culture change process, those that relate to analyzing and understanding the current corporate culture. This analysis is important, because many elements of the culture can be utilized as tools to help transform it—mission and vision, corporate communications, compensation, hiring and promotion practices, and performance management and development.

Creating Your Own Culture of Competence: Chapter 3—Exercises

EXERCISE 1—USING COMPETENCIES TO ANALYZE YOUR CULTURE

Culture can be studied in terms of organizational structure, belief systems, social status, socioeconomics, and so on. For our purposes, however, we are interested in how culture relates to competence. As stated earlier, Metamorphics has developed a methodology and a tool called CultureScope for analyzing corporate culture using behavioral competencies as a diagnostic tool. This approach allows us to directly link corporate culture with individual competencies, the result of which is an easy translation from one to the other. CultureScope is an employee survey instrument that reveals a depth of corporate-wide competency information that to a large extent defines the corporate culture. Try this simplified version of the instrument to analyze your corporate culture by filling out the worksheets in Figure 3.1.

INSTRUCTIONS PART 1:

Study the list of 24 elements of culture and their definitions. Think about how much of a strength each element is in your organization. Give your organization a grade of **A** for the **SIX AND ONLY SIX** cultural elements that it is the strongest in. Give your organization a **B** for six elements that your organization is moderately strong in. Give your organization a **C** for the six elements that it is less strong in, and a **D** for the weakest elements. **USE EACH LETTER ONLY SIX TIMES.** To help yourself keep track, cross off the letters at the top of the box as you use them. Write the grade in the blanks on the left. Notice that there are four sections.

A A A A A A	B B B B B B	C C C C C	D D D D D

Relationship Competencies	**Employees in our company:**
____Teamwork	Work together with others and help others to work cooperatively to accomplish objectives.
____Conflict Resolution	Use a variety of approaches to manage and resolve concerns, disagreements, and conflicts.
____Attention to Communication	Deliver clear, effective communication and take responsibility to understand others.
____Interpersonal Awareness	Elicit, notice, interpret, and anticipate others' concerns and feelings.
____Cross-Cultural Sensitivity	Use an understanding of cultural differences to communicate, influence, and manage.
____Organizational Savvy	Understand and utilize organizational dynamics to achieve objectives.

Figure 3.1   Exercise: Using competencies to analyze your culture.

Task Achievement Competencies	Employees in our company:
____Flexibility	Respond quickly to change and easily consider new approaches.
____Results Orientation	Focus on desired results, and set and achieve challenging goals.
____Innovation	Foster and initiate new ideas, methods, and solutions.
____Initiative	Proactively identify and act on problems and opportunities.
____Managing Performance	Monitor and evaluate performance against goals and make adjustments to achieve goals.
____Concern for Quality	Monitor work, systems, and processes and take action to ensure they meet or exceed standards.

Personal Attribute Competencies	Employees in our company:
____Integrity and Truth	Gain the trust of others by taking responsibility for own actions and telling the truth.
____Conceptual Thinking	Use concepts and theories to find similarities and put ideas together in new ways to solve problems, innovate, and better communicate.
____Self-Development	Take steps to ensure continued learning and professional growth.
____Service Orientation	Commit to satisfying internal and external customers.
____Continuous Improvement	Identify and implement ways to make job tasks or processes more efficient.
____Stress Management	Maintain performance and self-control under pressure.

Leadership Competencies	Managers in our company:
____Developing Others	Use a variety of approaches to help others develop their capabilities.
____Strategic Thinking	Use an understanding of competitive position to develop both short- and long-term strategy.
____Visionary Leadership	Develop, articulate, and implement a vision that leads the company toward its mission.
____Decisiveness	Make decisions in a timely manner.
____Establishing Focus	Align people and allocate resources consistent with organizational objectives.
____Motivating Others	Enhance others' commitment to their work.

Figure 3.1   (Continued)

INSTRUCTIONS PART 2:

Now record your grades in the table. The columns refer to four categories of culture: relationship, task achievement, personal attribute, and leadership. Write the names of the cultural elements from **PART I** under the appropriate column heading, and in the row of the grade you gave them. For example, if you gave the element **Stress Management** a **C**, you would write **"Stress Management"** in the third column (**Personal Attributes**) and the third row (**C**). Make sure that each column has only six elements in total.

	Relationship	Task Achievement	Personal Attribute	Leadership
A				
B				
C				
D				

Figure 3.1   *(Continued)*

Here are some questions to ask yourself following completion of the corporate culture worksheets:

- In which competency categories is your organization strongest?
- In which competency categories is your organization weakest?
- In what areas do your cultural strengths provide the most benefit to the organization?
- In what areas do your cultural weaknesses cause the most harm to the organization?

CHAPTER

4

The Role of Leadership

The important role leaders play in guiding organizations to achieve their highest potential and fulfill their missions—creating a culture of competence—has been proven over and over again. Leadership involves a complex set of capabilities that includes the ability to organize, analyze, conceptualize, plan, teach, train, strategize, evaluate, problem-solve, prioritize, affirm, reprimand, decide, heal, inspire, and even love. Each of these capabilities relates to one or more of the behavioral competencies described in Chapter 2. In this chapter we will discuss the key principles, functions, and competencies that determine the quality and effectiveness of leadership.

Metamorphics has developed a competency-based selection and evaluation process for the Chicago public school system. As a result of school reform, each school has an elected local school council, comprised mostly of parents and community members, that hires and evaluates the principal. Through this project, in some of the most difficult and disadvantaged neighborhoods in our country, we met principals who demonstrate what a person can achieve with the right position and the right competencies.

Dr. Gladys Jones became principal at a predominantly African-American elementary school in Chicago with all the problems of inner city

81

schools: low test scores, poor graduation rates, student hopelessness, and so on. Seven years later, banners are displayed in the neighborhood, proclaiming the school's commitment to global technology. Test scores have dramatically improved, and every student is taking English, Spanish, and Japanese.

Another principal, Kathleen Mayor, took over a school eight years ago that had been converted from a high school to an elementary school to relieve overcrowding. The school was opened with two days' notice and no books, little furniture, an average classroom size of 42 students, and demonstrations by parents in front of the school protesting their children's assignment there. During the first two weeks Kathleen drove her station wagon from school to school, begging for books, school supplies, and furniture. During jury duty two weeks later, she convinced a fellow juror who worked for a paper company to donate a truckload of paper to her school. Her initial school vision was simple: to have the school be a place where parents strive to enroll their children.

Kathleen built the school step-by-step, begging and borrowing and enlisting support from every place she could. Last year the school finally got a new building. Test scores have risen dramatically. Her original vision is today's reality: Parents campaign to get their children in the school. When President Bill Clinton came to Chicago to publicize the case for investment in education, her school was the one he visited to showcase what is possible in school reform.

Stories from corporate America also abound, and provide their own kind of inspiration. The U.S. subsidiary of one of the top British merchant banks was losing $3 million per year. A new general manager took over the operation, and three years later it was *earning* $3 million per year, with a workforce of happier, more satisfied, developing employees. These kinds of stories can be found throughout the world of business.

Leaders make a difference. In Chicago schools, they make the difference between lives of hope and lives of despair. In the world of business, they play a key role determining corporate culture and organizational success. Today almost every organization needs to hire the best possible leaders to help it succeed in this time of increasing competition and challenges. The ability of the organization to live its mission and values depends on the ability of its leaders to develop and execute the strategic plan. The cost of having ineffective leaders at the senior management level is great, in terms of missed opportunities, lost revenue, increased turnover, lower employee morale, and poor organizational alignment.

The critical elements of leadership that lead to or interfere with creating a culture of competence include:

- The motives for leadership.
- The principles of leadership.
- The functions of leadership.
- The competencies of leadership.
- The relationship between organizational needs and leadership competency.
- Leader as change agent.
- Leader as parent: dealing with authority issues.
- The need for personal development.
- Self-care for leaders.

The Motives for Leadership

THE NATURAL DESIRE TO LEAD

Many factors make up the motivation to take leadership, some of which lead toward effective leadership and some of which interfere with it. One universal positive element is the innate desire to take charge of the environment so that one's needs are met. If a baby is hungry and sees food, the baby will reach for it. People naturally go for what they want and need, unless going for it is punished to the point that the natural take-charge behavior is replaced with more limited behavior patterns. The environments of home and school frequently train children to do what they are told, not to disrupt, not to speak their minds, not to organize others, not to try to change things they don't like—in other words, not to lead.

People take leadership every day in many venues based on their desire to have workable lives. They do so with their children and spouses, at PTA meetings, while arranging social events, and in the course of doing their jobs. The natural desire to take charge and have things right is one of the best sources of motivation that we can draw on to encourage others to take more leadership. "You want things to be right—make it happen!" This invitation is sufficient to initiate leadership behavior in many people.

INSTILLED EXPECTATIONS

Why is it that so many CEOs and other leaders were the eldest child in their families? Once younger siblings join the family, the eldest is expected to take responsibility for their care and safety. This expectation of responsibility and leadership becomes internalized and a part of their self-image. As a result, many firstborn children often go through life expecting to take responsibility, and tend to assume leadership in situations with greater frequency than others.

Each family is unique and has its own particular set of values and beliefs. If those beliefs include responsibility and leadership, and the children don't reject the values in their acts of rebellion, they will be more likely to take on those beliefs as their own. This may explain why we see several generations taking positions of leadership in many families—doing so is a part of the family culture, its set of customs and beliefs that are passed on from generation to generation.

THE IMPORTANCE OF MOTIVATION

Understanding motivation is important when hiring, managing, and developing leaders. It will tell you where you need to be especially alert regarding their performance, and where they may need assistance and coaching. Leaders' needs for affirmation are only a problem if they cause poor judgment or their actions adversely affect the organization. These problems can often be managed if they are addressed directly.

It is also important for leaders to be aware and conscious of their own motivations. There is nothing wrong with having a need to be affirmed, or having a drive for financial security. There is every reason, however, for leaders to be aware of their needs and stay conscious to how they tend to influence their decisions and actions. By remaining aware of their needs, leaders can choose how those needs are met, rather than having their needs unconsciously control their choices.

The Principles of Leadership

There are several principles that underlie the role of leadership and transcend leadership style and function. Other things being equal, leaders who act in accordance with these principles will be more effective than those who do not.

THE PRINCIPLE OF INTENTION

We get what we intend. Intention is the principle by which people assert their will and create their experience based on their wants and desires. Intention takes two forms, reactivity and assertion. In reactivity, people react to the world around them. Reactivity is essentially negative in nature, and involves words or behavior that directly or indirectly says, "No." With assertion, people act on the world out of desire. Assertion is the positive expression of intention.

Intention is the principle behind the statement "I want . . . ," and the expression of will is its ultimate conclusion. What happens in people's lives is an expression of their will, either consciously or unconsciously. To the extent that people can operate from intention, they can assert their wills fully, accept logical consequences, and adapt their behavior while maintaining a sense that their experience in life is a result of their authorship or creation.

Effective leadership occurs when people operate with intention, asserting their wills to create the world as they desire it to be. To the extent that the motivations and actions of leaders are based on reactivity, their power to create positive change and results is diminished.

THE PRINCIPLE OF RESPONSIBILITY

The principle of responsibility is centered on the premise that people in every moment create and author their own reality. At every point we are free to choose one of two viewpoints—that we are victims to forces beyond our control, or that we shape our world by our actions. Both points of view are valid, but they lead to quite different conclusions. Victimhood leads to inaction, passivity, and complaints, because we are the acted-upon rather than the actors. From the principle of responsibility, in contrast, we see the world as a source to learn about our intentions and ourselves, for we have created what we intended. We take responsibility for the gaps between our vision and the reality we have created, and take action to narrow those gaps.

As author of our own reality, we are each responsible for everything. We are each responsible for every employee's success in the organization, for the successful delivery of the organization's products and services, and for the fulfillment of the organization's purpose. Any other perspective implies that we are not authors of our own realities.

It is from the perspective of responsibility that the greatest change occurs. Even if something happens that is 1 percent within my control and 99 percent outside my control, by focusing on how I determined the outcome, I am more likely to change results in the future than if I focus on the aspects of the event for which I could make no difference.

Leadership derives from responsibility and authorship. To the degree that victimhood is the chosen existential point of view, a leader's effectiveness will be diminished.

THE PRINCIPLE OF SERVICE

The principle of service is the foundation of all leadership activity. Leadership exists to serve the interests of more people than just the leader—it must serve a higher purpose. The higher purpose may be to win the basketball game, or it may be to improve the quality of education in the country, or it may be to reduce waste in the manufacturing process. It may be to improve the financial well-being of the shareholders, or to increase people's sense of connection with God. Whatever the particular purpose, it is larger than the individual leader. There is no greater source of satisfaction (in my opinion) than serving others and serving the greater good. The great world leaders have all led from the principle of service to others.

We can always orient ourselves toward service and set individual standards based on this principle. There are several key questions that can always be asked:

- Whom am I serving?
- How well am I serving?
- How can I serve better?
- How can I help others serve better?

Focusing on the answers to these questions will usually orient leaders toward decisions and actions that will benefit the group. The principle of service helps leaders keep their eye on the key question: "What is my job here?" The tendency to focus on self-interest and personal needs is balanced by the focus on whom and how well one is serving.

Service is an easier principle to orient others around than either intention or responsibility. The concept of service is rooted in the Judeo-Christian foundation of western civilization, and is a part of almost everyone's espoused value system. Focusing on service is one of the best ways to align a group around a common purpose or objective. In general, employees can find it within themselves to *want* customers to be served well. Managers can find it within themselves to *want* to serve their subordinates and their bosses.

What Is the Job? The Functions and Competencies of Leadership

Few people are formally trained to take on leadership. The job typically goes to those with the motivation and the leadership competencies required for being marginally effective. Just as employees and managers find it useful to have job descriptions to define the responsibilities and accountabilities for positions, it is helpful to establish the functions in the job of a leader. Articulating the critical functions of a leadership role along with associated leadership competencies can put leaders in a better position to examine the gaps between their current behavior and what they need to be able to do to guide the organization to higher levels of performance. The purpose of this chapter is to identify the critical leadership functions and to demonstrate the power of competencies in defining those functions as well as a framework for leadership in your organization. Table 4.1 shows the relationship between key leadership functions and the competencies associated with them.

MODELING THE CORPORATE CULTURE

Leaders model the corporate culture anew every day by what they do. The behavior they exhibit, the policies they draft, the emotions they express or suppress, the results they focus on or ignore, the commitment they display, the attitudes they communicate, and the values they live by all affect the attitudes and behavior of the organization. They create the culture by both their conscious and unconscious acts and decisions. It is daunting and humbling for people in leadership positions to realize how their behavior helps create their culture regardless of whether they intend it to do so.

I visited a manufacturing plant several years ago and met with the plant supervisors, who complained about how horrible it was to work for the plant manager. One of their biggest complaints was that the plant manager and his wife fought frequently, both at home and while he was at work. He would come to the office in a bad mood every morning. After speaking with his wife on the telephone he was always upset. After the call, he would immediately go through the plant and criticize every little thing he saw that wasn't perfect. The corporate culture the plant manager created was significantly influenced by his marital troubles and the difficulty he had keeping them from affecting his emotional state at work.

Leaders create their cultures whether they want to or not. Understanding how culture creation works, leaders can use their words and actions to

Table 4.1   The functions of leadership and their critical competencies.

Functions	Critical Competencies
1. Modeling the corporate culture	Every competency
2. Developing the corporate philosophy	Visionary leadership; change management; integrity and truth; Purpose, principles, and values; attention to communication; influence; building organizational commitment; teamwork; conceptual thinking
3. Establishing and maintaining standards	Integrity and truth, managing performance, concern for quality
4. Understanding the business	Analytical thinking, entrepreneurial orientation, strategic thinking
5. Determining strategic direction	Strategic thinking, analytical thinking, decision quality
6. Managing change	Change management, influence, decision quality, attention to communication, integrity and truth, building organizational commitment
7. Being a good follower: aligning with superiors	Conflict resolution; interpersonal awareness; service orientation; teamwork; integrity and truth; purpose, principles, and values
8. Developing workforce potential	Interpersonal awareness, developing others, empowering others, analytical thinking, concern for quality, decisiveness, managing performance
9. Inspiring and motivating	Motivating others; visionary leadership; purpose, principles, and values; building organizational commitment
10. Establishing alignment	Establishing focus, teamwork
11. Establishing focus	Establishing focus, managing performance
12. Holding ultimate responsibility	Managing performance, integrity and truth, results orientation, initiative
13. Dealing with authority issues	Conflict resolution, interpersonal awareness, integrity and truth
14. Determining successors	Decision quality, results orientation, managing performance, developing others
15. Managing ambiguity	Stress management, change management, analytical thinking, decisiveness
16. Optimizing organizational structure and process	Analytical thinking, change management, influence, managing performance

shape the culture consciously, rather than doing it unconsciously as in the previous example.

For modeling the corporate culture, every competency is relevant.

DEVELOPING THE CORPORATE PHILOSOPHY— MISSION, VISION, AND VALUES

It is the job of leaders to establish the corporate philosophy and make it the breathing, dynamic core of the organization's belief system. Corporate philosophy is a tool that leaders can use to their benefit or detriment. Like corporate culture, philosophy exists apart from its conscious creation. If leaders don't create it consciously, the philosophy will be created based solely on the observed behavior and the operating values underlying it. If a manufacturing company has problems with quality that are consistently overlooked by its leaders, the operating value that quality doesn't matter will guide employee behavior.

For developing corporate philosophy, critical competencies include visionary leadership; change management; integrity and truth; purpose; principles, and values; attention to communication; influence; building organizational commitment; teamwork; and conceptual thinking.

ESTABLISHING AND MAINTAINING STANDARDS

Leaders communicate their standards of what is acceptable and what is not every day. Like corporate philosophy, standards are often not consciously defined or openly verbalized, and are in those cases defined by the actions that leaders take and don't take in response to circumstances.

Historically, the word "standard" refers to an emblem or flag on a pole that an army used as the rallying point in battle. The troops could always see where the standard was and use it to become oriented on the battlefield. Today, standards play the same role in a different context. They provide an organizational rallying point and a means of measuring behavior against a quantitative or qualitative value.

Standards can be both personal and organizational. For example, several years ago I developed a personal standard that in every work contact, whether in person or on the telephone, I would serve the person in some way. I could serve in many different ways: I could be friendly and help others feel good, give them feedback that they might not get elsewhere, or offer my perspective and counsel. I do not always meet this standard, but I use it to evaluate my behavior and modify it so that I measure up more frequently.

By the nature of how authority works, employees naturally orient to the standards of their leaders. Low standards lead to low performance, and high standards lead to high performance. Leaders all have standards, although most of these remain below the level of awareness. Nevertheless, what bothers leaders and what doesn't is noticed by employees, and they respond accordingly.

A simple example of a common problem in many companies is that meetings start late. People who arrive on time for meetings wait for others, and soon learn that they should arrive late also if they want to use their time efficiently. One CEO I know changed meeting behavior in his company with a simple standard: All meetings he attended would start on time no matter what. When I first attended a meeting of the management committee, I was three minutes late. You can imagine how I felt when I walked into the conference room and everyone else was present and the meeting underway. I was never again late for one of their meetings. The CEO's standard set the norm for the organization.

For establishing and maintaining standards, key competencies include integrity and truth, managing performance, and concern for quality.

UNDERSTANDING THE BUSINESS

Leaders need to understand how their organizations function. They need to be able to answer some basic questions:

- What is our purpose?
- Who are our customers?
- What customer needs are we satisfying?
- How are those needs changing?
- What is our core capability?
- What is our business model?
- What are our strengths and weaknesses?
- What differentiates us from our competitors?
- Which leaders are effective and which are not?
- What are the key elements (market, sales and distribution, human resources, products and services) that determine organizational success or failure?
- What current and future trends in the industry might affect our business?
- What is our market strategy in response to those changes?

- How does our organization work from a financial perspective?
- What are our costs?
- What is working well and what is working poorly?

There aren't always easy and immediate answers to these questions. What is key is that leaders need to understand their organizations so they can act in its best interests, whether that be responding to competitive pressures, taking advantage of opportunities to expand into new markets, or developing innovative products and services. Equally important is the leader's ability to explain the rationale for business decisions and strategies to gain employee commitment to the changes and risks that often come along with doing business in a competitive marketplace. Another benefit of communicating the business purpose for decisions is that employees armed with that knowledge can begin to make similar decisions in their day-to-day work.

For understanding of the business, critical competencies include analytical thinking, entrepreneurial orientation, and strategic thinking.

DETERMINING STRATEGIC DIRECTION

Leaders chart the course for the organization. It is their job to identify relevant trends and organizational strengths and weaknesses, to analyze resources, and to determine organizational strategy. (It is not exclusively their responsibility, of course.) Employees look to their leaders to set the strategy and communicate it to them. They want to know that they are in good hands, and that the people running the ship know what they are doing.

The ability to accurately assess the situation and come up with appropriate pathways is not a simple skill. It is often not an easy one to learn. It requires a broad range of experiences, wisdom, and judgment, and an understanding of the relationship between cause and effect in extremely complex situations. It involves the ability to understand and utilize the concept of leverage, whereby leaders determine which actions will have the greatest positive effect. It involves an understanding of the importance of staying the course, and knowing when to stick to a strategy and when to abandon it.

Many CEOs are successful leaders without strong strategic leadership skills, particularly in situations in which a change in strategic direction is not necessary. This is often the case with second- and third-generation family members running the family business, who do a fine job so long as the basic dynamics of the business don't change. When the competitive landscape changes or when new environmental circumstances come into play, their ability to respond effectively is often limited. Do not assume that just because a leader was able to navigate through one set of circumstances successfully that he or she will be successful doing it under a different set of circumstances. The best leaders can do so, but in my experience such leaders are rare.

For determining strategic direction, key competencies include strategic thinking, analytical thinking, and decision quality.

MANAGING CHANGE

Managing change is a subset of strategic leadership, and represents the internal side of strategy. It involves understanding how the organization needs to change, and developing and implementing the plan to do so. It requires long-range perspective, strong influence skills, and a commander in chief's understanding of how to wage a war. Leaders need to develop allies, create communication strategies, develop campaigns, choose their battles, and consolidate gains.

Effective change leaders know they can't change everything at once. Change usually occurs through a series of incremental steps, few of which are by themselves revolutionary. From each step you take the next one leading you toward your ultimate destination. You choose different issues at different times, develop allies for the occasion, and develop policies that meet the particular need at the particular time.

A CEO took over a manufacturing company in West Virginia that had been marginally profitable for years. It had a unionized, aging workforce with a rigid management team and out-of-date manufacturing practices. One of his first actions was to take the vice president of manufacturing, who had been promoted into the job from purchasing (with no manufacturing experience), and give him a new job in charge of customer service. Customer service was not the right job for him, either; however, the CEO knew that he could get by with a weak customer service manager, but he definitely needed a strong manufacturing leader. Next, he offered early retirement to 39 of the workers, with a special inducement of reduced benefit costs to encourage them to accept it. Twenty-one did so in the first round, and he offered it again the next year to encourage more departures.

In addition to personnel changes, the CEO began planning changes in the manufacturing process. He reached out to the plant employees who seemed most progressive and elicited their suggestions. After analyzing the business's problems, he put together a plan that addressed many of the issues, including purchasing, waste, marketing, and sales. He didn't address all the problems at once, of course. Like his personnel policy, he did things in stages, tackling manufacturing and purchasing first, followed by marketing and sales.

For managing change, critical competencies include change management, influence, decision quality, attention to communication, integrity and truth, and building organizational commitment.

BEING A GOOD FOLLOWER: ALIGNING WITH SUPERIORS

It is the job of leaders to align with the person or people to whom they report. For CEOs, it is usually their boards of directors. For other leaders, it is their managers. While the concept of aligning with one's bosses seems to be an obvious responsibility of management, it is a common failing of leaders. Here is an example from one of our clients.

The chief financial officer for a distribution company was bright and aggressive, and had vast knowledge of the business. He capably led each of the business heads through the strategic planning process. He did so well, in fact, that the CEO began to feel as if his leadership role was being usurped. Important decisions were being made without his consultation, and he noticed that at senior management meetings the CFO was asking questions in a way that implied that the CEO didn't really understand what was happening in the business. The CEO went through some self-examination to see whether he was having trouble relinquishing control, or whether his CFO was really acting in bad faith.

It was through the secretary of one of the business heads that the CEO discovered that the CFO was openly subverting his authority and disparaging him to the business heads behind his back, accusing him of mismanagement and ineptitude. He made fun of the CEO, and communicated that he believed that he was smarter, possessed more savvy, and was a much better businessman than the CEO. After some soul-searching and a thorough investigation, the CEO terminated the CFO. After the CFO departed, the CEO discovered the extent of the damage the CFO had caused. While pursuing his leadership endeavors in the company, the CFO had disregarded his own department. Receivables had grown considerably, information technology (IT) projects were behind schedule, and most of the accounting staff were on the verge of quitting.

True alignment with superiors includes the following behaviors:

- *Communicating transparently.* Whatever your superiors need to know to do their jobs effectively, they know. Both good and bad news is shared as soon as is appropriate. They are kept informed of important developments so they can plan and take action accordingly. Any surprises to them are surprises to you also.

• *Owning their mission.* What they care about, you care about. What matters to them matters to you. If you do not understand why something is important to them, you ask them. You use the words "we" and "our" with respect to their agendas, both with them and with others. You act as if your best interest and their best interest were identical.

• *Committing to their success.* You contribute in any way you can to their success. You give them helpful feedback, you make suggestions, you identify problems and difficulties, and you carry your share of the load.

• *Compensating for their weaknesses.* Understanding their strengths and weaknesses, you know where they tend to fall down and what their blind spots are. Knowing this, you ensure that those areas are well covered by yourself or others, so that their weaknesses don't hurt either them or the organization.

• *Responding to attacks.* As we will discuss shortly, most attacks on leaders are rooted in childhood authority issues and produce much more damage than positive benefit. (By attack we refer to defamation of people's character or abilities, not disagreements with their policies, decisions, or actions.) The most effective attacks are those that strike at the places where leaders are most vulnerable and least likely to defend themselves well. Your job as follower is to defend them against attacks, and if at all possible to stop the attacks from occurring. No organization with a corporate culture that tolerates attacks on leaders will flourish anywhere near its potential.

• *Maintaining a higher vision for them.* You see them not just as they are but how they can be. You share your vision of them with them, and encourage them to stretch themselves toward that vision.

• *Communicating honestly.* You take the risk to tell them the truth as you see it, knowing that the truth will best serve the organization, them, and yourself in the long run.

• *Communicating respect and appreciation.* You let them know what you value in them, including their personal traits, values, skills, and behaviors.

• *Helping them tend wounds.* Strong leaders take risks, and people who take risks get hurt sometimes. Your job as a follower is to help them tend to their wounds, then help them get back on the horse again to go back into the fray. If wounds are not tended to, they interfere with effective functioning. We will discuss this further later in this chapter.

• *Serving them to your highest ability.* The principle of service applies fully to supporting your leaders to accomplish their missions. The job of the

CEO is to serve the board. The job of the CFO is to serve the CEO and the board to help the organization achieve its purpose and its objectives. This applies to every position at every level.

• *Clearing up any upset feelings.* You will be upset with your superiors at times, feel unacknowledged and unappreciated. It is your job to deal with your feelings and clear them out so that you can relate and interact in the ways that will best serve the organization. If you harbor those feelings, they will usually end up hurting someone—you, your superior, your employees, or your customers.

Leaders who cannot follow others will not reach their highest calling or have the greatest impact on the organization that they are capable of, because the reasons they don't follow well are the very same reasons they are unable to effectively lead.

For being a good follower and aligning successfully with superiors, critical competencies include conflict resolution; interpersonal awareness; service orientation; teamwork; integrity and truth; and purpose, principles, and values.

DEVELOPING WORKFORCE POTENTIAL

In the past the responsibility for managing the organization's investment in human capital has often been left to the human resources department. Given low unemployment levels, changing demographics, shorter employment cycles, less employee loyalty, and work that requires a more educated workforce, leaders are increasingly being held accountable to be more involved throughout the entire employment cycle, from hiring to retiring. A leader's success today is contingent upon the ability to select, evaluate, place, empower, and retain a team of individuals who can execute strategy and plans to ensure growth, profitability, and competitiveness. It also requires knowing the right time to terminate employees when they are no longer serving themselves or the organization. More specifically, this set of skills includes:

• *Selecting.* Leaders need to hire the right people. They have to know what they require, find qualified candidates, attract them, assess them accurately, make the best choice, negotiate terms, and successfully close the deal.

• *Evaluating.* They need to accurately assess the capabilities and potentials of their subordinates. This includes understanding subordinates' proficiency on important competencies, skill strengths and deficits, personalities, emotional barriers, career aspirations, motivations, emotional needs, effectiveness, and potential. Through this understanding leaders make the best use of their resources.

• *Developing.* Leaders use their ability to accurately assess subordinates' strengths and weaknesses to improve their competence and their performance. A leader not only analyzes subordinates' performance; a leader helps them to identify the root cause of their performance difficulties and works with the employees to generate effective, cost-efficient solutions. A leader thinks about career opportunities that may help people develop their competencies and their skills, and provides ongoing feedback to let people know how they are doing and how the leader wants them to improve.

• *Placing.* Leaders put the right people in the right jobs. They also look for special projects or temporary assignments within the organization to leverage employees' talents, maximize their contribution to the organization, and ensure they have development opportunities. Placement requires an understanding of the subordinate and the organization, as well as the ability to communicate and influence people in a way that benefits the organization, the leader, and the individual.

• *Empowering.* Leaders give as much responsibility to their subordinates as they can handle, and frequently reevaluate whether they can handle more. They expect their subordinates to make mistakes as they take risks to stretch themselves, and they use mistakes as learning opportunities to further their growth. They are thoughtful regarding the responsibility they delegate, and manage the risk to ensure that mistakes do not result in excessive damage to the organization.

• *Retaining.* Leaders make sure that valued subordinates stay in the organization. They serve their subordinates well and do their best to ensure that their personal and professional needs are met in the organization, including those for recognition, challenge, compensation, career opportunity, and growth and development.

• *Terminating.* Leaders continually weigh a complex set of factors to determine whether or when it is appropriate to terminate a subordinate. This includes a consideration of the following questions:

• What level of performance do we need for the job?
• What is the extent of the gap between the employee's current performance and what is required for successful job performance?
• What are the barriers to the employee performing adequately?
• What can be done and at what cost to overcome those barriers?
• How much of the problem is caused by others and not the employee?

- What can be changed to make the employee sufficiently effective?
- How much will in cost in time, money, lost opportunity, and so on to improve the employee? Is it worth the investment?
- Is there another job that the employee would do well at?

If the answer to these questions leads to termination, leaders handle the termination in a way that maintains the highest level of goodwill possible, is honest and open, and serves the employee to help him or her become more successful in the future.

For developing workforce potential, critical competencies include interpersonal awareness, developing others, empowering others, analytical thinking, concern for quality, decisiveness, and managing performance.

INSPIRING AND MOTIVATING

Leaders inspire and motivate their organizations. They help make it fun for employees to get up and go to work in the morning. They accomplish this in different ways and different styles. Some use mission and vision to motivate their workforce. Others use pep talks—"Win one for the Gipper!" Others use the desire to win—"We want to be number one in our industry." Others use camaraderie and the sense of belonging—"Do it the P&G way." I know one female senior executive who became the "mom" of her company, motivating employees with her warmth and emotional acceptance of them. They loved working there and would do anything for her.

When circumstances turn adverse and the organization is in crisis, inspiration and motivation usually require a different tone. Take Winston Churchill's speech to the House of Commons on June 18, 1940, at a time when England was facing its darkest moment during World War II. In the summer of 1940 German Nazism was flush from a string of victories and seemed invincible. Britain stood without allies, and invasion seemed imminent:

> *The Battle of Britain is about to begin. Upon this battle depends the survival of Christian civilization. Upon it depends our own British life, and the long continuity of our institutions and our Empire. The whole fury and might of the enemy must very soon be turned on us. Hitler knows that he will have to break us in this Island or lose the war. If we can stand up to him, all Europe may be free and the life of the world may move forward into broad, sunlit uplands. But if we fail, then the whole world, including the United States, including all that we have known and cared for,*

will sink into the abyss of a new Dark Age made more sinister, and perhaps more protracted, by the lights of perverted science. Let us therefore brace ourselves to our duties, and so bear ourselves that, if the British Empire and its Commonwealth last for a thousand years, men will still say, "This was their finest hour."

Employees working for troubled companies need frequent reassurance and encouragement in order for them to stay motivated and engaged in their jobs. In fact, a loss of employee confidence is sometimes sufficient to push an organization over the edge into bankruptcy.

For inspiring and motivating others, critical competencies are motivating others; visionary leadership; purpose, principles, and values; and building organizational commitment.

ESTABLISHING ALIGNMENT

It is the leaders' job to align the organization around common goals and objectives. They are tireless in their efforts to reinforce how the duties and responsibilities of each individual, unit, and department relate to the organization's overall goals and objectives.

Leaders also deal with nonalignment where it exists by allocating resources and establishing priorities to ensure that organizational activity supports business objectives. People know where the organization is going, they know their role in helping the organization get there, and they are provided the resources they need to play their part.

To develop the leadership role of establishing alignment, consider these critical competencies: establishing focus and teamwork.

ESTABLISHING FOCUS

Similar to establishing alignment, establishing focus refers to ensuring that the organization keeps its "eyes on the prize." The leader concentrates attention on the initiatives that will have the greatest impact on the organization's ability to achieve its key objectives. Critical questions that leaders need to be asking to ensure that employees are focused include: "What is the most important objective?" "What most needs to be done?" "Where should we be concentrating our resources?"

As with establishing alignment, communication and persuasion are key elements of this leadership function. Everyone in the organization needs to know and accept the organizational priorities and objectives as their own, and then take the initiative to execute them on that basis.

For establishing focus, critical competencies include establishing focus and managing performance.

HOLDING ULTIMATE RESPONSIBILITY

Leaders have the job of holding ultimate responsibility for the success of the entity they lead. This concept is epitomized by the saying "The buck stops here." Ultimate responsibility is most often associated with the position of CEO, whose job by definition is to take complete responsibility for the success of the organization. In most cases, however, responsibility for sales often resides with the highest officer in charge of sales and responsibility for a manufacturing plant resides with the plant manager.

Responsibility is a confusing and distressing word for many people, conjuring up unpleasant images and emotions. Look at some of its synonyms: "burden," "obligation," "duty," "load," "onus," and "liability." Who would want to take responsibility? No wonder we can't find enough leaders!

Earlier we discussed the importance of the principle of responsibility to leadership, using authorship as the foundation of responsibility. Each of us creates or authors our own reality. We are each responsible for our actions and the results we create. To the extent that we acknowledge and accept this axiom, we take ownership of our activity and expect to be accountable for our actions and the results that follow from them. We see and acknowledge the gaps between our ideals and the current reality, and develop and execute a plan to reduce the gaps. The contrasting position is that of victimhood. Instead of being actors we are the "acted-upon," the pawns subject to the whims of forces beyond our control and influence. This perspective robs leaders of their effectiveness.

Ownership, authority, responsibility, and accountability are inherent aspects of human nature. In fact, in many situations it is difficult to imagine true joy and satisfaction without them. What joy is there in winning a race or being on a winning team if you have no responsibility for and didn't at all author the result?

Leaders own the results of the entity they lead. They take steps to understand and assess the current reality of the entity. They establish a vision of their ideal or goal state, and develop pathways to get from here to there. They monitor and measure the entity's progress toward their vision or goal, and continually examine their strategy and tactics to see what does and does not work. They apply that learning and revise their plans accordingly.

Responsibility and ownership are not exclusive domains of the formal leader. It is possible for employees at all levels and in any position to take complete responsibility for the success of an endeavor. In fact, it is the only logical position that leads to successful attainment of goals and desires. Let's illustrate this with a stark example:

Imagine you are a member of a platoon in a jungle where the enemy might attack at any moment. You are not the platoon leader, and have no leadership responsibility. The survival of the platoon depends on every member; a lapse in attention of the part of anyone could result in the death of everyone. In this situation, suppose you see that the soldier guarding the platoon's right flank is daydreaming and not paying sufficient attention to his job. What do you do? Do you say to yourself, "It's not my job to get him to pay attention; it's the sergeant's job," or do you do whatever it takes to keep you all alive? Every soldier who has faced this situation knows what it means for *everyone* to take complete responsibility for the success of the group.

The more people taking responsibility for the success of the group, the greater the likelihood of its success. Any person can at any time make the decision to assume ultimate responsibility for the group or the initiative. Those who make that decision will lead from whatever position they inhabit.

For holding ultimate responsibility, critical competencies are managing performance, integrity and truth, results orientation, and initiative.

DEALING WITH AUTHORITY ISSUES

While it is natural for every person to take responsibility for the success of the whole organization, most people don't. Some of the biggest obstacles for many employees are the feelings they have about their leaders and their personal issues and behavior patterns related to authority figures. Leaders need to be alert to the fact that employees may interact with them in much the same way they related to their parents or other authority figures from their early childhood. Feelings of resentment, isolation, rebellion, or passive-aggressive behavior can often come to play in the workplace as the boss takes on the role of a parent figure and employees take on the role of children in responding to decisions, challenges, or conflict.

One company had a management team that demonstrated this kind of dysfunction. The heads of all the business functions including sales, manufacturing, engineering, research and development, and finance expressed loathing for the CEO. In a meeting with several of them, I was told that the CEO consistently made unreasonable demands and would scream and yell in response to problems. They felt the company would be better off without a CEO. They said that they were a great team who worked smoothly together to get things done. The only problem with the team was its leader, the CEO.

The CEO told a different story. The management team avoided conflict and accountability like the plague. If the CEO didn't point out organizational problems, they would never be mentioned. If he didn't insist that the budget be completed by a certain date, it would not get done. He saw his management team as a group of managers who couldn't do their jobs fully by themselves, forcing him to push them to do what they needed to do and to hold them accountable for doing it.

During a two-day off-site workshop on teamwork, this dynamic slowly became apparent as it manifested itself in various forms throughout the first day. At the end of the day I shared my observations and feedback with the team. They were operating like a dysfunctional family system in which the dad (the CEO) and the children (the management team) together created a family in which all the accountability resided with dad. The kids did nothing to hold each other accountable, and all the ill feelings and judgments they had toward each other were displaced and misdirected to dad. He was seen as mean, irrational, and uncaring; their world would be a better place without him.

What the management team did not see was that their belief system and their behavior encouraged the CEO to assume the role of the abusive father. By refusing to maintain and hold each other accountable for any standards of performance, they propelled the CEO into the role of disciplinarian. From the CEO's point of view, he *had* to hold the management team's feet to the fire, because they wouldn't do it themselves.

The CEO willingly played his role in cocreating the family dynamic in the management team. He was very comfortable in the role of the martyred leader, who had to ride herd on his irresponsible children to get them to behave. Their dislike of him reaffirmed his beliefs about their irresponsibility and his own victimhood as leader.

While the CEO and the other members of the management team complained about each other, in reality none of them wanted to change the situation enough to do anything about it. What they didn't talk about was the benefit they each received by maintaining the current dysfunctional dynamic. The CEO got to continue feeling superior to his team in competence, and got to maintain a stance of moral superiority as the long-suffering victim of their irresponsibility. He also avoided having to face the really tough job, that of changing the system to one in which all members of the team hold themselves and each other responsible and accountable for the success of the business. Taking that job on would challenge his leadership skills and make him uncomfortable in ways that he would probably find personally risky and threatening.

The benefit the other members of the management team received was that they got all the joy of being passive-aggressive as they watched those around them act out their anger and resentment. They also got to be the morally superior victims, in this case of a dominating tyrant who abused and berated them. They got to live in a make-believe world of good and evil, in which they were good and the CEO was evil.

This kind of dysfunctional management system is found in companies of all shapes and sizes, and demonstrates some of the dynamics of authority at its worst. In this particular situation, no one on the management team took responsibility for their dynamic, and two years later only one of the six members of the team remained. The CEO was replaced, and the rest of the team were either demoted or terminated.

The dynamics of authority need not be played out as though everyone were reliving their childhood relationships with their parents. Learning how to respond to subordinates when they are acting out their authority behavior patterns is a skill that is important for every leader to develop and continually improve. Handled poorly, it can turn a company into an unhealthy breeding ground for gossip, recrimination, and finger-pointing that lowers morale, reduces productivity, and harms everyone.

For managing authority issues, critical competencies include conflict resolution, interpersonal awareness, and integrity and truth.

DETERMINING SUCCESSORS

It is the job of leaders to plan for their succession. Succession planning is a leadership function that few leaders perform without active organizational support, in part because few of us feel secure enough to cheerfully select and develop people to be able to do our jobs better than we do them. Yet that is the job of succession planning. It requires a commitment to the organization's success that transcends our own fears and insecurities regarding our own position in the organization.

A common mistake many leaders make is to designate one person as their successor and decide they have done their job. Then for some reason the person leaves the organization or position and the leader is left with no prospects for replacing himself or herself. A great many small and middle-market businesses are sold or dissolved because their leaders have not ensured that there is at least one other person ready to take the helm.

To be reasonably sure that you will have one successor, you probably need to start with at least three potential successors. One of the most successful strategies is to identify (and hire if necessary) three people who are strong enough to potentially succeed you. Competency assessment is a critical aspect of that determination. Depending on your position, the three candidates could hold the same or different positions. Train and develop all three candidates to become as competent and as successful as possible.

From among the three of them it will usually become evident which will be your best successor, and you will also have backup candidates should something happen to your preferred candidate.

As leaders take responsibility for larger groups with multiple layers and levels of leadership, it is their job to ensure effective succession throughout their unit. The same process described for oneself needs to occur in every leadership position throughout the organization. When every leader is training three successors, you have a dynamic organization and a corporate culture committed to growth and development.

For determining successors, critical competencies are decision quality, results orientation, managing performance, and developing others.

MANAGING AMBIGUITY

A natural consequence of the inherent human desire to learn is the desire to know and understand things. Uncertainty is uncomfortable; not knowing and not understanding are upsetting. Unfortunately, despite our best attempts to understand the present and be able to predict the future, it seems to be inherently unpredictable. Physicists can approximate the average position of an electron, but cannot determine its exact path. Chaos is an inherent aspect of our universe.

It is the job of leaders to think, act, and manage in complex, ambiguous situations. In the complex world in which we live today, we cannot possibly know enough to control everything to our satisfaction. In the world of climatology there is the phenomenon called the butterfly effect, which is the notion that a butterfly flapping its wings in Japan can alter the weather in New York City through the effect of the tiny breeze its wings generate. The impact of a leader's actions can sometimes seem inconsequential in an ever-changing, complex business environment. Yet, it is those small day-to-day efforts that can have a far-reaching impact on the business. The ability to continue to assess a situation, make hypotheses, test assumptions, take a position and abandon it when it is no longer effective, along with the ability to maintain a sense of humor, are all skills to be called upon to manage ambiguity.

One other important facet of managing ambiguity is helping others do the same. Because the desire is so strong in many people to live in a world of black and white where the rules are defined and causes are known, leaders must be able to help others function well in the fluid, constantly changing reality in which we live.

For managing ambiguity, critical competencies are stress management, change management, analytical thinking, and decisiveness.

OPTIMIZING ORGANIZATIONAL STRUCTURE AND PROCESS

Work is accomplished through the organization of people and tools in ways that get things done. How people and equipment are organized helps determine efficiency, quality, and overall effectiveness. One of the functions of leadership is to think about and analyze process, reexamining and reengineering if necessary to make it easier for the organization to do its job.

One major manufacturer I know spent last year in a massive reorganization of the manufacturing operation. Over the course of the prior 50 years, decisions were made based on expediency rather than overall efficiency. If a plant one thousand miles from a customer had capacity and a plant a few miles away had none, the company produced the product in the plant one thousand miles away. While this may have been the right decision at the time, 50 years of expedient decisions resulted in an organization full of inefficiencies that dramatically affected productivity and profitability. When company leaders bit the bullet and embarked on their reengineering effort, they shut down one plant, moved manufacturing lines to plants geographically proximate to their customers, and relocated machines within the plants so that material moved through the manufacturing process efficiently. Thinking about process and organizational structure saved the organization millions of dollars per year.

How people are organized is another element of optimizing structure and process. The issue of centralization versus decentralization is one example of a process and structure issue. There is no right or wrong answer in general to the question of whether to centralize a function. It depends on the particular situation and its unique aspects. Leaders need to examine and analyze the current process, discover what works and what doesn't, and try to determine if a modification of the structure or process would improve it. If so, they then must create and execute a plan to make it happen.

For optimizing organizational structure and process, critical competencies include analytical thinking, change management, influence, and managing performance.

The Relationship between Organizational Needs and Leadership Competency

Theoretically, leaders could have sufficient competence to handle any situation with an equal degree of mastery. In practice, leaders are human beings with strengths and weaknesses, and those strengths and weaknesses make them more effective in some circumstances and less effective in others. By understanding some of the different kinds of needs that organizations face, you can better understand the demands on leaders and the capabilities and competencies they need to successfully lead their organizations.

KEY ORGANIZATIONAL VALUE DRIVERS

Through the work I've done with private equity firms I've learned about the concept of organizational value drivers. Private equity firms typically raise capital from institutional and private investors and create funds through which they invest in businesses. Many funds invest only in companies in which they can obtain a controlling interest, thereby having the ability to control the board and influence policy and leadership to maximize the creation of economic value. Because of the need for a high rate of return, the investment is frequently limited to a time frame of three to seven years. Many private equity firms have the philosophy that their job is to hire the right CEO, and they leave the rest of the job to that individual. Some private equity firms have a more active approach, and try to keep the CEO and the organization focused on the key organizational value drivers. These are the (typically) two or three factors in or elements of the company's situation that will most drive the company's value. They serve as the key points of leverage for improving the company, and are the places where organizational change produces the biggest results per resources invested. Here are a few examples:

- A retailer selling general merchandise with rapidly declining sales over the past several years determined that it had one key value driver: improving its merchandising practices. It needed to do a much better job of finding out what its customers wanted and needed and stocking the store with that merchandise.

- A packaging manufacturer determined that it had three key value drivers: First, it needed to focus on making products that were profitable. Second, it needed to focus its sales and marketing efforts on the high-volume, profitable customers. And third, it needed to reduce the length of the research and development cycle for new products.

- A company selling travel incentive packages to businesses for use in promotion had spent the prior year improving its customer service and information systems. Now the key value driver was sales. With the delivery capability for over twice its current revenue base, the company needed to acquire more reps, develop a more effective sales strategy, and execute it to increase the company's top line.

- A company distributing automobile parts to automobile repair shops recognized that its key value drivers were twofold: First, it needed to consolidate its backroom systems and operations, having recently made several acquisitions in the course of building its company. Second, it needed to use its size in the market to negotiate better terms with suppliers.

Leaders need to understand the key value drivers for their organizations, and put together and execute effective strategies based on that understanding.

ORGANIZATIONAL NEEDS

In addition to key value drivers, organizations have other needs based on their particular situations that require a particular set of skills, competencies, and experiences. Leaders managing the transition from an entrepreneurially run to a professionally managed organization need skills such as operating to a budget, developing policies and procedures, or standardizing processes.

Businesses in other situations also have special leadership needs. Here are some examples:

- *Companies in crisis.* Crisis managers are a unique breed of manager. They need to operate in emotionally stressful situations with resolve and a degree of dispassion that most people would find difficult. Operating in a world where there isn't enough cash, where suppliers have not been paid for months, where employee layoffs are necessary to keep the doors open, crisis managers need strong skills in:
  - Communicating clearly and openly.
  - Using their understanding of the essential dynamics of the business to stem the flow of cash, negotiate with lenders and creditors, and reorganize the business to return it to at least marginal profitability.
  - Negotiating.
  - Conveying confidence.
  - Acting quickly and decisively.

- *Growing rapidly by acquisition.* In today's world of increasing centralization of capital, more and more organizations are in an acquisition mode. Leaders involved in acquisitions need a set of skills related to the acquisition process and the process of integrating the acquired companies based on the need to merge the operations.

• *Industry consolidations.* More and more industries are undergoing consolidations, in which large companies are being formed by acquiring other companies within the industry. We have one client with annual revenues in the neighborhood of $300 million that is the result of the consolidation of 60 different family-owned businesses. You can imagine the peculiar set of problems the CEO has to respond to in that situation.

• *Industry contraction or stagnation.* Another particular set of problems occurs in industries that for a variety of socioeconomic reasons are not growing, or are contracting. For example, because of the improved quality of automobile manufacturing, the car repair industry has been and will continue to be flat for years. The mobile home industry has been stagnant for years. The aluminum can market has been shrinking for years, as aluminum cans are replaced by less expensive packaging materials. In each of these situations, leaders need to be able to come up with strategies and tactics very different from those in growth situations.

• *Family businesses.* Being a leader in a family-owned business has its own unique set of challenges, whether or not you are a family member. Imagine the complex dynamics of having 16 relatives, representing several generations, from three different families working in the same company in its third generation of family ownership. Or imagine that the owner's son reports to you in the sales department, and that you would be charitable to call his performance mediocre. To be an effective leader in this kind of situation requires a degree of proficiency in the competencies of organizational savvy and interpersonal awareness above that normally necessary. It also often requires a degree of patience and a sense of humor typically found only in people eligible for sainthood.

• *International operations.* A whole new dimension of problems arises when businesses cross national borders. Foreign currency risk, trade finance, different cultural customs, quality issues, expatriate compensation, and language translation are just a few of the issues that must be addressed.

FUNCTIONAL NEEDS WITHIN THE BUSINESS

Based on the overall needs of the business, the ability to take charge of specific functions may be critical. In the travel incentives business, for example, where expanding sales becomes a key driver for the business due to increased delivery capacity, the CEO must be capable of taking charge of sales, either directly or indirectly. In a manufacturing business where reducing cost is the key value driver, the CEO had better either have a strong manufacturing background or have an excellent vice president of manufacturing who can take complete responsibility for the success of the initiative.

The same functional needs may exist within a department. Within the finance area, the installation of a new accounting software package may be the critical issue that needs to be addressed. The CFO needs to be able to manage the installation process with sufficient expertise and knowledge, or bring in someone else to do so. Similarly, the vice president of manufacturing may need to be an expert in cost or hire an expert in cost to meet the strategic needs of the organization.

CUSTOMER VALUE APPROACHES TO THE MARKET

Michael Treacy and Fred Wiersema in their classic treatise, *The Discipline of Market Leaders*, developed a model of business management based on three essential concepts[1]:

- *The value proposition*, which is the combination of values (price, service, quality, etc.) that the company implicitly promises its customers.
- *The value-driven operating model*, which is the overall business system to deliver on the value proposition.
- *The value discipline*, the ways companies can be best in their markets through the combination of the preceding two factors.

Treacy and Wiersema identify three distinct value disciplines that can create market leadership:

1. *Operational excellence*, where price is the basis for market leadership. Large retail chains such as Wal-Mart are prime examples of operational excellence, where low prices are maintained through cost control and process efficiencies.
2. *Product leadership*, where having the best product is the basis for market leadership. Top performance is more important than price in this discipline. Lexus established its market position based on product leadership, as did Nike and Johnson & Johnson.
3. *Customer intimacy*, where serving the particular customer is the predominant focus. With the discipline of customer intimacy, satisfying the customer's need is more important than either price or product

---

[1]Treacy, Michael & Wiersema, Fred. *The Discipline of Market Leaders*. Reading, MA: Addison-Wesley, 1997, xii.

performance. Examples of market leadership based on customer intimacy include IBM in the 1970s, Airborne Express, and the major consulting firms.[2]

Leaders need to understand their organization's approach to the market with regard to customer value, and need to maintain rigor and consistency with respect to that value approach. Leaders who have a deep understanding of marketing are able to develop market disciplines based on the organization, the industry, and the opportunities that the market provides.

Leader as Change Agent

In business today we talk about the need for change as if it were a new phenomenon. In reality, change has been a basic condition of the universe since the beginning of time. The issue is not with change itself.

The real problem is that the *rate* of change is increasing, requiring organizations to respond quicker and more frequently to new and different circumstances than ever before. As a result, the need for people to change their behavior and become more proficient in the key behavioral competencies is greater than ever before. In addition, the required change in behavior is not just in degree but in kind. Exhorting people to "Do more!" does not work in today's business climate in which most employees feel stressed and think they are already pushing themselves hard for the company's sake. And telling people repeatedly that "You have to do things differently!" is simply not effective over time. It is like parents who, when children do not understand something, say it louder and louder until they are screaming at the top of their lungs. Of course, increasing the volume does not increase the child's comprehension. Similarly, repeating the message that employees need to change their behavior usually does not help people change much. What they do hear is the fear and upset in the message, that they had better change their behavior or else. This message seldom has the effect leaders desire, because the threat of negative consequences is insufficient motivation for long-term change in deeply ingrained patterns of belief and behavior. If fear and negative consequences worked, we would be a nation in which no one smoked cigarettes, no one drank alcohol, and few people were overweight.

[2]Ibid., 145–161.

The biggest problem leaders face as change agents is that it is as difficult for them to change themselves as it is for anyone else. Because one of the main organizational dynamics is that leaders create organizations in their own images, reflecting their own strengths and weaknesses, it generally does not work to try to change the organization without changing the leader. This is why it is usually easier for new managers to effect organizational change than for managers who have time and experience with the organization. It is not that the new managers are more respected or are more effective than those with organizational experience. It is because their behavior patterns and belief systems are not the ones that created the organization, so they will naturally change the organization to reflect their own set of patterns and beliefs. Given the challenges of changing both the organizational and leadership behavior, here are some guidelines that will help leaders function as more effective change agents.

Organizational change should be treated as if it were a revolutionary war. If you think of it as overthrowing the old order—the entrenched habits, behavior patterns, and beliefs that resist doing things the way they need to be done—you will more likely recognize the difficulty of the change process, and marshal your forces accordingly. It is not a war that can be won overnight. If we define "enemies" to be the elements of the culture including policies, customs, and beliefs, as well as resistance to change, then chances are you don't know all your enemies in this war. You must function as an excellent commander in chief, performing all the functions that come with the job. These functions include:

- Continually assessing and reassessing the situation.
- Developing and implementing strategy and tactics.
- Identifying allies and enemies.
- Identifying strengths, weaknesses, opportunities, and threats.
- Assessing your resources and those of the enemy.
- Evaluating the weapons (tools for change) at your disposal, and developing new ones to help you win the war.
- Developing and implementing a communications strategy to win the hearts and minds of the people (the employees).
- Inspiring and motivating the troops.
- Celebrating victories.
- Tending to wounds and recovering from defeats.

- Establishing milestones and time lines for the change process.
- Choosing your battles wisely.
- Consolidating gains and securing recently won ground before proceeding further.
- Keeping your eye on the vision you are striving toward.

This is a daunting list of functions and responsibilities for any leader, and it is easy to feel overwhelmed and frustrated. There are a number of positive elements that are important to remember. First, the more leaders practice these functions, the better they become at leading the change. They acquire skills and improve competencies that have wide application in both professional and personal areas of their lives.

Second, you have many allies, not the least of which are the hopes and dreams that reside in the hearts and minds of the very people resisting change. By working with the forces of shared goals and vision, you not only will be more successful but also will enjoy the process.

Third, unlike a revolutionary war that you either win or lose, in this war it is possible to make significant progress and never get close to your vision. You may change the culture in some important and meaningful ways that make a big difference in the organization, and also find elements of the culture that seem immobile and so resistant to change that you lose hope of it ever happening. The thing to remember is that *any* change that helps the corporate culture foster innovation, serving others, teamwork, results orientation, and the other important competencies will have made the organization a better contributor to its customers, its employees, and its shareholders, and to the society at large.

Responding to Attacks on Leaders

Here are some examples of what we are calling attacks on leaders:

- *Example One*: Employees talk among themselves about their manager, criticizing all kinds of little things she does, most of which have little to do with the job. They complain daily about what she does, but have no intention of communicating those complaints directly to her or doing anything about it themselves.
- *Example Two*: In a weekly staff meeting, employees angrily criticize their manager for the perceived unfairness of the work schedule for the

forthcoming week. They vent their anger on their manager, who was no more responsible for the heavy workload than they were.

- *Example Three*: Employees focus their attention on the weaknesses of their manager rather than the strengths. They are quick to blame the manager for anything that goes wrong, but seldom give the manager any credit when things go well.

People who have leftover resentments related to their childhood authority figures and who have the tendency to assume the position of victimhood rather than responsibility will generally have an unconscious desire to blame and punish the current authority figures in their lives, the most prominent of whom are their managers. We are using the term "attack" to include any behavior that blames, disparages, insults, or in other ways makes leaders wrong or bad. The underlying bad faith may involve any of the following:

- *The speaker does not take complete responsibility for co-creating the situation.* In the example of the management team described earlier, members of the management team blamed the CEO and took no responsibility for their refusal to hold each other accountable, thereby pushing the CEO into his role.
- *The speaker's motivations are to weaken rather than improve the leader's effectiveness.* It is common that when people don't feel good about themselves, they want to pull others down to their level to avoid feeling their own pain and upset. We have all known people (if not ourselves) who seem to take joy and satisfaction in pointing out the faults and weaknesses of leaders. It is as though they become better human beings because the leader is a worse one.
- *The speaker's motives include a desire to distract and divert attention away from more personally threatening issues.* Many people, when confronted with their own poor performance, respond by attacking their manager for issues that have nothing to do with their performance.
- *The speaker criticizes the character of the leaders rather than their behavior.* This may include ascribing motives that are solely in the mind of the speaker or are based on the assumption that the leaders are driven by some of the darkest motivations imaginable.

There is a place for criticizing the behavior of leaders and managers. Constructive feedback is one of the most powerful change tools we have to improve the quality of organizational leadership. While constructive feedback and attacks on leaders have a superficial resemblance, their effects are quite different.

Attacks on leaders seldom serve a useful organizational function. Allowing attacks creates a corporate culture in which it becomes unsafe to step up to leadership. People will avoid leadership because they don't want to be shot down as they have seen other leaders shot down. Leaders will become further and further isolated from the rest of the organization, creating a degree of divisiveness that will hurt the organization's effectiveness. Further, the whole concept of development is sabotaged by leadership attacks, because the credibility of the people who develop others is undermined.

In organizations with a culture of competence, attacks on leaders seldom occur, and when they occur they are responded to promptly in ways that keep them from continuing. Here are a few guidelines for responding to attacks:

Interrupt attacks on leaders whenever and wherever you see them. In hallways by the watercooler or in the boardroom, do not allow attacks to be expressed. If people are complaining about their manager, insist that they go talk to their manager about their dissatisfactions. If people are blaming their manager and not taking responsibility for their role, help them see how they have contributed equally to the situation in which they find themselves. Every time you allow an attack to continue without interruption, you are implicitly condoning and approving of that behavior.

Develop and publicize policies promoting feedback and eliminating attacks. Use the opportunity to educate the workforce and encourage responsibility and accountability.

Don't say anything about leaders that you wouldn't say to their faces. Model the behavior you want throughout the organization. Be direct in communication yourself, and when you are not, apologize and correct the situation.

If you express a criticism about a leader to another person and have not expressed it to the leader, go do so as soon as possible. Following this rule keeps relationships from being clouded by unexpressed judgments and feelings, and frequently removes the element of attack from critical communications.

Take swift action to respond to attacks as soon as you hear about them. Because of the insidious nature of attacks on leaders and the extent of feelings about authority throughout the workforce, it frequently does not work to ignore attacks in the hope that they will go away on their own.

They may in fact subside, but more often they gain momentum as the upset of different people adds to the emotional cauldron of blame and attack. Furthermore, allowing attacks to take place without response lets the organization know that making attacks on leaders is an acceptable behavior within your corporate culture—not a message you want to spread.

The Need for Personal Development for Leaders

It is both stated and implied throughout this book that for their organizations to change, leaders themselves need to change. It is obviously much easier to tell someone else to change than it is to change oneself. In the role of leader it becomes even more difficult, because people who subordinate to you in the organization tend to see you as an authority figure more than as a human being with strengths and weaknesses. Leaders tend to be as resistant to change as anyone else. Because of their roles as leaders, however, their resistance has a more powerful effect. After all, they have the power to terminate people below them who push them too hard to change. Regardless of whether they actually use that power, their power and influence inhibit subordinates from giving them direct feedback, making it more difficult for them to grow and change.

In addition, the higher the level of the leaders, the greater the economic value they add (at least theoretically) to the organization and the greater the economic cost of their leaving. Since personal change usually involves a certain amount of discomfort, the managers of leaders are often hesitant to press them to make important changes for fear that they will leave the organization. This is most evident in how boards of directors interact with their CEOs, often avoiding anything that the CEOs might interpret as criticism. Because they feel so dependent on their CEOs for their organizations' success, they don't want to upset them. As a result, the CEOs get no assistance to help them improve, neither from those above them nor from those below them.

Part of your job as a leader is to improve yourself. Not only will doing so improve the functioning of the organization, it will also help create a corporate culture that encourages professional and personal development. If you do not demonstrate a desire to change and improve yourself, your organization will follow your example more than any words to the contrary.

In future chapters we address how to develop process and structure to facilitate individual behavior change to improve professional performance. As a leader, however, you have to assume that you need to take complete responsibility for your own development, and that you cannot rely on anyone else in the organization to provide you with the help you need. This is actually the most workable point of view for *any* employee, but for leaders it is essential because of the dynamics of authority and leadership just described. Here are some guidelines for managing self-development as a leader.

GUIDELINES FOR MANAGING SELF-DEVELOPMENT

Perform an objective analysis of your organization. Preferably performed by an objective third party, this should include an analysis of the corporate culture, strengths and weaknesses of the management team, employee behavior and traits, quality issues, production efficiency, and so on.

Use the analysis of your organization as a mirror of yourself. Coming from the perspective that we each create our own reality and that you have created your organization to be how it is, what is being reflected back to you? (This assumes that you have led the organization long enough to have placed your imprint upon it.) Who is the leader the organization is mirroring? Let's take as an example a middle market company that manufactures dental equipment and examine some of its characteristics:

- It is profitable and is growing at a moderate pace.
- It makes quality products, and employees take pride in their workmanship.
- Production time lines are frequently missed for many different reasons.
- Within departments people work together well to get things done, but communication between departments is guarded and limited.
- Employee morale is moderate in the company. People don't feel particularly inspired and excited about coming to work, but neither are they disgruntled and upset.
- The engineering manager is an excellent engineer but a terrible manager. He has disempowered every other engineer in the company by criticizing and intimidating them, controlling information, and insisting that all significant decisions come through him.
- There is no focus on personal or professional improvement in the company.

- Employees work hard during their shifts.

- The communication style of supervisors is to command and control, telling their subordinates what to do.

Based on this description of the company, what is our portrait of the CEO? He is a hard worker who gets things done (as mirrored by the company's track record of making good products). His management style has two sides: When he cares about something he commands and directs (as reflected by his supervisors), but when he doesn't care much he lets people do what they want (as reflected by his tolerating his engineering manager's behavior). Whether or not he says he cares about meeting deadlines, he cares less about it than he does about avoiding conflict (as evidenced by time lines not being met). He doesn't fully attend to communication (as mirrored by the weak communication between departments), and spends little time and energy on his own professional development (as reflected by other employees' lack of commitment to development). He is probably fair in his dealing with people (as evidenced by the moderate employee morale), and he manages around conflict rather than taking issues on directly (as evidenced by his toleration of the engineering manager's behavior).

From a competency perspective, we can see that the CEO is probably strong in results orientation and integrity and truth, and moderate in managing rerformance, motivating others, and attention to communication. He is evidently weak in developing others, continuous development, and conflict resolution. Because competencies are behaviorally based, we can feel reasonably confident about the accuracy of our assessment if he has been in the position for a number of years.

The reflection of self that an organization offers to its leader is seldom completely pretty. The blemishes are usually easy to see, and provide leaders with an opportunity to observe how they have manifested themselves in the world and what areas of themselves they need to change.

Get both direct and indirect feedback from the organization. There are many different ways to get this feedback:

- Anonymous employee surveys about the organization, its culture, its management, and your own management in particular.

- Making direct requests for feedback from subordinates.

- Employing 360° feedback instruments.

- In-depth performance review processes.

- If you are the CEO, arranging annual or semiannual performance reviews with your board of directors.

Understand and articulate the competencies and the behaviors you want to improve. The clearer you are about the behavior, the easier it will be to stay focused on changing it. "I want to deal with problems and conflicts more directly, and stop avoiding them." "I want to encourage and motivate managers better, and come across as less critical." "I want to hold people more accountable to maintaining high standards of quality, instead of buying their excuses for shoddy quality." In the case of our example, the CEO understood that the competencies most important for him to develop were managing performance and conflict resolution.

Be clear about the consequences to the organization of the current behavior you want to change. You will be more likely to change your behavior if you remember the cost to you and to the organization of your *not* changing the behavior. Unfortunately, all you have to do is open your eyes and look at the organization's weaknesses to see the costs right in front of you. There are the service problems that won't go away, the weak managers in the organization, or maybe the lack of innovation—whatever the problems are in your organization. The CEO in our example clearly saw the relationship between his avoidance of conflict and the company's track record of not meeting deadlines. He also saw how his refusal to confront his engineering manager was hurting the company.

Understand the root cause of the current behavior you wish to change. Although it is not necessary to understand the causes of behavior in order to change it, there are two main reasons for doing so. First, understanding the roots of the targeted behavior tends to increase self-acceptance and decrease the amount of shame and self-denigration that people often feel when confronted with the consequences of their behavior. Second, by understanding the root cause of the behavior, you will often become clear about the positive intention underlying the barrier. For example, our CEO could easily see the roots of his avoidance of conflict from his childhood, and could understand why he had a difficult time confronting employees. He could also see that his avoidance of confrontation was rooted in a desire to have cooperative relationships with his employees, even though it had the opposite effect.

Identify personal barriers to change. People would have changed their destructive behavior long ago had there not been barriers that made the behavior change difficult to pursue. Awareness of these barriers will help managers plan how they will overcome them when they arise. The CEO recognized that one of his biggest barriers was the anxiety that arose when he thought about confronting someone. Another barrier was that he often did not even realize that he was bothered by someone's behavior—his avoidance of conflict was so strong that he blocked out his upset and concern.

Create goals and action steps to change your behavior. Develop specific, measurable actions that you will do to change the targeted behavior. When we discuss performance development in Chapter 11, we will explain how to develop action steps in much greater depth. Our CEO developed two specific action steps to help eliminate his avoidance of conflict:

1. Once per week he made a list of things his subordinates did that week that bothered him.
2. Within two days of making the list, he would meet with a subordinate to discuss one of the items on the list. After the meeting, he would write down what went well in the confrontation, what went poorly, what he learned, and how he felt.

Action steps as simple as these will begin the process of changing the behaviors that leaders wish to improve.

Establish a means for monitoring and tracking behavior change. The desire to avoid accountability for changing destructive behavior is strong enough that often people will even forget that they agreed to change the behavior or to keep track of it. One common example is the frequency with which people who commit to losing weight stop weighing themselves after a few weeks. Because changing our habits and maladaptive behaviors is uncomfortable and emotionally challenging, our unconscious minds perform all kinds of tricks to help us avoid facing the discomfort—including helping us forget. This is why keeping track of the behavior change is so important. You want to keep the behavior conscious so that you can use your conscious will and intention to overcome the old habits. To monitor his behavioral change, the CEO maintained a computer file in which he documented weekly times that he avoided conflict and times that he faced it and communicated directly with subordinates and employees. Through this process he was able to stay aware of his behavior, note his successes, and remind himself of the reason for changing his behavior.

Get outside help to support you in the change effort. It is not easy for many leaders to get outside help. Many consider it a sign of weakness to need help from others. You are supposed to be able to figure things out yourself. After all, that is you got where you are, isn't it? This delusion has the effect of keeping people isolated and living in denial of the difficulties they face.

Most managers have little difficulty bringing in outside experts when they perceive a need for help in an area in which the organization lacks sufficient knowledge and skill—a machine is broken, the pay plan needs to be updated, a new accounting system needs to be installed, and so on. Why shouldn't an outside expert help in the area of behavior change, an area outside the expertise of most managers? The CEO in our example utilized an external executive coach to assist him in his behavior change.

To change your organization, change yourself. Of course, the way you change yourself is to change your behavior, which directly impacts the organization. As you change, you will literally create the organization anew based on your changed behavior. It won't change overnight, but the more consistently and frequently you display the new behavior, the faster it will change.

Behavior change of this sort is seldom straightforward. It is difficult to replace a deeply ingrained behavior with a different behavior. "Two steps forward and one step back" is the rule more often than not. You exhibit the new behavior a few times, then you slide back into the old behavior. You catch yourself, and you try the new behavior again. Under stress, you fall back into the old behavior. This pattern of behavior change is to be expected. To maximize the speed and ease of change, plan it like you would plan a battle. Mobilize all the resources you can, utilize allies, recover from lapses, and keep your eye on the overall objective.

Self-Care for Leaders

Our final area of focus for leadership has to do with an area in which most leaders can use some help—taking care of themselves. Tremendous benefits with leadership come. You learn and grow; exercise your will; gain competence, skill, and experience; and impact the world to accomplish your purposes. At the same time, leaders experience many difficulties. When you lead you take risks, and when you take risks you get hurt sometimes. (They aren't risks if you always win.) You fail sometimes. You may make catastrophic mistakes sometimes. You will likely be attacked in one way or another or at least not fully supported by your subordinates.

The job of leader includes the job of taking care of yourself, both physically and emotionally. Exactly what this means is different for each person, but self-care includes celebrating victories and tending to wounds. Too many leaders deal with their emotional wounds by pretending that they don't exist. They adopt an attitude of stoicism, and are seemingly indifferent to the emotional distress they experience. Although in the heat of battle it can help to suppress pain to focus on the fight at hand, after the battle it is time to tend to the wounded. Stoicism keeps people from being tended to and wounds from being healed.

The job of tending to emotional wounds is more complex than putting a bandage over a cut. It includes:

- Being listened to and feeling heard.
- Expressing sadness, anxiety, fear, and anger to the point where the emotional charge has been released.
- Contextualizing and learning lessons from the experience.
- Feeling connected to and cared about by others.

Beware the "Everything Is Great" Syndrome

Several years ago I interviewed a senior executive to join my firm. He was an excellent candidate in many ways—he had the requisite technical knowledge, he was strong in most of the important competencies, and the two of us got along well. Things were going swimmingly until I asked him to describe his strengths and weaknesses. He described his strengths well, but when asked about his weaknesses, he said, after thinking for a few seconds, that he didn't have any. When I said, "Come on, everyone has *some* weaknesses," he continued to maintain that he really didn't think that he had any. I tried a variety of approaches to draw him out. I told him several of my weaknesses, and then invited him to tell me one of his. He still couldn't think of any. This continual assertion ended the interview process. Anyone who denies having any weaknesses does not possess the level of self-knowledge I want in an executive.

What is surprising is the number of leaders and managers who, like this candidate, deny having any weaknesses. It is not that they consciously lie about their weaknesses; they *really* believe that they don't have any. They have been successful in their careers, and have developed a sense of self that denies any blemishes. They need to look good to themselves and others.

It is the job of leaders to know themselves. They need to know their weaknesses as well as their strengths. They need to be as objective as possible about who they are and what motivates them. Without self-knowledge, there will be little self-improvement.

Creating Your Own Culture of Competence: Chapter 4—Exercises

EXERCISE 1—MIRROR, MIRROR ON THE WALL

Leaders have the single most powerful influence on an organization's culture. If you want insight into the culture, observe the leaders on a day-to-day basis. List the organization's cultural strengths and weaknesses based on your personal perspective or use the cultural assessment tool you completed in Chapter 3. For each strength or weakness, indicate, if applicable, how leadership behavior demonstrates your assessment. This is also an excellent exercise to do in a group setting to help leaders to see the link between their day-to-day conduct and the organization's ability to initiate and sustain a change effort in the long run.

Cultural Strength or Weakness	*Leadership Behavior*

EXERCISE 2—LEADING TO WHERE?

Leaders at all levels in the organization need to work together to clarify expectations around their role in the culture change process so that long-term effort and impact can be sustained. An open, guided discussion on leadership strengths and weaknesses can help ensure that everyone is clear on how current leadership behaviors might be impacting the organization and the individual commitment and accountability required to change them. Use the following outline as a focal point for a discussion with members of your leadership team. As you discuss each function, you may want to refer to the managerial and leadership competencies in Chapter 2 to clarify definitions and identify sample behaviors.

Step 1: Select from the following list those leadership functions found in this chapter that are most important to the organization:

Creating the corporate culture.

Developing the corporate philosophy.

Establishing and maintaining standards.

Understanding the business.

Determining strategic direction.

Managing change.

Being a good follower.

Aligning with superiors.

Developing workforce potential.

Inspiring and motivating.

Establishing alignment.

Establishing focus.

Holding ultimate responsibility.

Dealing with authority issues.

Determining successors.

Managing ambiguity.

Optimizing organizational structure and process.

Step 2: Ask the group to provide an overall assessment of leadership's capability in fulfilling each of the functions you identified. A simple scale might be: Ineffective, Effective, Proficient, and Masterly.

Step 3: For each of the functions you have selected, ask the group to describe the negative impact on the organization based on leadership's lack of effectiveness, proficiency, or mastery.

Step 4: With regard to each function and its impact on current or future business success, ask the group to decide whether they would like to:

- Reinforce the function as a strength;
- Focus on it as an area for improvement; or,
- Do nothing about it.

Create a list of those functions they wish to reinforce as strengths and those they wish to focus on for improvement.

Step 5: Based on the group's decision to change or reinforce a particular function, provide the group with the list of critical competencies that are linked to each of the functions in this chapter. For example, if they see a need to focus on "determining strategic direction," this is linked to the competencies of strategic thinking, analytical thinking, and decision quality.

Step 6: Based on the group's discussion of the critical competencies needed to be effective leaders, have them develop strategies for improving or leveraging those functions. For example, they may want to obtain training, utilize the performance management system, or develop group goals regarding the function.

EXERCISE 3—MY MOST ADMIRED LEADER

In order to change behavior, leaders need to know what it is they need to change. Often descriptions of leadership behaviors can appear to be no more than finely crafted words on paper authored by someone who is far removed from the trenches. This simple group exercise can help leaders identify more closely with the leadership competencies and show them how they might translate the competencies to their day-to-day role.

Provide the group with the list of leadership competencies along with sample key behaviors. Break them up into groups of three or four and have them describe leaders who they feel have effectively demonstrated these competencies. Have them describe specific behaviors and actions the leaders took that support the effective use of the competency. This list of behaviors and actions can be used as a model for how leaders in the organization might behave.

CHAPTER

5

The Changing Role of Human Resources in Building a High-Performance Organization

HR is a profession in great flux. In preparation for this book I went to the library to look at books covering the field of HR. As I scanned the books I realized that most of them were completely out of touch with the present state of the HR function. None of the issues at the top of the agendas of the HR professionals I know was even mentioned in the books. I looked at the copyright pages, expecting the books to have been written in the 1950s. I was shocked. They were all published in the early 1980s.

The concept and very purpose of the HR function is in the middle of a change process that makes the job difficult for many HR professionals. The questions they need to be asking today are fundamental:

- What is the business of the organization?
- How is it changing?
- What can the HR function do to enhance the company's success in the business environment?
- Who are my customers?
- What are their problems?
- What do they want from me or my group?

The degree of flux in the profession is exemplified by a recent executive search our search firm conducted for a major manufacturer for an HR staffing professional. The company was looking for candidates who could manage senior-level searches throughout the organization and interact on a peer level with the company's senior executives. Candidates needed to have a strategic perspective and be capable of acting as effective change agents, using the hiring process as a means of transforming the organization and its culture. It was an exciting position, offering candidates the opportunity to work with the company's leaders and to play a major role impacting the leading organization in its industry.

In contacting eight hundred HR professionals, the search consultants found only two qualified, interested candidates. There were many interested staffing professionals, but almost none were strong enough in the competencies necessary for them to make the impact the company needed in the position. And none of the HR professionals who did have the necessary competencies were interested in a position focused solely on staffing.

When a search produces so few qualified candidates we know that something is wrong. There are only a few possible explanations:

- The company has problems that cause candidates not to be interested.
- The location is extremely unattractive.
- The industry is extremely unattractive.
- The compensation is inadequate.
- The set of skills and competencies needed just doesn't exist in the candidate pool in sufficient quantity.

In this case, none of the first four potential causes applied. There simply were not enough HR professionals with the competencies to do the job.

The vision for HR in progressive organizations is changing faster than the professionals in the field realize or understand. While from the organizational perspective not having enough HR professionals to fulfill the role is frustrating and limiting, the situation provides tremendous opportunity for those professionals ready to take on the challenge.

The History of HR

The industrial revolution began in the late eighteenth century when extensive mechanization of production systems resulted in a shift from home-based hand manufacturing to large-scale factory production. This revolution brought about a broad range of radical socioeconomic changes, one of which was the demand for increasing efficiency on the factory floor. In the late 1800s the movement for efficiency began to gain steam, and the concept of "scientific management" became in vogue. Managers began analyzing jobs by identifying their component tasks, determining the best way to perform them, and establishing the employee traits required to do the job. Scientific management sought to maximize efficiency and production by identifying strengths and weaknesses and putting the right employee pegs into the right holes. Personnel departments developed as organizations grew in size and the need to manage the administration of the workforce grew commensurately. Recruitment, selection, and payroll administration required increasing systematization and control.

The next phase in the development of the HR function was the "administrative science" movement that began around 1915. Henri Fayol was one of the first to provide general principles for management and organizational structure such as span of control, centralization, and managerial authority. The personnel department became a powerful, centralized bureaucratic function controlling how people were brought into the organization and how they were managed.

Beginning in the late 1930s, during the post-Depression period, the human relations movement began to impact the personnel function. This movement was in part a response to the impersonal nature of scientific management, in which the effect of the work environment or conditions on the workers was ignored unless it lowered productivity and efficiency. The human relations movement demonstrated the value of teamwork, employee participation, and treating workers with respect. Supervisor training became an important part of the personnel function, and employee motivation was recognized as an important management duty.

In the 1950s and 1960s personnel administration tended to become more situational, with policies and programs dependent on the particular circumstances of the organization. Personnel research became a common function in many large organizations, which tried to develop their policies and procedures based on their own particular needs and requirements. Manpower planning, involving the forecasting of personnel needs and the supply and flow of workers in and out of organizations, became part of the personnel function.

With the passage of social welfare legislation in the 1960s and 1970s and the accompanying concern for the rights and well-being of employees, the personnel function began to change to reflect the changing social fabric. Organizations began to have less control over employment practices as social legislation exerted a stronger role. As the society attempted to deal with the legacy of racism, sexism, and other forms of oppressive behavior, managers could no longer hire or fire anyone at any time for any reason they chose. Personnel administration began to include compliance with social employment legislation as well.

In the late 1970s the term "human resources" began to be used, replacing "manpower" and "personnel administration." This change in terminology reflected the growing perception that people made the difference between organizational success and failure. This trend continues today with the increasing use of "human assets" and "human capital" to convey the value of people to organizations.

Over the past two decades five more trends have changed the landscape of human resource management: the globalization of business, the reengineering movement, information technology, increasing specialization, and the changing employment contract between organizations and their employees. In the new contract, performance is rewarded with opportunity, challenge, experience, and compensation. In the old contract, loyalty was rewarded with lifetime employment. These trends, in conjunction with those related to social welfare, have changed the nature of the job and the function of human resources.

The Role of HR in Corporate Culture

From this short history of the human resources function in organizations, it is clear that the nature of the job duties for HR professionals is largely determined by the current societal perspective regarding the nature and role of the workforce in relation to organizational success. Regarding the overall corporate culture, however, the role of HR in the organizational system has remained fairly constant: HR's job is to help the organization have the people and the personnel policies that will help the culture maintain itself. In other words, HR develops and implements practices and policies to create employee behavior that operates within the behavioral confines deemed by the organization to maximize organizational success.

Because the need for organizational change is recognized as so important today, HR professionals face a disconcerting paradox: While they desire to be agents of change, many of the main functions of their department operate to help the culture resist change and thwart behavior that falls outside organizational customs and norms. The process of standardization that is central to the HR function intrinsically serves to limit "abnormal" behavior. Policies regarding employee discipline, hiring and promotion, compensation, compliance, and employee appraisal typically communicate to employees that the behavior that is rewarded is the behavior that has led to success in the past.

The other aspect of most HR activities is that they are primarily either administrative or reactive. The administrative duties involve executing transactions according to established procedures that by their very nature are inertial. Examples of these activities include payroll processing, employee discipline procedures, wage and benefits administration, and compliance.

The other kind of activity that HR professionals engage in that consumes vast quantities of time is reacting to the immediate needs of managers and employees as they arise. It is not unusual for senior HR managers to spend most of their time answering employee questions, participating in impromptu meetings with managers, handling employee problems, and so on. Given the demands for cost control today and the resulting reduction in staff head count, most HR professionals feel as though they have little time to be change agents. Keeping up with the daily responsibilities seems frequently to be a big challenge by itself.

On the one hand we can see that the nature and character of HR positions today lead more toward the status quo than toward change. On the other hand, in almost every HR conference and journal we hear how important it is for HR professionals to be strategic partners for executive management and change agents for their organizations.

If you ask most HR professionals whether they would prefer to be HR administrators or change agents and strategic partners to executive management, most would say the latter. The job is more important, the prestige is greater, and it certainly sounds like it is more fun.

In my experience, many HR professionals do not function as change agents and are not perceived by executive management to be strategic partners. One of the reasons is that they are often not strong enough in critical competencies to effectively play the role and impact the organization.

HR Leadership Competencies

To understand why more HR professionals aren't effective change agents and strategic partners to executive management, let's examine the competencies important for leadership HR positions.

Knowing that the women and men who go into HR tend to be people-oriented, we might expect them to be stronger at relationship competencies than people in most other professions, and perhaps weaker in some of the other competency categories.

In Figures 5.1 and 5.2, you can see the relative competency strengths and weaknesses of HR professionals compared to other professionals in a typical organization (a Metamorphics client). As we expected, HR professionals are stronger in relationship competencies and considerably weaker in task achievement competencies than the non-HR professionals.

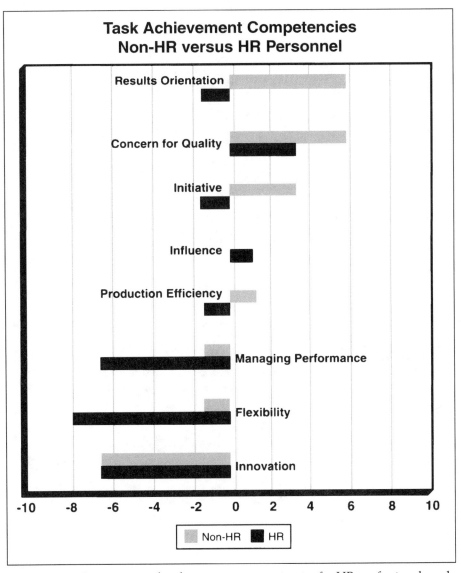

Figure 5.1 Comparing task achievement competencies for HR professionals and non-HR professionals in a typical organization.

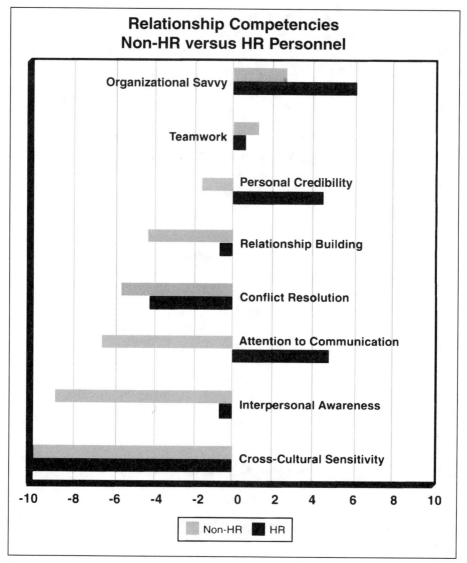

Figure 5.2   Comparing relationship competencies for HR professionals and non-HR professionals in a typical organization.

TASK ACHIEVEMENT COMPETENCIES

- Results orientation.
- Managing performance.
- Initiative.
- Influence.
- Concern for quality.
- Continuous improvement.
- Production efficiency.
- Flexibility.
- Innovation.

All nine of these competencies require significant proficiency on the part of HR leaders. As change agents they need to set challenging goals and take responsibility for their achievements. They initiate projects and manage them from start to finish. They ensure that HR functions are performed with the highest quality, and help line managers improve the quality of their operations. They focus on production efficiency, ensuring that HR functions such as payroll and benefits are delivered promptly and accurately while minimizing costs. They are also flexible and innovative as they respond quickly and creatively to the changing situation in the organization.

The competency in this set that is most critical to success of HR leaders is that of influence. Because the role of HR involves persuasion more than command and control, HR professionals have to be able to persuade effectively and to be adept at utilizing the advanced key behaviors associated with influence: building alliances, enlisting third-party support, building evidentiary documentation to support a position, persuading key influencers, anticipating objections and designing a plan to overcome them, and structuring presentations and situations to achieve desired results.

Examples of HR Task Achievement Competencies in Action
Strong Influence
Mary is the vice president of human resources for a manufacturing company. The CEO is a strong executive who knows the industry and business and develops effective strategies, but who has a problem remaining open-minded. He forms opinions quickly, and once they are formed he tends to ignore contrary evidence. This causes a number of problems, including a failure to develop people because they made a mistake or said the wrong thing.

Mary has known the CEO for many years, and has a repertoire of tactics to help address this problem. She maintains lists of accomplishments and contributions made by managers, and uses the information to immediately point out to the CEO when his appraisal of a manager runs counter to the overall behavioral assessment. When the CEO ascribes fault to the manager inappropriately, Mary will sometimes lead the CEO through a process of analyzing the situation to establish a more accurate picture of where the responsibility really falls. One of the more effective tactics that Mary uses is to preempt the CEO's emotional response by expressing the CEO's position more strongly than the CEO himself would express it. Mary will say, "Mark did a terrible job in managing that situation. I can't believe that he would misread it so badly." The CEO's response is inevitably more tempered than it would have been otherwise. Finally, Mary has the capability of standing up directly to the CEO, facing his wrath squarely, and firmly insisting that he alter his opinion about the manager. While she doesn't do this very often, she will do so when she believes it is necessary and in the best interest of the company.

Weakness in Influence

Bob works in a company with a CEO who had a similar habit of forming and holding strong opinions about people, some of which hurt the organization when they are inaccurate. Unlike Mary, however, Bob is ineffective at changing the CEO's point of view. Bob prides himself on being a calm and reasonable person, and expects others to behave similarly. When his CEO develops a negative emotional response to a manager based on partial or inaccurate information, Bob is offended, but he doesn't feel secure enough to express his own opinion about the manager and about the CEO. His desire to avoid conflict serves to keep him from confronting his CEO or challenging his opinion. As a result, good people leave the company and end up working for its competitors.

Weak Results Orientation

Four members of an HR consulting group of a utility company went into a meeting with the corporate treasurer that had been set up by the team leader. The subject was the reorganization of the treasury function of the company so that it would better meet the corporation's strategic goals. The treasurer opened the meeting by asking about the purpose of the meeting. The lead member of the HR consulting team responded by launching into details describing the proposed compensation levels for people in the treasury area. Another member started worrying out loud about how two clerical employees were going to be dropped from the organization. A third team member started brainstorming about opportunities for those clerical employees elsewhere in the company. The head of the HR consulting department, to whom the team reported, sat in the meeting in silence. Finally, 15 minutes into a 25-minute meeting, the fourth team member, who had said nothing to that point, asked the treasurer what his issues were in the reorganization. It came out at that point that the treasurer was concerned about how his direct reports were handling the reorganization. The team had gone into the meeting with no clear objectives, and demonstrated little capability in helping him address his concerns and issues.

Strong Concern for Quality, Results Orientation, and Managing Performance
An organizational development team developed a set of goals for the year in cooperation with their internal clients. They created a set of measurement instruments to ensure that the goals were accomplished to the satisfaction of their clients. They looked over their own skill sets to ensure that they were able to accomplish their goals. Where some members of the team had skills that others lacked, they trained each other to improve delivery capability. They were specific in their contracting with their internal clients, including process and expected outcomes.

Strong Initiative
The head of HR for a division of a global corporation headquartered in France understood through some conversations with HR in the corporate headquarters that there was an increasing concern and focus at the top of the organization on the need for more leaders and more high-potential employees in the company. Two months before any initiative was announced, he contacted all the search firms the company used and began educating them about its need for "high-potentials," a process that included defining the term and laying the groundwork for the changing candidate specifications that he believed were going to ensue. When the high-potential initiative was announced two months later, he was able to present a plan to senior management outlining the steps that needed to be taken, as well as addressing the organizational impediments to hiring and retaining fast-track employees. Prior to this initiative, it was highly unusual for employees to move quickly from one job to another or to move from one job function to another. By bringing up the issues at the beginning of the process, the head of HR greatly improved the probability of successfully hiring and retaining new employees with high levels of competence.

RELATIONSHIP COMPETENCIES

- Attention to communication.
- Conflict resolution.
- Cross-cultural sensitivity.
- Interpersonal awareness.
- Service orientation.
- Political know-how.
- Relationship building.
- Teamwork.

While we might expect HR professionals to be particularly strong in relationship competencies, there is a wide variation of proficiency within the HR profession. Human resources professionals are often effective at most of the basic key behaviors for the relationship competencies, but few are strong in the advanced key behaviors. For example, most HR professionals cooperate well on a team, but few are willing to engage in the kind of confrontation necessary to ensure that a team functions at its best when someone is not contributing fully. Regarding service orientation, most HR professionals want to satisfy their internal customers, but few of them adopt the "whatever it takes" attitude usually required to completely satisfy senior management's needs.

Examples of HR Relationship Competencies in Action

Strong Service Orientation

Sharon was the HR manager for a division of a financial services company. It was obvious to everyone involved in the division that she was dedicated to its success. She was among the first to arrive in the morning and the last to leave at night. The division head treated her as a trusted adviser, consulting her regarding personnel matters almost daily. She advocated for the division to corporate headquarters, and was known to have taken unpopular stands on behalf of the division. She operated throughout her workday as though her own personal success was identical to the division's success.

Weak Cross-Cultural Sensitivity, Interpersonal Awareness, and Service Orientation

A nuclear power station was having serious operational problems that were causing frequent unplanned power outages that cost the company one million dollars per day. Human resources was charged with the task of helping address the organizational problems, which seemed to involve the relationship between the plant management and the workforce. At this almost all-white mainly male rural power station, the HR department sent in an organizational development team comprised of an external African-American male consultant and an internal white female consultant. Both of the consultants were experienced, competent professionals, and the team worked well together. Unfortunately, they never managed to gain any significant level of trust and acceptance within the system, and they were basically ignored. Within three months the external consultant had quit the project, and a month later the internal consultant was transferred to another plant. As a result of the fiasco, it had become more difficult for *any* HR consultant to make an impact on the plant, because employees no longer trusted the motivations of HR.

The problem in this situation was not with the consultants' competence or experience. The problem lay with the vice president of HR, who demonstrated poor judgment regarding customer needs, sensitivity to cross-cultural issues, and interpersonal awareness. He created failure by not assessing the situation and its needs, instead trying to improve cross-cultural sensitivity on top of a myriad of other critical problems.

PERSONAL ATTRIBUTE COMPETENCIES

- Integrity and truth.
- Self-development.
- Decisiveness.
- Decision quality.
- Stress management.
- Analytical thinking.
- Conceptual thinking.

Among personal attribute competencies, we have little reason to believe that HR professionals are more competent than non-HR professionals. The reasons people go into HR have little to do with any of these competencies, either positively or negatively.

However, all of the competencies in this category are critical to the role of HR. For example, a loss of credibility can destroy the effectiveness of HR professionals, who depend on an appreciation of their expertise and goodwill for their influence. Because of the authority of their positions, CEOs and vice presidents of manufacturing will be listened to and followed even if they are considered untrustworthy. Human resources professionals who are considered untrustworthy will be ignored and ineffectual.

The two thinking competencies—analytical thinking and conceptual thinking—will contribute to HR professionals being viewed as trusted advisers to line management. These competencies are critical to designing and implementing change management processes, for which HR should play a key role.

Examples of HR Personal Attribute Competencies in Action

Strong Self-Development

Carol is the head of HR for a middle-market technology consulting firm. She is dedicated to improving her performance, and invests considerable time and effort every year to obtaining feedback regarding her performance. She enlisted the support of an executive coach to help her improve her relationship with her CEO. She has improved her communication skills, and has become a much more results-oriented partner for him. Carol has made self-development a habit, and has become a model in her company of someone committed to learning and self-improvement.

Weak Integrity and Truth

Harry was the vice president of human resources for a large consulting firm and had joined the firm two years earlier. He had a strong relationship with the CEO, but was despised by most of the workforce. He had demonstrated over and over again that he would say and do things to curry favor with the CEO, and would say and do the opposite when the CEO wasn't around. Employees believed that he was operating in his own self-interest rather than that of the company. He was effective at keeping his job so long as the CEO remained with the company. He contributed little value to the company, however, and was terminated a few months after a new CEO was installed.

Strong Analytical Thinking

Joseph is excellent at breaking problems down into their component parts, and has been helpful in solving a wide variety of problems in his manufacturing company. When the plant in Kansas was experiencing production difficulties, the CEO sent him and the vice president of manufacturing to investigate the problem and determine its causes. This skill in diagnosing problems has established a degree of credibility that has given him influence in many matters in which he would otherwise have little say.

Weak Influence
Martha has opinions about people and policies throughout the organization, but she doesn't trust her judgments and will not take stands for fear of displeasing others. As a result, she is viewed as a lightweight by the senior line managers, and she is continually frustrated by her lack of influence. She has several good ideas about how to improve the organization, but they remain unheard.

MANAGERIAL COMPETENCIES

- Motivating others.
- Empowering others.
- Developing others.

In my experience, HR professionals are not any better managers than other professionals are, but the importance of these competencies is greater because of the role of HR in establishing personnel policy and providing leadership and supervisory training. Human resources leaders need to understand how to and be able to motivate, empower, and develop employees in order to lead the organization in its change management strategy to transform its corporate culture.

Examples of HR Managerial Competencies in Action
Strong Empowering Others and Developing Others
Elaine is a master at developing the people in her department. Her enthusiasm and confidence in others are infectious, and people put in extra effort not because they have to but because they want to. Elaine has taken special interest in the management team, and regularly meets with each manager. She invites them to talk to her about their personnel issues, giving them feedback as a part of the process. She has become the coach to the management team. Her leadership in developing others helped convince the CEO of the importance of this skill, and she has created and implemented a competency-based appraisal and development process that has been recognized as representing some of the best practices in the field.

Weak Developing Others
Jerry, vice president of human resources, is one of the most knowledgeable HR professionals I have ever met. He has demonstrated an understanding of organizations that has served the company well. He has led a restructuring of the organization, and played a key role in helping the chairman of

the board resolve some critical relationship issues with the CEO. However, Jerry is quite intellectual, and prefers not to deal with issues that involve emotions. As a result, he does not pursue discussions with his subordinates about the barriers affecting their performance, and does not really help them improve. It is not surprising, therefore, that his organization has a weak and ineffective appraisal process that does little other than to provide a justification for compensation decisions made by the management team.

LEADERSHIP COMPETENCIES

- Visionary leadership.
- Strategic thinking.
- Entrepreneurial orientation.
- Change management.
- Building organizational commitment.
- Establishing focus.

Like most line managers, few HR professionals are strong in many of the leading competencies. The truly visionary and strategic HR professionals are easy to recognize. They will typically become spokespersons for their organizations, spreading the gospel of organizational change—the need, the challenges, the benefits, the costs, and the change process. They are also extremely articulate and can paint a picture of the present and future that helps employees understand and accept organizational strategy.

Entrepreneurial orientation is another competency that does not come naturally to most HR professionals. (Few people go into the field because they want to become entrepreneurs.) They tend to be weak at the skills and inclinations associated with looking at new business opportunities and assessing risk. This weakness tends to limit their influence and involvement in many of the key decisions affecting the business.

Examples of HR Leadership Competencies in Action
Strong Visionary Leadership
Barry is the head of HR for a large utility that is experiencing a difficult time transitioning to a deregulated marketplace. He is eloquent in explaining the difficulties that the company faces, and makes no attempt to whitewash the situation. He maintains a positive attitude, and describes a vision of the future toward which the company is headed: "We can no longer operate like a protected monopoly. We have to compete on the basis of the price of our products and the quality of the services we provide. We need to

create a new organization in which all employees work together to determine how we can deliver energy as inexpensively as possible with the highest quality of service and customer satisfaction."

Weak Change Management
John does not think well strategically about how to manage a change process in his organization. He seems unable to anticipate potential outcomes, and adds little value in discussions about change strategy. His CEO brought in a consulting firm to advise the management team and help develop a strategy for reorganization. The consultants suggested substantial staff cuts that would save the organization millions of dollars. John took part in the design primarily by answering questions asked by the consulting firm. The reorganization was accomplished and the staff reductions were made. Unfortunately, the consulting firm vastly underestimated the effect of the staff reductions; too many people were let go. There simply weren't enough remaining employees to perform the job functions of the company, and the firm had to hire back a significant number of terminated employees. Morale was decimated, and the process unnecessarily cost the company millions of dollars. Because John played no part in planning the change process, the organization did not receive the benefit of his knowledge and experience, instead relying entirely on a consulting firm with no long-term knowledge of how the firm functioned.

Aligning with Organizational Purpose: The Challenge for HR

The challenge for HR today is to function in strategic and tactical partnership with senior management to help the organization achieve its mission and vision. This is a difficult and complex task, given the administrative and bureaucratic nature of the HR function. Nevertheless, most HR professionals didn't join the profession because they wanted to become bureaucrats. It is the desire to work with people and organizations to help them function well that HR professionals respond to—the same motivations behind being a change agent to help create a culture of competence.

Organizations need HR professionals who will provide the critical leadership they need to help transform the behavior and beliefs of their employees. At the same time, the resistant and reactive nature of organizational culture serves to thwart HR professionals from functioning in the ways organizations need in order to flourish in these times of accelerating change.

To do what their organizations need, HR professionals must be more than merely capable—they must be adept at almost every behavioral competency described earlier.

Here are some guidelines to help HR professionals succeed in meeting this challenge:

1. *Align with the CEO.* Too often HR professionals view the CEO as someone they have to serve, rather than their partner to achieve the organization's mission and goals. This lack of alignment can have a number of causes. Their own feelings about authority figures may cause resentment or apprehension. Listening to and empathizing with upset employees many times per day may encourage them to forget the big picture and take the side of disgruntled employees against the CEO. Or, particular behaviors or communication styles of the CEO may trigger feelings that make it difficult for the HR professional to *want* to align with the CEO. Nevertheless, indulging in those feelings or allowing any of these reasons to prevent alignment will damage the organization and HR professionals' success.

2. *Take responsibility for the entire organization's success.* The most meaningful and inspiring frame of reference for HR is, "What will most help the organization achieve its mission and purpose? What are we trying to accomplish? How can I help?" Weaker HR professionals focus on protecting their turf and their span of influence. By focusing on the good of the whole organization, HR will add the greatest value and at the same time be perceived as a more valued resource to the organization.

3. *Focus on production efficiency regarding the administrative HR functions.* Do not neglect the basic HR functions in order to play a bigger role in the organization. The foundation of credibility is based on doing the basics well. The administration of payroll, benefits, appraisal, and selection needs to be performed according to high standards of quality and efficiency.

4. *Become outstanding at results orientation and managing performance.* Unless you are recognized as a "get it done" kind of person, you are unlikely to play a significant role as an organizational change agent. Set challenging goals, monitor performance, and accomplish the goals on time. Nothing builds credibility more than taking on tough assignments and accomplishing them.

5. *Begin by identifying purpose, objectives, and needs.* Helping your organization focus on purpose is a way to contribute immediately. Whether it is a meeting, a project, or a new initiative, by asking the question, "What is the objective of this [meeting, project, initiative, etc.]?" you will help everyone orient toward the larger purpose and improve organizational alignment.

6. *Focus on process.* Too often line managers have great ideas but fail in their implementation because they use ineffective processes to implement them. By helping the organization focus on *how* to make things happen, you can contribute to the change process and to organizational success in every area of business.

7. *Solicit feedback on how you are perceived.* You can ask for direct feedback, perform employee surveys, or gather data from managers, peers, and subordinates, obtaining 360° feedback. How others perceive you is critical to success for HR professionals. Once you have the feedback, you can formulate a plan to improve yourself and your impact on the organization.

8. *Develop yourself.* Ultimately credibility and integrity come from practicing what we preach. Human resources professionals need to be models of developing human beings, people who are continually growing and learning. Every occasion is an opportunity to exercise talents and competency, experiment with new behaviors and processes, and learn from mistakes and successes. It is unlikely that you can create a culture of competence without exemplifying the desired behaviors yourself.

Bob Wright, consultant to many business leaders, has described the purpose of HR as "having the right people in the right place at the right time in the best possible shape." While this is a daunting statement, it is one that can serve as an inspiring vision of possibility that is available to every HR professional.

Creating Your Own Culture of Competence: Chapter 5—Exercises

EXERCISE 1—INFLUENCE

Given the critical role HR has in gaining support and commitment for culture change, influence is a key competency. The following list of development activities can be helpful in designing a plan to improve HR influence and impact on the organization:

- Rather than immediately present your case when eliciting support for a project, first develop and ask questions that will identify or confirm your client's issues and concerns.
- Identify an individual in your department or elsewhere in the organization who demonstrates effective influence skills. Observe and

monitor his or her behaviors. Incorporate those behaviors in your approach.

- Tape-record or videotape a presentation you make to a group. Observe your speech and behaviors and compare them to the following (or ask someone else to view the video and provide you with feedback).

Presents one's point of view in a way that enlists others' support.

Demonstrates how one's position benefits the audience.

Elicits and responds to objections.

Develops and presents persuasive arguments to address the concerns, wants, and needs of others.

Anticipates reactions and objections and plans how to overcome them.

Uses new information or approaches to overcome major resistance or objections.

- In planning for a presentation, develop specific examples or analogies to which the group will relate. If it happens to be a group of high-level managers, be sure to incorporate results-oriented language.

- Identify a key manager within the organization who will serve as your coach to help you influence the organization. Specifically ask for that manager's help.

EXERCISE 2—HOW IS HR DOING?

Use the following to open up discussion on the HR department's ability to align with organizational purpose.

Ability to Align with the CEO
Does the CEO view HR as a partner in achieving the organization's mission and goals?

Taking Responsibility for the Entire Organization's Success
Does HR avoid tactics that communicate self-interest and turf protection?

Focus on Production Efficiency
Is HR able to balance quality administration of payroll, benefits, appraisal, and selection with knowledge of business strategy?

Being Outstanding at Results Orientation and Managing Performance
Does HR have a reputation for setting challenging goals, monitoring performance toward those goals, and delivering results in a timely manner?

Identification of Purpose, Objectives, and Needs
Does HR consistently communicate a clear purpose or rationale behind projects or initiatives?

Focus on Process
Does HR use effective, well-understood processes for accomplishing work?

Soliciting Feedback on How HR Is Perceived
Does the HR department regularly ask for feedback on its impact and performance and act on that feedback?

Develop Yourself
Do HR professionals proactively pursue development opportunities for themselves and others?

6

Using Vision and Corporate Philosophy to Create a Culture of Competence

One of the key attributes of human intelligence is the ability to create and use abstract concepts to explain reality and to imagine a reality different from the current one. We also have the ability to use these concepts to guide our behavior toward that imagined reality.

It is in this context that vision and corporate philosophy play a key role in creating a culture of competence. They give people a framework to help them make decisions and choose actions. Vision and philosophy are powerful tools to build corporate culture and to develop people to become their best.

The Elements of Corporate Philosophy

Corporate philosophy is the system of norms and beliefs that guides how people think and act at work. Corporate philosophy includes the vision, mission, values and principles, and operating agreements that guide the organization. Corporate philosophy may be broadly inclusive and heterogeneous—"In our company, anything goes"—or it may involve a singular, specific set of beliefs, like Procter & Gamble's. Every organization has a corporate philosophy, whether or not it is overtly articulated.

VISION

A vision is a statement of what you want to become, a conceptualization of an idealized future state that people can take action toward achieving. A vision is different from a goal in that it tends to be more general and to incorporate a bigger picture. Visions tend to be moving targets, states to which we aspire but which we never achieve. By the time we get close to achieving the current vision, our vision will have evolved into one with greater challenges based on new perspectives and perceived possibilities.

The use of vision is important because it helps determine what people strive for. Many people's hopes and expectations are limited by a poor self-image that usually has resulted from past experiences. If people believe themselves to be lazy and incompetent, they will tend not to be the quickest, most capable workers. Their self-image is likely to be the internalization of the messages they have received. However, if they begin internalizing a different message, a reflection of a vision in which they see themselves as capable and competent, they are more likely to strive to achieve competence.

Vision raises possibility. It gives hope and motivates people to go for bigger and better things. It encourages people not to settle for smallness and mediocrity. People feel better about who they are and what they can achieve. Vision can lead to motivation, action, and change that would otherwise not have occurred.

One of the best examples of vision in recent times is the "I have a dream" speech delivered by Martin Luther King Jr. on the steps at the Lincoln Memorial in Washington, D.C., on August 28, 1963. I was there and heard that speech. The vision of freedom, unity, and acceptance put forth by Martin Luther King Jr. on that day helped shaped my beliefs and my lifelong work. It has become a part of my vision, in which all people are cherished and are challenged and supported to learn, grow, and become the best they can be. This book is one of the results of that vision.

An example of an inspiring vision for a company is the one Johnson & Johnson first codified as their credo in 1943. The current version of the credo is as follows:

Credo

We believe our first responsibility is to the doctors, nurses, and patients,
to mothers and fathers and all others who use our products and services.
In meeting their needs everything we do must be of high quality.
We must constantly strive to reduce our costs
in order to maintain reasonable prices.
Customers' orders must be serviced promptly and accurately.
Our suppliers and distributors must have an opportunity
to make a fair profit.

We are responsible to our employees,
the men and women who work with us throughout the world.
Everyone must be considered as an individual.
We must respect their dignity and recognize their merit.
They must have a sense of security in their jobs.
Compensation must be fair and adequate,
and working conditions clean, orderly, and safe.
We must be mindful of ways to help our employees fulfill
their family responsibilities.
Employees must feel free to make suggestions and complaints.
There must be equal opportunity for employment, development,
and advancement for those qualified.
We must provide competent management,
and their actions must be just and ethical.

We are responsible to the communities in which we live and work
and to the world community as well.
We must be good citizens, support good works and charities,
and bear our fair share of taxes.
We must encourage civic improvements and better health and education.
We must maintain in good order
the property we are privileged to use,
protecting the environment and natural resources.

Our final responsibility is to our stockholders.
Business must make a sound profit.
We must experiment with new ideas.
Research must be carried on, innovative programs developed,
and mistakes paid for.
New equipment must be purchased, new facilities provided,
and new products launched.
Reserves must be created to provide for adverse times.
When we operate according to these principles,
the stockholders should realize a fair return.

This vision serves as the core of the Johnson & Johnson culture. On J&J's web site, the credo is presented in 36 languages, including the native languages of such countries as Morocco, Israel, China, Malaysia, and Bulgaria. Here is how the web site describes the role of the credo in J&J culture:

> *General Robert Wood Johnson, who guided Johnson & Johnson from a small, family-owned business to a worldwide enterprise, had a very perceptive view of a corporation's responsibilities beyond the manufacturing and marketing of products. . . . Johnson saw to it that the Credo was embraced by his company, and he urged his management to apply it as part of their everyday business philosophy . . . .*
>
> *The Corporation has drawn heavily on the strength of the Credo for guidance through the years, and at no time was this more evident than during the TYLENOL® crises of 1982 and 1986, when the company's product was adulterated with cyanide and used as a murder weapon. With Johnson & Johnson's good name and reputation at stake, company managers and employees made countless decisions that were inspired by the philosophy embodied in the Credo. The company's reputation was preserved and the TYLENOL® acetaminophen business was regained.*
>
> *Today the Credo lives on in Johnson & Johnson stronger than ever. Company employees now participate in a periodic survey and evaluation of just how well the company performs its Credo responsibilities. These assessments are then fed back to the senior management, and where there are shortcomings, corrective action is promptly taken.*
>
> *Over the years, some of the language of the Credo has been updated and new areas recognizing the environment and the balance between work and family have been added. But the spirit of the document remains the same today as when it was first written. . . . Its principles have become a constant goal, as well as a source of inspiration, for all who are part of the Johnson & Johnson Family of Companies. . . . About fifty years after it was first introduced, the Credo continues to guide the destiny of the world's largest and most diversified health care company.*

The power of vision to change and guide organizations and influence the lives of its employees is profound. The vision for an organization may not be as inspiring as that offered by Martin Luther King Jr. but it can have just as powerful an impact. The advantage organizations have that Martin Luther King Jr. didn't have is that they can use the vision repeatedly in a multitude of situations and environments, and can combine it with policies, programs, and initiatives to keep it alive in the hearts and minds of employees, as J&J does.

To be utilized effectively, vision should have some key characteristics:

- *It should be easily understandable.* Employees need to be able to grasp it easily upon hearing it, and they should be able to recall its essential message without great difficulty. This is important if the vision is to be used in a multitude of contexts to support organizational change.
- *It should be desirable.* Employees should read or hear it and respond by saying to themselves, "That sounds good. I like that. I would feel good if we were like that." No vision at all is better than an undesirable one.
- *It should be inspiring.* The more inspiring the vision, the more power it will have to motivate employees and influence their behavior. Visions provide inspiration to the extent that they increase people's hopes that their most important wants, needs, and dreams can be fulfilled.
- *It should lead to a set of standards.* It should be possible to evaluate a decision, option, or action by asking whether it is consistent with the vision. One of the key benefits of vision is that it can be used to help keep behavior aligned toward a common end.
- *It should be possible to operationalize it.* You should be able to use the vision to create initiatives and programs to help achieve it. By identifying the current reality and the gaps between it and the vision, you can create a change strategy to move the organization on a path toward its fulfillment.

The difference between vision and goals warrants further comment. It is easier for many people to think in terms of specific goals—the results they want to achieve. While goals are important to help people establish objectives and construct a plan to achieve them, they do not inspire and guide as vision does. A powerful vision is a source of motivation and a consistent reference point for all kinds of actions in different arenas. In a company without an inspiring vision, goals will tend to feel less important and fulfilling.

MISSION AND PURPOSE

If vision is what we want to become, mission is the answer to the question, "Why?" It is the organization's purpose. It provides the ultimate reason for all organizational activity. Every organization has a purpose—otherwise it wouldn't exist.

Table 6.1 lists some examples from James C. Collins and Jerry I. Porras's *Built to Last* of core purposes for some well-known entities.

Mission and purpose form the ideological foundation of organizations. Every policy, procedure, strategy, and tactic of the organization should fit within the mission. (Otherwise, why would the organization do it?) Mission provides the ultimate source of inspiration and motivation for all employees and all activity.

Table 6.1 Examples of core purposes for well-known entities.

Cargill	To improve the standard of living around the world
Fannie Mae	To strengthen the social fabric by continually democratizing home ownership
Hewlett Packard	To make technical contributions for the advancement and welfare of humanity
Israel	To provide a secure place on Earth for the Jewish people
Mary Kay	To give unlimited opportunity to women
McKinsey	To help leading corporations and governments be more successful
Merck	To preserve and improve human life
Pacific Theatres	To provide a place for people to flourish and to enhance the community
3M	To solve unsolved problems innovatively
Sony	To experience the joy of advancing and applying technology for the benefit of the public
Telecare	To help people with mental impairments realize their full potential
Wal-Mart	To give ordinary people the chance to buy the same things as rich people
Walt Disney	To make people happy

Source: James C. Collins & Jerry I. Porras, *Built to Last*, New York: HarperBusiness, 1994, 224.

The formal organizational mission is usually developed by senior management, sometimes with the assistance of a consultant and sometimes with the involvement of other employees. Because they are in vogue today, it is common for organizations to create and publicize mission statements that are inspiring and powerful. Unfortunately, many of them do not truly reflect company behavior and actions. The espoused and the actual mission of an organization may be quite different. The key question to determine whether a mission statement is espoused or actual is: Does organizational behavior demonstrate the mission? Are the goals, agendas, and initiatives manifested throughout the organization consonant with it?

Many manufacturing companies, for example, have mission statements that state something akin to "Our mission is to be the #1 manufacturer of widgets in the world" or "to provide our customers with the highest-quality products and the best service at a fair price," and so on. If you take a look under the hood, however, you typically find that business practices do not reflect the stated mission. The commitment to quality is mediocre at best; they don't measure customer service to learn how good it really is; and their pricing policy has nothing to do with fairness. They are currently nowhere close to being #1 and have no strategy to improve their position in the market. Furthermore, the attitudes and behaviors of their managers demonstrate no particular desire or motivation to be better than they currently are.

Another less-than-inspiring commonly expressed corporate mission is "to maximize shareholder value." While it is appropriate to include shareholder value as a part of a mission statement, focusing entirely on the value to owners excludes every other stakeholder. Which employee who doesn't own stock is going to wake up in the morning and say, "Boy, am I excited about going to work today! I can't wait to make our owners wealthier!" Contrast this with the Johnson & Johnson credo, which lists shareholder value as the last of four responsibilities, following customers, employees, and the community.

The true purposes of many companies would be embarrassing to admit. Here are some examples of how the mission statements of some companies would read if they were written to reflect actual organizational behavior. They would say, "Our mission is . . .

"To increase the short-term value of our stock."

"To provide the extended family of the founder with ongoing income."

"To make enough profit to stay in business while not working too hard."

"To keep the current leadership team in their jobs."

"To make as much money as we can."

An inspiring mission can play a key role in a culture change strategy. To the extent that employees believe in and care about the mission, they will dedicate themselves to its achievement. We will discuss shortly how to create and utilize mission toward this end.

VALUES AND PRINCIPLES

Values and principles provide the set of basic norms and beliefs that guide organizational behavior. They answer these questions: "What matters?" "What is important?" "What do we believe in?" "How should we act?" Like vision and mission, values and principles provide a set of guidelines for making decisions; determining policies, strategies, and tactics; and choosing behavior. Here are some examples of organization values.

3M[2]

- Innovation: "Thou shalt not kill a new product idea."
- Absolute integrity.

[2]Collins, James C. & Porras, Jerry I. *Built to Last.* New York: HarperBusiness. 1994, 68.

- Respect for individual initiative and personal growth.
- Tolerance for honest mistakes.
- Product quality and reliability.
- "Our real business is solving problems."

IBM[3]

- Give full consideration to the individual employee.
- Make customers happy.
- Go the last mile to do things right; seek superiority in all we undertake.

Procter & Gamble[4]

- Product excellence.
- Continuous improvement.
- Honesty and fairness.
- Respect and concern for the individual.

At Zwell International and Metamorphics we use principles as the key tool to define the core values guiding organizational behavior. In the description of each principle we include a detailed explanation to provide all employees with a picture of how the principle relates to behavior. The principles are service, commitment, responsibility, play, truth, and self-improvement. This set of principles has guided our company since 1991, and has been the center of our culture change process. We have used it to define and communicate the essence of our vision for our corporate culture, and I have watched these principles take hold in our employees. I knew we had succeeded when during the interview process our employees started rejecting candidates because they weren't close to the standards inherent in our principles. I was told that in their interviews, candidates made excuses and wouldn't take responsibility for things in their career that didn't go well. I was told that some candidates weren't committed to our standards of service. I could see that our principles had been internalized and that they had gone from being *my* principles to being *our* principles.

Every organization has a set of values and principles that determine what behavior is acceptable and what is not. Cultural norms and customs reflect

[3]Ibid., 69.
[4]Ibid., 70.

these values and principles. In fact, the best way to determine the values and principles that operate in an organization is to identify the norms and customs and to observe the rationale for decisions. Through this approach we will once again find the difference between espoused and actual values.

One company, for example, espouses the value of employee development throughout the organization. However, the CEO regularly criticizes members of his management team in front of others, insulting and disparaging them in a way that causes humiliation and discouragement. As a consequence, the espoused value of employee development is significantly less important in the culture than the actual value of covering your tail and protecting yourself from the CEO's wrath.

Values make a difference. John P. Kotter and James L. Heskett, in their study relating corporate culture to financial performance, found that higher-performing firms significantly outscored their lower-performing counterparts on every measure pertaining to values.

> We also found considerably more evidence at the higher performers of a value system that really cared about all key constituencies. Which constituencies were stressed the most varied: stockholders at ConAgra and Golden West, customers at Albertson's and Anheuser-Busch, employees at Hewlett-Packard and Springs Industries. But no group was ignored, and fairness to everyone was a standard feature—a commitment often described as an emphasis on "integrity" or "doing the right thing."
>
> Again, [the focus on values] was sometimes striking. At Albertson's, there was a "Corporate Creed" stating the firm's responsibility to customers, employees, community, shareholders, and society. At ConAgra, something similar was written in four-inch-high letters on a wall near the executive offices. At Dayton Hudson, we found the same proclamation in its "statement of philosophy." At Anheuser-Busch, the commitment to constituencies was in its "mission statement." At Springs Industries, the very first line of its 1989 annual report opens with a similar statement. At American Airlines, a strong commitment to all their constituencies was written in its statement of "Corporate Vision."
>
> Although a few of the lower performers had somewhat similar statements, these tended to be more recent and to list fewer key constituencies. Often they seemed artificial, as though they were the product of a single individual or a single meeting, and not the real priorities of most managers. At the lower-performing firms, managers seemed to care more about either their own careers or perks or specific products and technologies.[5]

[5]Kotter, John P. & Heskett, James L. *Corporate Culture and Performance*. New York: Free Press, 1992, 52.

OPERATING AGREEMENTS

Operating agreements are an element of corporate philosophy that is less common than vision, mission, and values. Operating agreements literally refer to a set of specific agreements with which employees agree to operate. They define acceptable behavior clearly enough so that people can be held accountable. Here are some examples of operating agreements:

- Show up for meetings on time.
- Do what you say you will do.
- Treat others with respect.
- Proofread every document before customers see it.
- Acknowledge the truth in criticisms before disagreeing with them.
- Respond to customer complaints within 24 hours.

Operating agreements provide a vehicle for translating vision, mission, and values into behavioral norms and rules. They provide a mechanism that helps employees hold each other accountable to operate in accordance with the corporate philosophy. Take, for example, the situation in which an employee consistently shows up late for meetings. If you confront him with his lateness, he might defend himself by saying, "I wasn't the only one late, or even the latest." Without the operating agreement, there is no easy way to explain why you are talking to him about it rather than someone else who was late. With the operating agreement, however, it is irrelevant whether others were late. He had an agreement to be on time regardless of whether others were.

A manufacturing client of ours demonstrated the use of operating agreements to change an important element of the corporate culture. Part of its management practice was a three-day quarterly meeting of the top 40 managers in the business that was looked forward to by most managers with the same enthusiasm they had for major dental work. Most managers seldom spoke up in the meetings, reports were represented in the dullest possible manner, and it was left to the general manager to ask the challenging questions.

Plant managers had a similar problem at their monthly meetings. The plant managers did not interact with each other, and any feedback to a plant manager had to be given by the vice president of manufacturing. To remedy the situation, I led them in an exercise at an off-site meeting to develop a set of operating agreements to cover how they wished to interact with each other. Agreements they came up with included full participation, showing up on time for meetings, telling the truth, expressing disagreements, challenging each other for the benefit of the business, and so on.

These operating agreements transformed the monthly plant manager meetings. Managers began talking to each other in the meetings, going so far as to question each other's projections. They began contributing to discussions, sharing solutions to common problems, and offering assistance to each other. After a few meetings they began to talk about the quarterly management meetings, and one of them said, "Wouldn't it be great if those meetings ran like our plant manager meetings?" It took them seven months to get up the nerve to propose using operating agreements at the quarterly meetings, but when they did they obtained general agreement to do so. The result was the best quarterly meeting that they ever had, one in which the level of participation and real communication among senior managers significantly contributed to the business.

The concept of operating agreements is simple; yet they are not used as frequently as they should be. By explicitly obtaining agreement to be honest, communicate openly, give constructive feedback, show up for meetings on time, and so on, more can be done to align employee behavior with higher values than with the more typical unstated values of "Avoid conflict at all costs" and "Keep your head down."

The Relationship among Corporate Philosophy, Motivation, and Competency

With the evolution of the brain and human intelligence, the relationship between thought, motivation, and behavior has become very complex. Not only can humans think, we can even think about thinking—what is called awareness or consciousness. The motivations that shape behavior and affect competency come not only from the desire to satisfy basic visceral needs but also the desire to serve higher, ideological purposes. Visceral motivations are based on physical, mental, and emotional needs, while ideological motivations are based on norms and beliefs.

VISCERAL MOTIVATIONS

Innate physical needs and wants. Physical needs such as hunger and sleep affect decisions and the rationale behind those decisions. Tasks considered to be extremely important when you are fresh early in the day can lose much of their significance by 11 o'clock at night when you are exhausted and ready to go home after a long day. Behavior, perceptions, and beliefs are all affected by physical needs.

Needs are not just physical, however. People have emotional needs for love, affirmation, acceptance, and belonging. They also have needs for challenge and stimulation, to satisfy the innate desire to learn and grow. These needs exist in all individuals, and they influence decisions and behavior. We have all seen people put in unbelievable effort and hours at a task, just for a few words of appreciation from their boss or a customer. People stay at jobs with lower pay and benefits and undergo considerable hardship in order to experience the satisfaction of an intensely challenging work environment.

Learned wants. Because learning is so essential to human development, it can be expected that what is wanted is shaped by family, friends, peers, authority figures, and the larger culture. The desire for wealth, for example, is a learned want. I know of no research showing that wealthy people are happier than the general population. Yet our culture tells us that money is the road to happiness, and people do things for money that betray their values and integrity.

Habits and distress-based behavior patterns. People take on habits and rigid behavior patterns from past distressful experiences that function as behavioral tape recordings.[6] These behavioral tape recordings "play" when they are triggered in certain situations that somehow are similar to the past experiences in which the behavior was recorded. For example, someone who was bitten by a dog when young may experience fear and shy away from dogs as an adult. The fear and resultant behavior in the present is a rigid response not to the present but to some experience that occurred long ago. The same process of behavior pattern formation often occurs in relation to many work situations and behaviors—relationships with managers, attitudes toward work, interactions with customers, and so on.

The natural desire to heal from physical and emotional wounds.[7] There seems to be an innate desire for people to want to heal the wounds from past distressful experiences, both physical and emotional. Each person deals with it in his or her own way, but the desire to heal forms the underlying unconscious motivation for more behavior than most of us realize. For example, the source of the emotional high in the dating and courtship process is often related to painful feelings we have about our parents, usually the parent of the same sex as the dating partner. Often the dating partner represents the opposite polarity from the parent, and our ecstasy

[6]Jackins, Harvey. *The Human Situation.* Seattle: Rational Island Publishers, 1973, 1–7.
[7]Ibid.

reflects our unconscious desire to avoid our childhood pain. It is fascinating to see, however, how many of us then create a relationship in marriage with this person that causes us to feel the same way about them that we felt about that parent. This can be seen as an unconscious attempt to resolve childhood issues through a current relationship. This same dynamic occurs in the work environment every day.

The desire to experience pleasure and avoid pain. If you burn your finger on a hot surface and a bucket of cold water is available, you will put your hand in the water to stop the pain. This basic motivation influences most human behavior.

IDEOLOGICAL MOTIVATIONS

Ideological motivations are rooted in the moral precepts of right and wrong, good and bad. The concept that some behaviors are intrinsically better than others is based on moral judgment, or philosophy. Every time someone reacts emotionally and thinks, "That was a bad thing to do," the person is responding to an ideological system. There are several different types of ideological motivations: norms, beliefs, and vision and purpose.

Norms. Norms represent the lowest level at which visceral motivations are replaced by ideological ones. Norms are the rules of conduct people learn through the socialization process, and form the behavioral library from which people choose appropriate behavior. These rules are mostly unconscious, and reach our awareness only when someone breaks them. Some examples are using a knife and fork incorrectly; failing to offer to shake someone's hand; speaking too directly in Tokyo; or not speaking directly enough in Amsterdam.

We consider norms the lowest level of philosophy because they are not attached to a philosophical or value system based on higher purpose. The power of norms is not based on any higher values beyond "This is the right way because this is how we do it." Conformity prevails, and the underlying rule is that what is different is wrong.

Beliefs. Here we begin to address the relationship between values and action. It is a uniquely human capability to base decisions and actions on a belief system involving moral precepts. People have died for their country, starved rather than stolen food, and done all kinds of things because of their core beliefs. The power of belief systems is that they can override all the previously listed behavioral motivations. The desire to do the right thing—to live in accordance with a set of beliefs rooted in higher purpose—has literally changed the face of the planet and human society as we know it.

Vision and purpose. The highest levels of philosophy, vision and purpose, allow people to base their behavior on their highest vision of possibility for themselves and others. The greatest, most revered leaders of our times, such as Gandhi and Martin Luther King Jr., accomplished what they did because they led others to act not on short-term self-interest but on their highest ideals. People are often willing to sacrifice their well-being and sometimes their lives for the values of equality and human dignity.

PHILOSOPHY AND COMPETENCY

If we are trying to create a culture of competence, we should in our strategy devise as many ways as possible to align employee motivation with competency. Every way we can help employees *want* to be proficient in competencies will help them learn and execute the behaviors that will bring them and the organization ongoing success. It is in this light that corporate philosophy helps. Mission, vision, values, and operating agreements all help employees orient toward a set of behavioral standards that have greater moral and inspirational power than the motivations of greed, selfishness, and short-term gratification.

Mapping Values to Competencies

It is in this light that values and competencies are linked together. Without higher values, the motivation to improve competency is valid but not particularly inspiring. If bettering one's influence skill or analytical thinking will result in making more money or getting promoted, a person may be sufficiently motivated to improve him- or herself. If one receives an extra bonus of 5 percent of salary for increasing proficiency at service orientation, one may become more attentive to customers. Unfortunately, however, personal gain is often not sufficient to motivate behavior change. Most people already have motivation to improve their behavior—they know that if they performed better at their jobs, they would earn more money and receive more recognition and career opportunities.

The problem is that self-interest is often not a strong enough force to overcome habitual behavior patterns. If common sense and self-interest were adequate motivation, none of us would smoke cigarettes or be overweight. Everyone would take more initiative, be deeply concerned about quality, and easily admit mistakes without defensiveness.

Values and vision provide a level of inspiration and motivation that helps people overcome the addictive pull of old habits and customs. The desire to live in accordance with higher purpose and principles can make the difference between change and inertia. By linking competencies with corporate philosophy, people have a better reason than mere personal gain to become more competent employees.

An effective corporate philosophy will be easily mapped to the behavioral competencies. In this light, let's take another look at Johnson & Johnson's credo and some of the competencies embedded in its vision:

- **Statement:** "We believe our first responsibility is to the doctors, nurses, and patients, to mothers and fathers and all others who use our products and services."

  Competency: *Service Orientation*—The company is saying from the outset that it exists first and foremost to meet the needs of its customers. Further, it is defining its customers not as the buyers but as the users of its products, the people who benefit from its products.

- **Statement:** "In meeting their needs everything we do must be of high quality."

  Competencies: *Service Orientation* and *Concern for Quality*—What matters is meeting customer needs and providing quality.

- **Statement:** "We must constantly strive to reduce our costs in order to maintain reasonable prices."

  Competencies: *Production Efficiency*—Operate as efficiently as possible. *Continuous Improvement*—Focus on continually striving to improve, in this case for cost reduction.

- **Statement:** "Our suppliers and distributors must have an opportunity to make a fair profit."

  Competency: *Strategic Thinking*—This statement encapsulates a strategic tenet, that J&J will partner with others in the supply chain and build mutually beneficial relationships.

- **Statement:** "Everyone must be considered as an individual. We must respect their dignity and recognize their merit."

  Competency: *Interpersonal Awareness*—Every employee is to be treated with respect.

- **Statement:** "Employees must feel free to make suggestions and complaints."

  Competencies: *Stress Management*—Employees need to be able to express their frustrations. *Concern for Quality, Production Efficiency,* and *Continuous Improvement*—Employees should be able to help improve things.

- **Statement:** "There must be equal opportunity for employment, development, and advancement for those qualified."

  Competencies: *Cross-Cultural Sensitivity*—No matter what the background, race, and so on, everyone will have the same opportunity. *Developing Others*—The company is committed to developing people and providing advancement opportunities to those qualified.

- **Statement:** "We must provide competent management, and their actions must be just and ethical."

  Competencies: *Integrity and Truth*—Managers will be fair and operate with integrity. The phrase "competent management" implies a number of competencies without detailing them: *Motivating Others, Empowering Others, Establishing Focus, Managing Performance,* and so on.

- **Statement:** "Our final responsibility is to our stockholders. Business must make a sound profit."

  Competencies: *Results Orientation* and *Managing Performance*—The company will focus on achieving financial objectives that include bottom-line profitability.

- **Statement:** "We must experiment with new ideas. Research must be carried on, innovative programs developed, and mistakes paid for."

  Competencies: *Innovation*—Innovation must be supported. *Strategic Thinking*—Recognizing that there will be mistakes that may be costly in their consequences, these costs should be planned for and paid for.

- **Statement:** "When we operate according to these principles, the stockholders should realize a fair return."

  Competency: *Visionary Leadership*—Rather than focusing on shareholder return as the primary objective, the credo sends a message based on trust and good faith: If we live by higher purpose, the company will make a sufficient profit.

We have listed a number of competencies that are embedded in J&J's credo. The credo provides an excellent foundation for aligning employees behind the competency paradigm. The way for J&J to live by its credo is by employees being proficient in these competencies.

From the organization's perspective, employee competence is the path to achieve its vision. From the employees' perspective, competence is the path to achieve personal fulfillment, through both professional success and personal contribution to a purpose bigger than oneself.

AMERICAN NATIONAL CAN'S USE OF VISION AND COMPETENCIES

Several years ago, American National Can's Flexible Packaging business launched a change process to improve organizational effectiveness and profitability. At the time the business was fairly typical of long-established manufacturing companies. Employees worked hard, were loyal, and did as they were told. Managers told employees what to do, followed orders themselves, and also worked hard. Throughout the culture there was a clear need to increase the amount of employee contribution, from both managers and other employees, of their talents and abilities. The organization needed people to innovate, take responsibility, and work together to figure out how to succeed in an increasingly competitive environment.

Through the combined initiative of executive management and human resources, the business developed a change strategy that included the two key elements we have been discussing to change the mind-set and behavior of employees: corporate philosophy and competencies.

The business defined its corporate mission as follows[8]:

BUSINESS MISSION

To be the preferred supplier through Total Customer Satisfaction *by providing*:

High-quality products

Excellent service

Low-cost products

Innovative products and services

Embedded in this mission statement are the competencies of concern for quality, service orientation, results orientation, and innovation. To further ground the change process in terms and language that employees could relate to, the business developed a broad vision statement[9]:

FLEXIBLE PACKAGING VISION

We are a business where our customers' total experience in dealing with us—quality, service, cost, innovation—causes them to prefer us over our competition.

We are a business where our people work in teams, are not bounded by organizational walls or layers, are thinkers and participants, take responsibility and ownership for how our business operates, know where they stand, have the opportunity to learn and advance, and know how to take advantage of those opportunities.

---

[8]Presented by permission of American National Can.
[9]Presented by permission of American National Can.

We are a business where our owners want to invest in us because we consistently deliver on our commitments, grow faster than the industry, and improve more rapidly than our competition.

Like the J&J credo, ANC's Flexible Packaging vision statement includes customers, employees, and shareholders. It is not as inspiring as J&J's credo regarding service to the wider community, but it paints a clearer and more inspirational portrait of the kind of behavior the company wants to see in its employees. Here the competencies of teamwork, initiative, results orientation, managing performance, self-development, innovation, service orientation, and concern for quality are emphasized.

Who wouldn't want to work for a company that wanted its employees to work well together, improve themselves, take initiative, serve their customers well, and operate with high standards of excellence? By stating the vision so clearly, the business has laid the groundwork for competency assessment and development. The mission and vision statements are prominently displayed in every Flexible Packaging facility, and serve as the launch point for many company initiatives, including the use of competencies.

Later in this book we will talk more about how ANC has used competencies to change its corporate culture and impact the business's bottom line. What is relevant here is that the business has consistently explained its use of competencies in relation to corporate philosophy: It is through developing our competencies that we will achieve our mission and vision. The business developed a set of competency models for each major job function, with five competencies common to all: teamwork, fostering new ways (innovation), results orientation, managing performance, and influence skill. Each of the job models includes the other competencies underlying the corporate philosophy.

Guidelines for Using Corporate Philosophy to Change Corporate Culture

Most change strategies that successfully transform organizations are rooted in philosophy. It is a key leadership task to utilize corporate philosophy to communicate organizational values and mobilize and motivate the workforce toward the organization's objectives. Toward that end, here are some guidelines to follow.

1. *Include others in formulating corporate philosophy, but don't take too long.* Leaders make mistakes in each direction. Some CEOs develop mission and values statements on their own and impose them on the organization, obtaining lip-service approval by others. In these situations the espoused corporate philosophy usually has little relationship to the philosophy that really runs the culture. Unless CEOs obtain agreement from the other leaders whose job it is to bring that agreement into the organization, the ideologies they develop often cause more harm than good. This happens because they contribute to a cultural norm of denial and hypocrisy, where what people say has little in common with what they do. In this kind of culture, leaders typically have little personal credibility among the workforce, effectively disempowering themselves.

On the opposite side of the spectrum, some leaders go so far as to include so many others that changes in corporate philosophy either never get approved or get so watered down that they lose their power as a tool for change. This is a common phenomenon in large, decentralized organizations in which power and control is diffused throughout regional fiefdoms. Large accounting firms, associations, school systems, and health-care organizations often exemplify this kind of structure. Any effort to lead change is emasculated by the cultural norm that requires consensus among all the affected parties, essentially giving everyone veto power over the change process.

2. *Make sure that your philosophy truly reflects your long-term organizational goals.* For many organizations, their stated mission and vision do not represent what they really want in the long term, and are instead statements describing how they would like things to be only over the next few years.

3. *Corporate philosophy should be inspirational.* If employees are not interested in achieving the mission, if they don't find the values meaningful, and if they find the vision uninspiring, the philosophy won't do the job. Investigate employees' reactions before spending time and money pushing it. Being #2 and trying harder was an inspirational vision for Avis, but it served little purpose for the big accounting firm whose mission in Chicago was to be #2. Likewise, increasing shareholder value isn't even inspirational to most shareholders, let alone the average employee.

4. *Focus on the key drivers of value and change.* Where are the leverage points? What are the behaviors and customs that, if they change, will most likely lead to other changes in the direction of your ideal culture? If every desired behavior and trait is included in the corporate philosophy, employees won't be able to distinguish which are more important than others. The likelihood of losing focus is great.

5. *Use the same concepts and terminology in corporate philosophy that will be used in competency applications.* The consistency will help employees understand and embrace the philosophy and the competency concepts, making it easier for them to apply both to their behavior on the job.

6. *Make sure that the language is simple and understandable.* People should understand it without deep concentration, and they should grasp the concepts quickly.

7. *Make sure that the elements of the corporate philosophy are clearly translatable into behavior.* Employees should be able to see how what they do relates to the mission or values statement, and picture the behavior that exemplifies the corporate philosophy. If the philosophy is too far removed from their everyday experience and they cannot relate to it, it will serve little useful purpose.

8. *Communicate the message over and over again.* This lesson has been learned by every effective CEO I know. The strength of television and radio advertising is not in the brilliance of the message but in its repetition, so that when people go to the store to buy coffee, the brand that comes to mind is the one stuck in their brains. The same benefit is accrued by repeating the corporate philosophy in different contexts and situations. Put it on posters on the wall. Say it in speeches. Put it in newsletters. Publish testimonials. Distribute articles that provide additional support. Share success stories. The more the message is communicated, the more deeply it will take hold.

We have been discussing how corporate philosophy plays a critical role in organizational transformation, by providing a common vision of a potential reality that is different from the current one. Vision can also play a key role on the individual level to help people change.

7

Using Vision for Individual Competency Development

Developing others is one of the weakest competencies for most managers. It is also a competency that becomes more important as managers rise in seniority and responsibility, because the ability to develop an effective management team is a key factor in determining organizational success. One valuable tool that managers can use to develop their subordinates is to use vision to increase subordinates' expectations of themselves.

Vision is important because people weak in a competency usually have little conception about what it means to be strong in the competency. They also often don't conceive of the benefits of being strong in it. If you ask executives who are weak in strategic thinking, for example, what they would be doing differently if they were strong in the competency, their typical response is, "Well, what I would do is. . . ." The sentence trails off with the question unanswered. These mental lapses on the part of otherwise bright people result from a set of beliefs about themselves and their capabilities that is often derived from much earlier experiences.

People adopt beliefs about themselves that say that they are limited in capability or potential. Often because of early experiences, they limit their sense of self and their behavioral responses to those they developed in childhood. Further, they actually stop thinking clearly in the areas outside these limits. For example, if you ask someone who believes he is dumb to solve a problem that looks difficult, his initial response is likely to be, "I can't." He won't even try solving the problem, even if he is capable of doing so. Only after considerable patient prodding will he apply his mind to it.

The relationship between behavior and vision can be summarized as follows:

> *Under most circumstances, what people do is limited by their self-image and their beliefs about their capabilities.*

In other words, people generally do what they think they can do, or less. The assumption underlying this book and indeed the entire concept of competency development is that people are capable of much more than they are currently doing. And because behavior mirrors belief, their performance can improve as their self-defining beliefs change to include a greater sense of possibility.

It is understandable why people don't think clearly in areas in which their competency is low. Their sense of self and their belief systems simply do not allow their intelligence to fully engage in the area. People low in initiative usually have had their initiative punished out of them when they were young. They may have learned not to take leadership or aggressively assert themselves, and their self-image reflects their nonassertiveness. They will long ago have stopped thinking proactively, and they will not naturally respond quickly when prodded to think in this manner.

Vision and Competency

Now we can see the importance of the role of vision in competency development. Because people are limited in their own thinking in areas of competency weakness, they need help envisioning themselves strong in the competency. Because their weakness in the competency is usually associated with childhood behavioral training, they also need help motivating themselves to improve the competency. After all, most competencies are like mom and apple pie—everyone wants to be strong in them. (Who doesn't want to be a good team player, a strong analytical thinker, an innovator, etc.?)

Vision plays the same role with individuals as it does with the organization. It provides people with a picture of their destination—in this case, high proficiency in the competency—and inspires them to want to achieve it. It also helps managers communicate to their subordinates in a positive context. Feedback has the purpose of helping people move toward a desirable state, rather than simply communicating ways in which employees are not performing well.

The steps for using vision for competency development are as follows:

- Identify the employee's competency strengths and weaknesses.
- Elicit the employee's own vision.
- Create your vision for the employee.
- Communicate your vision to the employee.
- Go for alignment.
- Invite the employee to transform the vision into reality.
- Develop pathways together.
- Continually hold the vision and communicate from that perspective.
- Reiterate these steps.

An Example of Vision in Action—the Manager's Point of View

Several years ago I hired a recent college graduate for a clerical position. I could tell that Lisa was bright because she learned each task in her job quickly, and she was highly verbal and articulate. Through the course of our interaction, I began to find out who she was—her strengths and weaknesses, her ambitions, and her self-image. My judgment was that Lisa was a strong conceptual and analytical thinker, and was strong in interpersonal awareness and service orientation. She took genuine pleasure in helping others, and effectively communicated her caring. Two of her biggest weaknesses were influence and managing performance. Other people did not seem to recognize or take advantage of her contributions. She also had a difficult time prioritizing her tasks appropriately, tending to put the least pleasurable ones at the bottom of her list and the most stimulating at the top. When I asked Lisa about what she wanted for herself—her personal vision—she said that she didn't know. It was clear to me that she had no career plans for herself, and that her current job was not the focus of her attention.

Over her first 18 months of employment, I gave Lisa more challenging tasks to accomplish as she succeeded in performing her previous assignments. Every six months or so I talked to her about her career, verbalizing my vision like this:

You have so much talent and ability organizing information and improving process. I can see you running the business side of our company, taking responsibility for all the activities in running a small business—accounting, purchasing, HR, and so on.

Lisa's response was that she was happy to help, but that she had no particular long-term interest in what I was describing.

Over the next year, Lisa, with my assistance, developed a database management system for the candidates and clients in our search practice. She learned on the job, and built a workable database. I continued to coach her on improving her ability to focus on task completion and manage her priorities (managing performance). I also gave her feedback on how to be more effective when dealing with vendors (influence). Her job skills grew, but when I talked with her she resisted any vision larger than that of doing her job well.

Over the next 18 months Lisa continued to contribute to the company in new and different ways. She helped write articles and assisted me in product development and the development of training materials. We hired someone to work under her, so she had the opportunity to train someone. During this time I started experimenting with different visions for her: Maybe she would like training; maybe selling; maybe product development; maybe marketing. None of these excited her. I grew frustrated, knowing that she would not be staying with the company if we didn't find something that truly engaged her.

The shift occurred when I finally decided to talk with her about her career and her interests from the perspective that I wanted the best for her, regardless of whether it was with our company. (This was difficult for me, because she had become a key contributor to the company, a highly trained partner to me in product development, my sounding board for many issues, and a close friend.) I met with her one day and said, "Let's forget about the company for a while. What matters to you? What really interests you? I'm committed to supporting you to fulfill your deepest heart's desire, even if it means your leaving here. I'd rather us figure out how you can do it here, but right now let's put that aside."

The conversation that followed was difficult for each of us—difficult for me because I didn't want to hear anything that might involve her leaving the company, and difficult for her because she wasn't clear about what she really wanted. It did become clear that she loved the database development and enjoyed the teaching and helping aspect of her job. We talked about other possible career options for her outside the company.

Over the next few weeks Lisa explored her interests and desires regarding work and career. She thought about leaving the company to become a full-time programmer and looked at the current and future needs at our company to see if there was a role that excited her. Meanwhile, as I was hearing her talk about her interest in information technology, I kept looking for how we could create a job that would fully engage her and serve the company and our clients. One of the vision options I proposed for her to consider was that she become our director of technology, which would become a real job a year later when we began development of our Internet applications to manage and administer our selection and performance development systems.

Two or three weeks after I proposed this vision, Lisa came into my office and announced to me that she had decided that the "technology track" that I had described to her was exciting, and that she wanted to do it. I was thrilled to have found something that engaged her, and her development and contribution have grown rapidly since then. Now she is helping to manage our software development, participating in leadership training for herself, and supervising two others, and has taken on the company mission as her own. She is beginning to function as a true partner in the business.

An Example of Vision in Action—the Employee's Point of View

I asked Lisa to write down her version of the development of her vision, to demonstrate the process from the employee perspective:

I came out of college not really knowing what I wanted to do, but knowing I wanted to work in the "real world" for a while to try it out. After spending a couple of months temping and looking at reception/administration jobs, I was sent by the agency to an interview with Mike. The job sounded like a basic administration job, but with the potential to grow.

My first big challenge in the job was learning how to work and communicate with Mike and receive feedback from him. Whenever Mike would give me feedback, suggestions, or constructive criticism, I would take it as an attack and an indictment. I was either upset or defensive a lot of the time. Mike tried many different tactics to find a way to coach me and give me feedback in a way I could hear. When we were finally able to set up rules of communication and feedback, our relationship solidified. What we finally settled on is that he would ask my permission before he gave me feedback ("Can I give you some feedback?"). This alerted me to get into a "receiving feedback" space, so I could hear what he was saying. It opened the way for me to be much more open to feedback than I had been.

I was pretty happy in an administrative, office manager role for quite a while, until I started nearing my internal two-year deadline for having a job just to try out the working world. Although I was learning a lot of skills, I felt that nothing I did was intensely challenging or satisfying, and I began to feel rebellious. I kept an attitude that I would do anything Mike asked me to do, but I wasn't going to take full responsibility. I said to myself repeatedly, "I just fell into this job—it doesn't have anything to do with what I want for my life." This victim stance showed up in everything I did—my main desire was to please Mike, but I had little investment in the projects I worked on beyond that.

Mike wanted more from me. I think he sensed that although I was not fully committed to the company, I was getting uncomfortable with "playing small." I had a desire for a bigger definition for myself, but did not see the role in the company that would fulfill that. Mike kept suggesting possible roles for me, but none of them seemed right, and I also did not trust that he was looking for the best thing for me, but looking for how he could use me the best.

During this period, I feel like I was saying "no" all the time. Instead of being compliant, I was being resistant. I kept digging my heels in for a long time, about issues big and small, making saying "no" part of my job. I was able to receive feedback from Mike, or at least put a good face on it, but I still was taking it as criticism and disapproval.

I started talking to other people about my career options. Mike was supportive of this exploration, but I knew he was afraid of it, too. The turning point that I remember was at a performance review, where Mike said to me, "Let's just say you were going to leave the company in six months. What skills would you want to take with you at the end of that time that you don't have now?" By taking the risk and asking this question, Mike freed me from my sense of obligation, and I realized that I had chosen and could continue to choose to work at the company, and that Mike would still value me as a person whatever I chose to do.

Since then, I have been continually in the question of what I like to do, and what engages me the most. I feel like I have the power to create my own job in the company, and I am looking at what will serve the company the best and serve me the best.

I have deliberately used this example to make the point that employee development can occur at every level of an organization, not just among senior managers. In a culture of competence, competency development is used to make *every* employee more effective, resulting in an organization that benefits from everyone's increased competence.

The Benefits of Broadening Vision

As Figure 7.1 depicts, people tend to take on more responsibility more successfully as they expand their vision of themselves. The supervisor on the

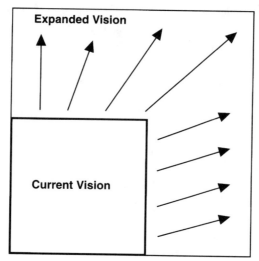

Figure 7.1   As people expand their vision of themselves as well as their job duties and responsibilities, they will tend to expand their functioning to match their vision.

shop floor who believes that his job is to ensure that his crew "does their job"—meaning they are on their machines when they are supposed to be—will likely accomplish his task. Another supervisor for the same company who believes that his job is to see that his crew produces the highest quality products they can, does it faster than any other crew, produces less waste, and has the most enjoyable time doing it will accomplish much more. Company productivity is a direct result of the quality of the vision of its employees.

How to Create a Vision for an Employee

Creating and holding a vision for subordinates is a difficult task for most managers. In the training we offer, we find it to be the management skill at which they are weakest. It requires using the imagination to create a picture of people not as they are now functioning but as they could be functioning if they were operating at their full potential. A vision can include any and all aspects of human functioning, including behavior, health and fitness, emotional state, intellectual capability, relationships, career development, wealth, community relations, and spirituality.

Here is an example of a typical vision statement for a subordinate:

I see you taking complete responsibility for every project in which you participate. You work well with everyone else on the project team, and notice how well each is doing on his or her piece of the project. When you see that anyone is having trouble, you either help them or make sure that they get the help they need. It doesn't matter whether you are the project lead or not; you still act as if the responsibility was yours.

Notice that in this vision statement I am not criticizing the employee or complaining about her behavior. I am also not promising any rewards for success or punishment for failure. What I *am* trying to do is to paint an enticing picture of a reality toward which she would like to aspire. The test of good visions is that they should inspire employees to raise their expectations of themselves and motivate them to invest more time and effort in improving themselves and succeeding at their jobs.

The following guidelines will help develop and verbalize effective vision statements for employees:

HOW TO USE VISION WITH EMPLOYEES

Begin by using words that make clear you are talking about a future state that the employee might reach. Some examples:
   "My vision for you is . . . ."
   "I can see you . . . ."
   "I think you can really do a lot here. I can imagine you . . . ."
Lead with their strengths, and refer to them frequently. By talking about their strengths, you not only help people feel good about themselves, you also help them see how their strengths can help them achieve the vision.
   Speak to your vision for the person, not for the job. People need to feel as though the vision is personalized for them, not just for anybody in the position. While your vision might be similar for anyone in the job, theirs should emphasize their strengths and their uniqueness. The more special and appreciated they feel, the more effective the vision will be.
   Inspire. Your vision should relate to their values and their wants and needs. They need to personally benefit in the vision, and the benefits need to be important to them. When I was working with Lisa in my company, until I found a vision that offered her benefits that she desired—gaining expertise in technology—the vision had no power or utility.

In your vision, imagine them considerably stronger in competencies in which they are currently weak. If influence is an important competency for their position and they are weak in it, include in your vision a picture of them being much stronger in the competency. Describe what their behavior would be if they were strong in the competency, relating it to the specifics of their jobs.

Use the terminology and concepts in the competencies to help articulate your vision. It will make it easier for you to create and verbalize the vision in terms of specific behavior that will help the employee understand and see it. The key behaviors associated with the competencies can help provide a framework for the words and the concepts. For example, the following are key behaviors for the competency of influence:

- Uncovering the concerns, wants, and needs of others.
- Developing and presenting persuasive arguments and cases to address those concerns, wants, and needs.
- Demonstrating how one's position benefits the audience.
- Presenting one's point of view in a way that enlists others' support.
- Eliciting and responding effectively to objections.
- Identifying key decision makers and key influencers of decision makers.
- Enlisting third-party support and outside resources.
- Anticipating reactions and objections and planning ways to overcome them.

A vision statement for a project manager who you believe needs to improve in influence might be verbalized as follows:

I see you, when you begin a project, getting to know your client deeply. You meet individually with every member of the client's team, and solicit their problems and issues. You get their viewpoint and uncover their hidden agendas. You also find out their "hot buttons," the things that they each really care about.

You investigate to determine the organization's decision-making processes. You discover the procedures through which decisions are made, and who the players are in key decisions. You learn who the key influencers are, and who has the ability to veto decisions. When it comes time for them to make important project decisions, you use this information to help the organization make the decision that best serves its long-term interests.

In this example, the vision statement paraphrases the key behaviors for the influence competency. By repeatedly verbalizing the vision, you will help employees weak in the area internalize the concept. Then, when they are in client situations, they will find that occasionally thoughts that are unusual for them pop into their consciousness: "I should ask them what their most important concerns are." Your vision slowly becomes their vision, and they transform that vision into behavior that benefits them, the client, and your company.

Include generalities and specific examples. You want to ground the vision from a number of different perspectives. Employees should see themselves in specific situations and should hear the general characteristics that describe the envisioned behavior.

Go for alignment with the employee. Ask them if your vision appeals to them. Listen to their answers, and find out what they care about and what they want. Keep modifying your vision until it is aligned with their values and desires.

HOW NOT TO USE VISION

Don't criticize in the guise of communicating your vision. You will be tempted to use the opportunity to complain about the employee's behavior: "Instead of being lazy half the time, you could be one of the most dedicated employees." If you slip in a complaint about their behavior, the vision will lose its power. They will feel defensive rather than excited, and threatened instead of inspired.

Don't lecture. Vision statements are effective to the extent that they elevate employees' personal hopes and dreams. The more you imply that the employee is bad if he doesn't do something, or should do it for your sake or the company's, the less empowering it will be. Statements like, "You would be much better off if you took more initiative," will not inspire so much as create resentment.

Don't tell them what they are doing wrong or what they should be doing. If you do so they will hear the criticism and not the positive potential in the vision. An example of what not to say: "You have been making lots of mistakes lately. My vision for you is that you are paying more attention to the quality of your work and making fewer mistakes."

Don't tell them they need to change their behavior. If you do so, it will be a disciplinary session rather than one that inspires employees to greater heights. An example of what not to say: "I really need you to take more initiative. Your not doing so is costing us a lot of business."

Don't offer inducements or rewards for achieving the vision. The vision should be motivating in and of itself. The dangers of inducements or rewards are twofold: First, the vision is not really theirs to own so much as yours to bribe them to achieve. Second, you may be making commitments that you will later regret. An example of what not to say: "I see you taking initiative to help the whole team succeed. If you do so, I see you being promoted to team leader, and eventually to project manager."

You can use the questions in Exercise 1 at the end of this chapter to help build a vision for employees. By doing so and continually trying to orient toward that vision in your communication with them, you will help lead them toward their own goals and aspirations, while benefiting your organization and your customers at the same time.

Holding the Vision

As is the case with corporate vision, the more often employees are reminded of and encouraged to move toward their personal vision, the more they will use it to guide their behavior and change their habits. It is one of the best ways I know to turn situations that would ordinarily be critical and discouraging into ones that provide coaching and encouragement for behavior change. Let's illustrate:

Barry was an intelligent, aggressive, and customer-focused project manager with a consulting firm. His attention to communication was spotty, and sometimes he forgot to pass information on to people who needed to know it in order for projects to proceed smoothly. While managing a project, Barry failed to give the client an important piece of information that resulted in a significant delay in the project. His manager was furious and felt like screaming at Barry and calling him every disparaging name he could think of. An excellent communicator of vision, his manager instead said this:

> *Barry, you screwed up the management of that project, and I'm really upset about it. It cost our client a week because you didn't let them know early enough that we needed the figures for the last five years. It has hurt them and our reputation with them.*
>
> *You are smart and you want to serve your clients well. In my vision for you, you are also well organized and compulsive about client communication. Instead of relying on your memory, at the beginning of every project you establish a list of all the information you are going to need from clients, along with the project time line. You*

update these weekly, and include them in your client reports. Your clients are the best-informed clients in the firm, and always know exactly where they stand.

The dilemma for most managers in this kind of situation is that they are upset and want to vent their frustration on their employees who are at fault, yet they know that disparaging their employees is demotivating and demoralizing. So, depending on their emotional makeup, managers tend to either go ahead and blast their employees or shut down their emotions and not give the employees appropriate feedback. When managers yell at their subordinates, the subordinates usually remember the emotions more than the content of the message. And when managers don't communicate when they are upset, their subordinates often lose the benefit of their managers' complete feedback.

The power of a vision statement like the preceding one is that it can be delivered even with the emotion of the moment and still have a positive effect. Because the context of the communication is positive, employees are more likely to hear the constructive nature of the criticism, and are less likely to respond entirely from their resentment for being criticized. The message is clear: "You made a big mistake; it hurt; this is how I expect you to do better in the future." This is the kind of feedback and help employees need.

Employees want to know that their managers are on their side and want the best for them. They want to perform at their best. They want to improve themselves. They want to be seen as bigger and better than they see themselves. By creating and holding such a vision, you can benefit your subordinates and the business, and achieve a level of satisfaction that most managers don't even imagine.

Learning to use vision is a slow and awkward process that requires practice. Most managers feel embarrassed when they begin creating visions for their subordinates and are hesitant to do so. In my experience, mastery of the skill takes years, but the benefits begin to accrue as soon as one starts practicing. Relationships with subordinates will begin to improve immediately, as they recognize and appreciate the desire for them to succeed and become more accomplished.

As we said in Chapter 2, the competency of developing others is one of the weakest among managers. Developing the ability to use vision to help employees see greater possibilities for themselves will almost automatically place you among the managers best in this competency. And once you develop the skill, you will use it everywhere. You will find that it improves every relationship and helps spouses, children, and friends perform better and feel better about themselves. Try it.

Creating Your Own Culture of Competence: Chapter 7—Exercises

EXERCISE 1—CREATING A VISION FOR AN EMPLOYEE

Answer the following questions to help develop a vision for an employee. After doing so, express the vision to the employee, and ask for his or her response. Use the opportunity to explore his or her own vision. This can be a good way to help employees begin to develop their own developmental strategies.

1. What is your vision of your employee's potential in his or her job if he or she were to grow and develop maximally over the next three years?

_____

2. Describe what his or her behavior would look like in general terms.

_____

3. Imagine examples of behavior that the employee would exhibit in the vision.

_____

4. What competencies does the employee most need to improve?

_____

5. Imagine behavioral examples demonstrating those competencies. Describe the behaviors as if you were talking to the employee directly.

_____

6. What would the employee be like if he or she were functioning at maximum capability in all aspects of the job?

_____

8

How to Use Competencies to Transform Your Culture

To improve the overall competence of a workforce, there are three basic approaches:

1. Bring more competent employees into the organization.
2. Improve the individual competence of the current employees.
3. Change the culture to increase the frequency and impact of competent behavior.

The most effective strategic plan to transform an organization includes all three approaches. Do everything possible to ensure that new managers and employees have more of the competencies that will help create a culture of competence. Implement a meaningful communication and performance development program that will educate the employees and provide them the conceptual framework and the training necessary to help them improve their competence. Rigorously examine the policies, procedures, and practices—the corporate culture—that affect performance, and change them in ways that will better facilitate, encourage, and reward behavior consistent with the desired culture of competence.

The competency paradigm provides a structure for supporting the change strategy. In this chapter we will address the key issues and elements needed to use competencies effectively to achieve these objectives. This includes:

- The importance of workability.
- How to set the stage for introducing and implementing competencies.
- The process for bringing competencies into your organization.
- How to develop competency models.
- How to structure competencies to maximize utility.
- The key principles of competency training.
- Employee expectations that accompany competency implementation.

The Key Concepts: Workability and Leverage

There are many consulting firms and individual consultants who offer products and services that are competency related. Most of what they offer is conceptually valid and would, if successfully implemented, add value. Successful implementation is the key, however. A major professional services firm recently spent millions of dollars developing software to improve and standardize its hiring process. The partners responsible for its development were excited by its potential value, and added more and more features to it to increase its range and power. They ended up with a tool that could greatly improve the selection and hiring process. Unfortunately, no one used it. People saw it as too complex and too difficult to learn, so they kept doing things the old way.

The most important question regarding any competency application is not how conceptually valid it is, but rather how *workable* and how *leveragable* it is. These principles involve many different aspects of functionality that are based on two main themes: Will people use it, and will it work when they do use it? These themes can be broken down into their components.

THE APPLICATION SHOULD BE EASY TO SELL TO USERS

For a competency-based application to be workable, it should represent a compelling value proposition that is easy to communicate to potential users. They need to see that the value they will receive is significantly greater than the cost of training and the time spent utilizing the application. In the example just described, potential users were not sufficiently sold on the benefits of the application to cause them to change their behavior and utilize it.

In addition to having a compelling value proposition, a competency-based application should be accompanied by a carefully designed and executed communication strategy. This communication strategy should include presentation materials that explain the need for the application, the theory behind the application, the benefits it provides, and how easy it is to learn and use.

THE APPLICATION SHOULD REQUIRE MINIMAL TRAINING

Some consulting firms require participants to undergo several days of training for them to be prepared to conduct the competency-based process. I remember many years ago when a senior human resources professional with a major bank asked me how long it would take to be trained in the process. I answered, "One day." She laughed and said that we could never get their managers to sit down for a full day of training. I then said, "How about four hours?" She replied, "They won't sit down for four hours, either." I asked, "Will they sit down for two hours?" She said, "I think we can get them to sit down for two hours." I replied, "Great! We have a two-hour training program." We do offer training sessions longer than two hours, but the point is that two hours of training to start people using a better selection process is much better than a longer training program in which managers won't participate.

THE APPLICATION SHOULD BE EASY TO UNDERSTAND AND EASY TO USE

People should be able to grasp the concepts quickly and easily, and the application should use language that is easily understood. The level of the language should reflect the literacy level of the users. If it is to be utilized by non-English-speaking users, it needs to be translated into other languages.

There are many software and paper-based applications that are too complex or too time-consuming for many people to use. It is amazing how many millions of dollars are spent every year developing tools and systems that work for the developers but not for the typical user. The basic steps of product development, including test-marketing, focus groups, and so on, aren't followed, resulting in the creation of a product that won't be used.

There tends to be a polarity between rigor and ease of use. Regarding competencies, for example, it can be argued that for any executive position there are at least 30 competencies that are key to success on the job. To assess those competencies in either a selection process or a review process is simply not feasible under most circumstances. We have to sacrifice rigor in order to make the process easier to use so that it *will* get used. The trick in development is to balance maximizing rigor and ease of use so that the product adds the most value while being easy to use.

However, there is a point at which the process becomes so watered-down that there is little reason to use it at all. Executives today are looking at returns on investment, a more formal way of saying that they are looking for the biggest bang for their buck. How will results improve because of the application? How can they obtain more benefits from the application? A competency-based appraisal process that helps improve future employee performance, for example, is more beneficial than one that merely assesses current performance.

PEOPLE SHOULD EXPERIENCE IMMEDIATE BENEFITS

The more quickly users experience benefits from the use of the application, the more easily it will become accepted as a standard practice in the organization. In one of our first installations of our competency-based selection process, the general manager of the business used the process on a Saturday to perform a telephone screening interview of a candidate. He learned more about the candidate than he ever had before in a telephone interview, and was so excited that he talked to his wife about it for half an hour immediately thereafter. He became the application's greatest advocate, assuring its successful implementation. When people have a positive emotional response along with the thought that, "This is good—it will make my life easier," then its likelihood of acceptance rises significantly.

THE APPLICATION SHOULD PROVIDE CROSS-FUNCTIONAL UTILITY AND CONSISTENCY

Many companies have competency-based applications for selection and appraisal that do not complement each other. They use different competencies and different means of measurement, and require users to learn two different systems. In this case the two applications actually diminish each other's effectiveness, because the confusion resulting from the dissonance between them reduces enthusiasm for their use.

The same conceptual framework should be used for every usage of competencies within an organization. The consistency will help weave the language of competency into the fabric of the corporate culture. Competency terms will become part of the thought process of employees, and will help create a set of behavioral expectations that leads to more competent behavior and higher performance.

MEASUREMENT SHOULD BE AS OBJECTIVE AND SPECIFIC AS POSSIBLE

If a policeman gave us a speeding ticket and had not measured our speed other than to declare that we were "going too fast," most of us would be quite upset. We would demand a more objective and definitive means of measuring our speed. We would want to know exactly how fast we were going, and what the speed limit was on the road on which we were traveling. We would be offended, indeed outraged, at the idea that we would suffer consequences at the whim of an officer's subjective judgment.

In the world of assessment and evaluation, standards and expectations for measurement are not quite so rigorous as on the highway. Nevertheless, employees experience a similar level of emotional outrage when they receive reviews that they view as highly subjective and based more on the feelings of the reviewer than on their behavior or the results they have produced.

Competencies will never be measurable to the degree of accuracy that automobile speed can be measured. That given, there are a number of benefits to making the measurement of competencies as objective and precise as possible. People will be less upset with their evaluations from others, because they will better understand the basis on which they received those evaluations. There will be less variability between evaluations of the same person, because the scale of measurement is clearer and better defined. It will also be easier to compare people to each other. Finally, measurement becomes a better tool for development, because employees can use the measurement scale to benchmark their current rating and help them set goals for future improvement.

THE EFFECT OF THE USE OF THE APPLICATION SHOULD BE NONDISCRIMINATORY

Everyone in HR and most executives are aware that it is illegal to discriminate against legally protected classes of people. Discriminating on the basis of age, gender, religion, race, ethnic background, or disability is unlawful. Unfortunately, it still happens.

In the mid-1990s Zwell International performed a search for a chief financial officer of a start-up biomedical company that transmitted patient information over the telephone lines. One of the candidates had a common Jewish last name, and one of the company's board members was interviewing the candidate. The conversation went something like this:

> Board member: "With a last name of Greenberg, I assume you are Jewish, it that right?"
>
> Candidate: "Yes, I am. Why do you ask?"
>
> Board member: "Well, I am an evangelical Christian, and I want the company to send Bible messages from the New Testament on our system to the bedsides of patients. Is that something that you would have a problem with?"

Fortunately for the company, the candidate had no interest in pursuing litigation. This kind of incident occurs more often than we would like to think.

Regarding any application associated with employment, it is important to examine whether and how it affects protected classes. One of the benefits of the competency paradigm is that it is founded on the most nondiscriminatory of concepts, the idea that hiring, appraisal, and development should be based on an assessment of the behaviors and traits that best predict performance—*behavioral* competencies.

THE APPLICATION SHOULD BE SUSTAINABLE

The initial implementation of almost any application is likely to have a positive effect if the users expect it to help. In the world of medicine it is known as the placebo effect. In medical experiments, the health of the people who take placebos usually improves even though the supposed medicine has no medicinal value. Over time the positive effect of the placebo often subsides as the newness wears off. In the world of social science, we know that almost any new way of doing things improves productivity for awhile so long as the people involved have positive expectations.

The ultimate value of a competency application resides in its sustainability, or the ability of the application to continue providing substantial benefits long after the honeymoon period has ended. Sustainability of an application depends on a number of factors that are peripheral to the basic function of the application. For example, there needs to be a process that broadens sponsorship for the application and transfers it from one leader to another. Otherwise it will die a slow (or not so slow) death after the sponsor either leaves the organization, loses interest, or shifts priorities.

There also needs to be an efficient and convenient mechanism for developing new trainers and advocates to keep the application alive and vital. Ideally, internal trainers can train other internal trainers. If external training is required, it should be easily accessible and reasonably priced. There also should be cultural processes in the organization—practices, policies, and customs—that involve the use of the application.

Setting the Stage for Competency Implementation

The best competency-based application on the planet will fail if it is not installed well. Whether a new competency-based selection process or performance development system will succeed depends on the efficacy of the implementation strategy and how well it is executed. The steps in the implementation process follow. It is not absolutely necessary to perform all these steps in order to successfully implement a competency-based application, but skipping a step could lead to problems in either acceptance or quality.

UNDERSTANDING THE CURRENT STATE

What is the current situation of HR practices prior to implementation? Regarding the hiring and selection processes, the following questions apply:

- What is the process flow of the typical hiring process?
- How standardized is the hiring process?
- What aspects of the selection process does the organization typically do well?
- What aspects of the selection process does the organization typically do poorly?
- What is the role of job descriptions in the hiring process?
- What competencies is the organization generally weak at?
- What competencies is the organization generally strong at?
- What are the common mistakes managers make in the hiring process?
- In the stated objectives and priorities for the organization, how much emphasis is placed on hiring the right people?
- Who in the organization cares about whether the best people are hired?
- Who has high standards for hiring and who has low standards?

- What is the role HR plays in hiring?
- What is the relationship between HR and line managers regarding hiring and selection?
- How easily does the organization adapt to new practices and processes?
- What kind of people does the organization usually hire?
- What are the characteristics, traits, and competencies of the demographic population from which the workforce is drawn?
- What has the organization done to date to expand or develop the population from which it draws its employees?
- What kind of people should the organization hire that it doesn't?
- What kind of people is the organization hiring that it shouldn't?
- How good is the organization at attracting candidates?
- How well does the organization know what it needs when it hires?
- How well does the organization recognize or acknowledge the need to improve the quality of the people it hires?
- How well does the organization see the potential benefits of improving the quality of the people it hires?
- What are the reasons the organization *does not want* to improve the quality of the people it hires?

This last question is particularly critical. When an organization hires people who are less than the best, there are reasons—benefits it receives from hiring mediocre performers. Some of those reasons typically include that current employees won't be "shown up" or challenged; pay practices won't be disrupted; the current ways of doing things won't have to be changed; and so on.

Regarding the performance review and development processes, the following questions apply:

- What is the structure and flow of the current review process?
- What role does the job description play in the current review process?
- On what are employees reviewed? Goals they set? Goals that are set for them? Skills? Traits and characteristics? Competencies?
- How long does it take for a manager to fill out the review form?
- Who reviews the employee? The manager? The employee him- or herself? Others?

- For what is the review used? Compensation? Succession planning? Development? Nothing?
- How seriously do managers and employees take the review process?
- How many employees do most managers review?
- What is the largest number of employees that a manager reviews?
- What percent of employees don't actually have an annual review?
- How useful is the feedback provided by the review process?
- How is the review process used to assist employee development?
- How is the review process used to help set goals and plans for the next review period?
- What are the forces in the organization and its culture operating to resist change in the review process?
- How does the organization respond to accountability?
- How strong is the corporate culture in the following competencies: Results orientation? Managing performance? Developing others? Interpersonal awareness?
- What is the attitude of employees and managers toward the review process?
- Who would benefit from a more effective process?
- How interested are employees in being developed?
- What is the current level of trust between employees and their managers?
- How much would managers benefit from improved performance of their subordinates?
- How prepared are managers to be effective coaches for their subordinates?
- Who in the organization would sponsor and advocate for a more effective review and development process?
- Who would ally with those sponsors?

These kinds of questions will elicit information about the current state of HR practices in the organization that you need to know in order to develop effective tactics to change the current practices. Without this analysis, you are likely to miss some key elements that could either make the implementation easier or sabotage its effectiveness.

One manufacturing company, for example, performed an employee survey throughout the entire organization in the early 1990s regarding employee satisfaction, needs, concerns, and performance issues. It found an overwhelming desire on the part of the workforce to be developed. It also found a high degree of dissatisfaction with the perceived arbitrary nature of the current review process and its lack of relationship to compensation. Using the employee survey data as the starting point, the company decided to implement a competency-based performance management system that included both competency assessment and an employee development component.

MODELING THE IDEAL STATE

To develop an appropriate pathway, it is just as important to establish where you want to be as it is to define where you are now. By taking the time to articulate how you envision your organization with regard to hiring, appraisal, development, and other HR practices, you will make the change process much easier to design and implement.

Regarding hiring, here are some of the key questions:

- What caliber people do you want to bring into the organization?
- Which competencies are most important for new hires to be strong at?
- What role would you like HR to be playing in the selection process?
- What role would you like job descriptions to play in the selection process?
- How consistent do you want selection practices to be in the organization?
- Is quality important in the hiring process?
- How do you want the hiring decision to be made?
- What should the relationship be between the assessment process in hiring and the assessment process in appraisal?
- Who should be involved in the candidate assessment process?
- What role should technical skill assessment play in the selection decision?
- How important is it to develop a diverse workforce?
- Is it important to hire people who can be promoted to more senior positions?
- What will be the financial consequences of hiring higher-caliber employees, in terms of productivity, payroll costs, and so on?

- If quality is important, what kinds of processes do you need to ensure that standards are maintained for the selection process?
- In your vision, what is the organization doing to ensure that it has a sufficiently strong population from which to draw candidates?
- What will the organization be doing to attract the candidates it needs?

For the employee appraisal and development process, there is a similar set of questions:

- On what basis should employees be reviewed? Competencies? Technical skills? Achievement of performance objectives?
- What role would you like job descriptions to play in the review and development process?
- What is your vision for employee development?
- Which employees do you want to have development plans?
- What should the relationship be between employee review and development?
- Who should review an employee?
- What should be the relationship between the review process and compensation? Career planning? Succession planning?
- What role would you like employee development to play in attracting new employees?
- In what job functions should people be developing and using performance plans?
- What should be included in performance plans? Performance objectives? Competency development goals? Technical skill development?
- What role should employees play in the establishment of their performance plans?
- How should performance plans fit into the broad strategic and business plans?
- What role should managers play as coaches of employee development?
- Should the organization provide mechanisms for reinforcing the behavior change necessary to improve employee competence?
- Does the organization want to reward only results, or will it reward employee improvement as well?

The answers to these questions will not only help define the strategy for implementing competency-based HR solutions, but they will also establish the framework for the solutions themselves. You will develop a different strategy and speed of implementation depending on how easily the workforce accepts new ideas and processes. A resistant and reactive workforce will require an extensive internal sales process and a slower implementation than one that eagerly supports management's desire to bring in strong performers.

ESTABLISHING PURPOSE AND OBJECTIVES

Once the current and the desired states have been defined, you are ready to establish the purposes and objectives of competency-based applications. As with the previous steps, it is important to identify what specifically you intend to accomplish by implementing the application. There are as many different purposes as there are benefits resulting from utilization of the applications. Here are examples of some purposes and goals:

- To hire strong performing employees.
- To transform the corporate culture.
- To change the organization's competitive position in the marketplace.
- To improve productivity.
- To improve employee retention.
- To shorten cycle time in the hiring process.
- To standardize the hiring process.
- To make the review process serve a useful function.
- To increase employee satisfaction.
- To reduce turnover.

Once the broad purposes are established, specific objectives can be defined that are measurable and time-bound. If the goal is to improve the quality of the workforce, how will you know if you are succeeding—that is, how will you measure improvement—and by when do you expect to accomplish how much improvement? The more specific you are about your goals and the more accountability you create for yourself, the more thought and focus generally go into the design and implementation of the solution. If one's goal is to increase revenue by 10 percent—a clearly quantifiable measure—through the implementation of competency-based selection and performance development, you are likely to put more effort into and attention on its implementation than if the goal is simply to successfully install the application.

The other benefit of defining objectives is that the act of doing so will often change how the application is implemented, and it may change the nature of the application itself. For example, if one of the intentions is to increase the alignment of employees with the organizational mission and goals, you may decide to include more employees in the candidate assessment process than would otherwise be the case. If one of the goals is to use employee development as a recruitment tool, it would make sense to develop an employee newsletter focused on developmental successes to be able to show job candidates. As you can see, defining goals can lead to the creative modification of processes so that the goals can be better accomplished.

BUILDING A CASE FOR THE NEED

Installing a competency-based hiring or performance development system is a significant organizational change. In the case of hiring, it involves standardizing a process that was not previously controlled. In the case of performance development, it brings discipline and accountability to the employee review and planning process that is challenging and disquieting to many employees. Prior to beginning the process of employee communication, it is important to build the case for the implementation. This is comprised of the typical elements of a sales process.

Identify the Problems
What are the organizational problems that the competency-based application is helping to solve? In selection, typical problems are that:

- Turnover is too high.
- The selection process takes too long.
- The quality of the managers and employees being hired does not consistently meet the standards necessary to be competitive in the market or to meet the organization's goals.
- The organization is intentionally changing, and it needs to bring in employees with different characteristics than those hired in the past.

These problems should be supported by facts, figures, graphs, testimonials, and whatever other evidence can be generated that demonstrates the nature and extent of the problem.

Diagnose the Problems
The next step is to show the extent to which HR processes—hiring and selection, performance management, the lack of an effective employee devel-

opment process, and so on—contribute significantly to the problems. For example, in analyzing the causes of employee turnover, one must make the case that much of the turnover is the result of people being hired who don't seem to have what it takes to succeed at the job. You might also demonstrate that many hiring managers don't know which traits and characteristics predict success on the job, and therefore are not assessing candidates on the important traits.

For the problems related to performance development, there are many different ways to draw the connection between the problem and the deficiency in processes that provide employees with meaningful feedback and help them improve their ability to perform and succeed at their current and future positions. For example, if one of the problems in the organization is that employees seldom come up with new and creative solutions, it is not difficult to make the point that the organization needs a better way to help employees improve their ability to innovate. If employee morale is low and many managers are not trusted by their subordinates, it is easy to state that managers need to improve their ability to motivate employees, and that the company has done a poor job of training and developing managers in this area.

Recognize the Consequences of the Problem

The next step in building the case for the application is helping people understand the consequences of the problem. An extra 5 percent in turnover results in substantial direct costs and even greater indirect costs. Hiring the wrong person for the job can have big consequences. One rogue trader, for example, caused Barings Bank to lose all its capital and forced its demise. Another indirect cost is the amount of management time that is spent dealing with weak performers, those employees and managers who should never have been hired in the first place. How much more productive would the organization be if managers spent more of their time helping the strong performers produce even better results? There are plenty of other indirect costs (the negative public relations that poor performers convey to customers and prospects, the interdepartmental friction that weak employees engender, etc.) that can be identified and associated with the problem.

The depiction of the pain caused by the problems is critical to building the business case. If employees do not understand how painful the consequences of a problem are, they will have little motivation to implement a solution, particularly if the solution involves changing personal habits and behaviors. Tony Rucci, then senior vice president of administration for Sears, used to give speeches in which he described the need to convince Sears employees of the need for cost reductions.[1] At the time of these initiatives, of every dollar a customer spent at a Sears store, approximately one and a half cents went to the bottom line. In a survey that the company performed of Sears employees, however, the company found that employees believed that of every customer dollar spent, over *40 cents* went to shareholders! No wonder employees were upset when their health insurance benefits were cut. Once employees understand the real situation, most will respond with acceptance and understanding as long as they are treated with respect.

Identify the Features of the Solution

You need to understand exactly how the competency-based practice will operate, and be able to describe each feature of the process in great detail. These include how long it will take to perform each step in the process, who will administer it, how the training will occur, and how success will be evaluated. New systems and processes get derailed mostly because details weren't fully understood and mapped out.

Identify and Document the Benefits of the Solution

Managers and employees need to clearly understand how they and the organization will benefit from the new HR practice. If they don't see how the practice will solve the problem and don't perceive other significant benefits, they simply won't do it unless forced to, and then only so long as the force remains in effect.

Most managers can see the benefit to them and to the company of their having more productive subordinates on their teams. Their goals will more likely be achieved and their jobs will be easier and more enjoyable with more help and participation from their subordinates. The same is true from the perspectives of coworkers and subordinates. Few employees prefer having a boss who is weak and ineffective to one who succeeds and helps them succeed.

One of the most compelling benefits of performance development is the personal benefit to employees themselves. They gain in skill and competence, increase their productivity and potential compensation, and gain opportunities for advancement and challenge that would otherwise be unavailable to them.

Just like Tip O'Neill's saying, "All politics is local," all meaningful benefits are local—that is, they need to be experienced by the employees as benefiting them personally in some way. The benefit need not be financial, but it needs to be heartfelt. For example, helping to end world hunger benefits

---

[1]Presented in a speech to the Human Resources Management Association of Chicago, September 1996.

humanity, but unless people perceive some personal benefit, most won't contribute to the effort. The benefit may be entirely emotional—"I feel better about myself because I helped other people in need"—or moral—"I did the right thing"—but there still is a clear benefit. In the corporate world, the personal benefits of implementing a competency-based HR practice fall into several categories:

- *Financial gain.* "If I do this, I will make more money." People will receive bigger bonuses, salary increases, and other perks when they hire more competent people who are more productive.
- *Career advancement.* "If I do this, I will succeed at my job, receive praise and recognition, and be promoted." The motivation associated with the benefit includes financial reward, but it also includes the desire for challenge and affirmation.
- *Power, prestige, and status.* "If I do this, I (or we) will be bigger and more powerful." Team or group affiliation can play a large role with this benefit. Either staying or becoming #1 can be a benefit that provides considerable emotional nourishment and self-affirmation.
- *Ease.* "If I do this, my job will be easier." This is a powerful benefit not because people are lazy and want to avoid work. Ease is a shorthand expression for a whole complex of concepts that include efficiency, productivity, leverage, satisfaction, and the avoidance of unpleasant tasks and interactions. If people are convinced that an HR application will make their work lives easier, they will usually be quite willing to try it.
- *Accomplishment.* "If I do this, I will achieve more." With regard to this benefit, achievement is its own reward, whether or not it results in increased compensation, recognition, or career advancement. For managers who gain personal satisfaction from developing others, doing a better job of developing people can be a sufficient benefit by itself to enroll them behind a new performance development program.
- *Development, growth, and learning.* "If I do this, I will learn, grow, and develop." For people whose natural desire to learn and grow has not been snuffed out by the educational system, the opportunity to improve themselves and gain new skills and capabilities can be enough of a benefit for them to support a new competency-based application.
- *Social.* "If I do this, I will enjoy being with people more." Job satisfaction will increase because employees will feel a deeper sense of belonging and connection to one another, and the need for affiliation will be better met. Part of the desire of CEOs and senior managers to improve the quality of their staffs is rooted in the hunger to have "playmates," or other professionals who will partner with them and with whom they can share the ex-

perience of growing and building. To the extent that HR practices increase employees' sense of belonging and acceptance by others, they will be perceived as having meaningful benefits to employees who are motivated by those needs.

- *Community-oriented.* "If I do this, the world will be a better place." While this is not the most common set of perceived benefits, it does play a role in some situations. For example, in organizations whose missions are directly related to higher purpose (religious organizations, day-care centers, foundations, etc.) the ability to serve the broader community better by improving HR practices can be a motivating benefit. In any organization in any position, people can take the stand that their job is to serve, and that anything that helps them serve better is a significant benefit.
- *Security.* "If I do this, I'll keep my job." The threat of job loss and organizational failure is used throughout the business world as a motivational tool to change employee behavior. The benefit of keeping one's job is not particularly inspirational, but it can be effective if employees really believe it. In order for job retention to be perceived as a benefit, employees usually need to know that the threat is real—they need to see employees terminated who don't perform up to standards or sufficiently change their behavior.

When an organization asks its employees to change their behavior, it is important that it be ready to show them how they gain from the new behavior. This preparation will pay off in spades once the implementation is underway.

Anticipate and Prepare for Objections and Questions

It is easy to get excited about a new HR practice such as competency-based selection or performance development. After all, it is the dream of most HR professionals to powerfully impact their organizations in ways that maximize organizational success and individual employee satisfaction and growth. Let me give you an example of an installation failing because of a failure to adequately anticipate and prepare for objections.

Our client was the sales department of a large utility. Utilities are not known for being the most progressive of organizations, and this company's development practices were consistent with the industry's reputation. The impending deregulation of the industry impelled the company's CEO to attempt to address the need for fundamental change. No longer would the company be able to compensate for inefficiency by obtaining rate increases from regulatory agencies populated with sympathetic colleagues.

The CEO demanded a substantial increase in revenue from the sales department, and threatened to replace the entire sales force if this did not occur.

The HR professional responsible for the sales department wanted to support the effort and saw performance development as a great tool to help increase sales. The performance review process in the past had been a relatively meaningless administrative exercise, and he wanted to use the current sales crisis to add power to the process. A relatively recent employee, he had been frustrated by the slowness of the organization to change and by the resistance of the sales force to taking responsibility for "making things happen." He also was disappointed by the degree to which employees' self-perceptions were inflated in the absence of any kind of behavioral standards.

Because of the urgency of the need and the time-critical nature of the situation, the HR professional decided to rush the implementation of the performance development application. Without doing the kind of preparation that was described earlier, he arranged a telephone conference call with the sales managers on a Tuesday and a conference call with the salespeople the next day. Neither group had any preparation prior to the phone calls except an e-mail announcing that a new program for improving performance would be presented.

The telephone calls did not go smoothly. The Tuesday call with the managers received a mixed response. Some of them were cautiously open to the idea, and others were openly resentful, skeptical, and suspicious. "Our salespeople are already under the gun. They have had to learn a new computer system. They have had their quota increased 25 percent. They are under a ton of pressure. They don't need something else to learn right now." By the end of the call they all agreed to support the program, although it was clear that some of the support was reluctant.

The call with the salespeople the next day was openly rebellious. "I don't care what you say, I am not going to learn another system!" "If they want us to sell more, why don't they give us more product to sell?" "Is management trying to build a case for letting us go?" "Why do they always blame the salespeople and make us the guinea pigs? If they really wanted to increase sales, they would make our support staff and the marketing department do it, not us!" For 75 minutes the salespeople vented and complained, communicating a level of upset and distress that surprised the department's leadership. They also manifested a degree of victimhood and blame that revealed a deeper problem in the organization. In the 75 minutes of venting, not once did any salesperson take any responsibility for any problem the sales department had. It was the fault of their information systems, their support staff, the purchasing department, their computers, the economy, the CEO, and so on. The attitude of the sales force assured the failure of the new performance development initiative. Their attitude also exposed a weakness in their sales managers in the competencies of motivating others and building organizational commitment. Managers had obviously not done a good job of leading employees to a position of responsibility and ownership of their behavior and their results. The most likely explanation is that the managers themselves felt as though they were victims, and therefore refused to confront their salespeople. The behavior displayed in the two conference calls only serves to underscore the need for the performance development system they were resisting.

For a new performance development application to be successfully installed in the company, much more preparation was needed than was done. At the very least, the HR professional should have anticipated the concerns and objections of the salespeople and their managers and prepared responses that hopefully would satisfy them and gain their acceptance and support. If he thought gaining their support was problematic, he should have planned to have the vice president of sales present and prepped to use his authority to obtain at least token support for trying the program and seeing if it helped them achieve their goals. By failing to anticipate their objections, the HR professional created even more barriers to organizational success than were present before the attempted introduction of the program.

OBTAINING MANAGEMENT BUY-IN

Managers deserve special attention in the implementation process. As leaders, their support is critical to the success of the application. The more heartily they endorse it, the greater the likelihood and ease of implementation. However, because weakness in the managerial competencies is often one of the reasons for installing a performance development system, the influence strategy needs to be well thought out. The competency of motivating others is essential to this process. The following key behaviors apply:

Help your managers uncover and identify their wants and needs, and then relate those wants and needs to the competency-based application. The more the managers are in touch with their job and career aspirations and see how the application can help them achieve those, the greater will their support be. This kind of interaction is most effective when performed on a one-to-one basis, during which time the manager receives individual attention and encouragement.

Acknowledge managers' achievements and contributions in a way that encourages them to support the initiative. When people feel acknowledged and affirmed, they are more likely to cooperate and join the effort. If they feel that they are seen as part of the problem you are trying to fix, they are likely to resist or even sabotage the implementation, in part because it reminds them of their own weaknesses and failings.

Create reward and recognition systems that encourage managers to promote the program. When installing a competency-based selection process, give public acknowledgment of times when managers did an excellent job of hiring by using the process. If installing a performance development system, create opportunities for employees to recognize and acknowledge their managers for providing them with helpful guidance and coaching. Use newsletters, bulletin boards, and so on—be creative. Bring in managers and employees to brainstorm ways to provide ongoing reward and recognition. Finally, to put teeth in the application, include the success of its implementation as one of the criteria for determining managers' bonuses.

Tackle morale problems directly by identifying and addressing managers' concerns and issues. If managers have trust issues and dissatisfactions with the organization itself, they will rarely wholeheartedly support new competency-based applications. Instead, they will often use their subordinates as their mouthpieces, allowing them to verbalize the same frustrations and complaints that they themselves feel. Talk to managers directly, encourage them to express their frustrations and criticisms, let them know that you hear their concerns, and respond honestly and directly to them.

Communicate about the organization in a way that motivates people to want to work and be proud of working there. It seldom works for long to tell employees that they have a terrible organization. By implication, they too are terrible. If you instead communicate a positive vision of how the organization could look if the application had its intended effect, and the benefits to the organization that could result from its implementation, employees are more likely to support it and change their behavior.

Help them take ownership of the implementation. Give them responsibility for implementing the application or for evaluating and improving its effectiveness. It is similar to what the wise teacher does when he or she has a disruptive student—gives the student an important job to do that defines him or her as part of the solution rather than part of the problem. The more people feel included in the project the more they feel like it is theirs, and the more they will take responsibility for its success.

Ask for their help. It is amazing how much people will do if they are only asked. They feel affirmed and valuable when they are treated as though they are important, which they are, and they will often become significant contributors as a result. For the implementation of competency-based applications, a high level of commitment on the part of managers is critical to its success. Ask them for their help, and thank them every chance you get.

COMMUNICATING THE PROGRAM TO EMPLOYEES

How a competency-based system is communicated to employees is important to determining its success. It is easy for employees to hear the implied criticism in the message if it is not crafted well. You don't have to be a genius to translate the statement "We need to do a much better job of hiring" to "We have been doing a poor job of hiring." If you were recently hired, you know what the organization thinks of *you*. If you were the one doing the hiring, you know what the organization thinks of your judgment!

There are a few rules that should guide your communications effort:

Focus on the main themes. Keep the message consistent and focused on the key elements that are most important for employees to hear and understand. People need to understand why you are changing the process, as well as the benefits to them, the organization, and your customers.

Use graphics wherever possible. For some people, comprehension is greatly improved when visuals are included. Pictures, graphs, simple charts, and so on, all help people understand the concepts, the process, and the benefits to an HR application.

Keep it simple. Avoid the use of complicated words and complex sentence structure whenever you can, and avoid jargon unless you plan to have it become a part of the common organizational vocabulary.

Create opportunities for questions to be asked and answered. Many employees are embarrassed to ask questions when it appears that they are expected to already know the answer. Assume that people don't understand things, and provide plenty of opportunities for them to ask questions. You may even want to plant questions—arrange to have an employee ask particular questions that you want to have asked, in order to encourage others to ask questions. You should assume that everything will be misunderstood by somebody, and be prepared to explain everything using language and examples that all your employees will understand.

EDUCATION AND TRAINING

The basic principles of training that apply to any HR practice apply to competency-based applications. These include:

- Tell them what you are going to tell them, then tell them, then tell them what you told them.

- Provide them with the theory and the reasons behind the practice.
- Present the information from several different perspectives.
- Make it entertaining.
- Give them the opportunity to observe the use of the skills in action, and to learn the difference between using the skills well and poorly.
- Prepare them for common pitfalls and mistakes.
- Give them the opportunity to evaluate use of the skills.
- Provide follow-up training to receive feedback and answer questions.
- Evaluate the training.

ASSESSING EFFECTIVENESS

One of the common problems we have seen in competency-based selection and performance development systems is the lack of regular evaluations so that problems with the systems can be improved. There are several ways to regularly evaluate the system. You can provide an evaluation form to be returned to HR that answers specific questions and gives employees the chance to give their feedback and suggestions.

One of our clients has adopted a practice of annually auditing its performance development practices. Every fall they bring in a consultant and take him to each plant to meet with different groups of employees. The consultant asks the employees to talk about the performance management process, including what is going well and what is not. These focus groups serve to provide senior management with a depth of information that they would otherwise not receive.

It would be wonderful to validate and quantify the effectiveness of a competency-based application in terms of effect on revenue, productivity, or profitability. Few organizations, however, are willing to adopt the rigorous practices required to scientifically validate its value. It is a difficult thing to do, because it is usually almost impossible to establish a legitimate control group that differs from the experimental group only in the use of the HR practice—the condition needed to demonstrate that differences in performance are caused by the use of the practice.

Nevertheless, the use of pilot projects can help organizations assess the effect and the value of a competency-based practice. At the very least you can obtain the opinions of managers and employees on the benefits of using the application as well as its associated costs.

Bringing Competencies into Your Organization: The Process

We have looked at setting the stage for competency implementation and some of the principles and practices that facilitate successful installation. Now let's look at the process of bringing them into an organization. This includes:

- Establishing the organization's competency methodology including potential uses, defining what a competency is, establishing the library of competencies from which competency subsets will be selected for different purposes, and determining the structure of a competency.
- Establishing the order in which applications will be implemented.
- Maintaining organizational consistency regarding competency usage.
- Determining which persons to include at which stage in the implementation.

ESTABLISHING THE COMPETENCY METHODOLOGY

It is worthwhile spending time planning for competency implementation and basing the design and strategy on how competencies will be used and for what purposes. The purposes should impact many aspects of competency development, from how they are defined to how they are measured. For example, if employee development is one of the purposes of competency implementation, it will be important to measure competency in a way that helps employees visualize what a higher level of proficiency in the competency might look like.

Potential Applications Utilizing Competencies

The following HR practices can utilize competencies to improve their functionality:

- *Job descriptions.* Job descriptions can include a list of the competencies that most differentiate superior performers in the position. They can also include threshold levels of proficiency required to succeed in the job, and the competencies required for the next logical position in an employee's career progression.

- *Selection.* If utilized in selection, you should be able to measure the competency proficiency of candidates in the interview process with a reasonable degree of consistency among interviewers.
- *Employee review.* If used for performance reviews, competencies should be easy to assess relatively quickly. (One manager may have more than 20 direct reports to review at the same time.) They should also relate to performance objectives and overall job success. Depending on whether employees assess themselves, they should be able to measure their own proficiency on relevant competencies.
- *Use of 360° feedback.* If competencies are to be used for 360° feedback or any other multiple rater feedback process, they need to be structured in ways that facilitate quick and easy measurement with minimal training.
- *Development.* If competencies are going to be used to help employees improve their performance, then the competencies should provide a structure that not only helps them assess their proficiency, but also helps them create a plan to change and improve their behavior.
- *Succession planning.* For use in succession planning, as many competencies as possible should be common across positions, so that employees in different positions can be compared to each other and to other positions.
- *Career planning.* Competencies used here should address the full range required to fulfill the career aspirations of all employees.
- *Reorganization analysis and planning.* If you are going to use competencies to help make personnel decisions when strategizing reorganizations, competencies should cut across positions so that employees can be compared to one another.
- *Job restructuring.* When thinking about how to restructure positions, competencies can be used to help determine whether the employee population has the proficiency to fulfill the needs of the restructured positions. Competencies should be measurable to accomplish this analysis.
- *Downsizing.* As with reorganization analysis and planning, as many competencies as possible should be common among different positions, so that employees can be compared to each other.
- *Compensation.* If competencies are used to help determine compensation, there needs to be a means of establishing an overall measure of employee competence.
- *Mergers and acquisitions.* If competencies are used to assess the management teams of organizations that are going to be merged or acquired, they need to be easily and quickly measurable.
- *Leadership development.* If competencies are utilized to help develop leaders, they need to be able to provide sufficient in-depth feedback to help people improve their leadership ability.

Establishing the Competency Library
Before determining what competencies will be used for different positions
and for different purposes, you need to create your library of competencies.
In Chapter 2 we provided a set of competencies that we use in our competency consulting. Different consulting firms have their own sets of competencies. Most of the competency sets that we have seen will function
effectively in the service of most of the HR practices just listed.

The important characteristic of competency libraries is that they contain
competencies that cover the range of characteristics and behaviors that determine superior performance for the organization's positions. The names of
the competencies are only important as communication tools for conveying
the concepts and behaviors to employees; otherwise, they are merely labels
to group those predictive behaviors together into the broader categories,
the categories called competencies.

One problem with some so-called competencies is that they are so broad
in concept that their utility is diminished. Leadership, for example, is sometimes considered a competency, yet in the context of our approach, it is a
concept that includes a whole cluster of competencies—visionary leadership, strategic thinking, change management, building organizational commitment, and establishing focus, to name a few. The problem with such a
broad "competency" is that it includes too many different characteristics
and behaviors to provide meaningful distinctions.

Developing the Structure of a Competency
Once the sets of competencies have been defined, it is necessary to define
and develop the structure of the competencies themselves. This structure is
defined by the answers to the following questions:

- How are competencies defined?
- How are they categorized?
- How are they weighted?
- How are they described?
- How are they broken down into components?
- How is competency proficiency measured?
- How will competencies be utilized for each potential application?

How Are Competencies Defined?
How you define competencies is a key element of the implementation strategy, and is an important part of communicating the concepts to employees.

First, it is worth pointing out that competencies should be defined, as the competency name itself is likely to mean different things to different people. Even a common word such as *initiative* means "volunteering for tasks when asked" to some people and "taking complete responsibility for projects from start to finish" for others.

Competencies are typically defined by simple phrases, by a paragraph of descriptive text, or by sets of behaviors and characteristics that describe them. Take, for example, the competency that we call *service orientation*. Here is how Lyle and Signe Spencer define the competency in *Competence at Work:*[2]

> *[Service orientation] implies a desire to help or serve others, to meet their needs. It means focusing efforts on discovering and meeting the customer or client's needs. . . . [H]ere the focus is on first, understanding the others' needs (rather than general understanding of others' thoughts, feelings, or behavior) and then doing something to help or serve the others. . . .*

Here is how Daniel Goleman defines a similar competency in *Working with Emotional Intelligence:*[3]

> *[Service Orientation]—Anticipating, Recognizing, and Meeting Customers' Needs*
> *People with this competence:*
>
> - *Understand customers' needs and match them to services or products.*
> - *Seek ways to increase customers' satisfaction.*
> - *Gladly offer appropriate assistance.*
> - *Grasp a customer's perspective, acting as a trusted advisor.*

Both definitions work. The important point is that the end users, in this case employees, need to be able to use the definition to relate the concept to their own common experience, so that the competency takes on a meaning that is understandable and hopefully appealing.

How Are Competencies Categorized?
The urge to classify and categorize data seems to result from the human desire to understand and control the environment. While the world does not always conform so well to discrete taxonomies—for example, many so-

---

[2]Spencer, Lyle M. & Spencer, Signe M. *Competence at Work.* New York: John Wiley & Sons, 1993, 40.
[3]Goleman, Daniel. *Working with Emotional Intelligence.* New York: Bantam Books, 1998.

called domestic products have foreign-made components—it is often useful to create categories into which to place an organization's competencies.

We use four categories: task achievement, relationship, personal attribute, managerial, and leadership. PDI (Personnel Decisions International), a consulting firm,[4] uses nine categories: administrative, communication, interpersonal, leadership, motivation, organizational knowledge, organizational strategy, self-management, and thinking. Daniel Goleman's taxonomy has two levels of classification.[5]

It would be easy to criticize any of these classifications, because human behavior and competencies don't fall into neat categories. For example, Goleman places the competencies of Self-Control and Innovation in the same category, when they involve quite different mental and emotional processes and largely unrelated behaviors. However, the criticism has little point unless the classification interferes with how usable the system is. If the categories help people understand and use competencies more effectively, then use them. If they make it more confusing or difficult, then change or abandon the categories.

How Are Competencies Weighted?

Both the competency research and common sense tell us that some competencies are more important than others for predicting job performance and success. Is it important then to weight some competencies more than others in assessing candidates and employees? Since we know that for salespeople, influence, results orientation, and initiative are more important differentiators of performance than concern for quality or analytical thinking, should we give them a multiplier in any calculations to reflect their greater significance?

While some organizations do so, we generally suggest not weighting competencies in competency scoring systems. First, because of the nature of statistics, if you average ratings on eight or ten competencies in the competency model, increasing the weight of a competency even four- or fivefold results in only a minor change in the average rating. Let's look at the example in Table 8.1.

In Table 8.1 we can see the effect of averaging competency ratings when the competencies are all rated equally and when they are weighted according to the frequency with which they differentiate superior performers. While the difference between the two averages is significant, it is not significant enough to justify the cost of validating the relative competency

[4]Davis, Brian L. *Successful Manager's Handbook*. Minneapolis: Personnel Decisions International, 1992, 16.

[5]Goleman, Daniel. *Working with Emotional Intelligence*. New York: Bantam Books, 1998, vii.

Table 8.1　This table compares sample weighted and unweighted competency rating of a candidate.

Competency (Weight)	Unweighted Rating	Weighted Rating
Influence (10)	7	70
Results orientation (7)	7	49
Managing performance (6)	6	30
Initiative (5)	5	25
Interpersonal awareness (4)	6	24
Service orientation (4)	4	16
Relationship building (3)	4	12
Concern for quality (3)	6	18
Analytical thinking (2)	6	12
Organizational savvy (2)	4	14
Average	5.50	5.87

weightings for each position in the organization. Furthermore, as much as we would like it to be otherwise, the competency assessment process as performed by most managers and employees is just not accurate enough to base decisions on fractional differences in averages.

The more important use of highly weighted competencies in assessment is in terms of *threshold levels* of proficiency needed to perform the job well. For example, successful salespeople almost always demonstrate a proficiency in the competencies of influence and results orientation at or above a certain level. Salespeople who cannot influence others to adopt their point of view and who do not set and go after achieving goals will seldom be strong performers. It doesn't matter how strong they are in the remaining competencies—they cannot compensate for a lack of drive and influence ability. In the selection process, therefore, you may want to require a minimal level of proficiency on the most important competencies, no matter what the average competency rating is.

How Are Competencies Described?

In addition to competency definitions, what expanded descriptions will help employees understand the concepts and related behaviors and traits? Providing employees with appropriate reference material can only improve their comprehension and effective use of the concepts and related HR tools for selection, appraisal, development, and so on.

Behavioral examples describing instances of the competency in action are also important elements of competency descriptions. The combination of brief competency definitions, expanded descriptions, and behavioral examples gives the organization the best chance of successfully implementing competency-based practices to produce the intended positive impact.

How Are Competencies Broken Down into Component Parts?

Telling employees that they should improve their initiative or their results orientation is not particularly useful by itself. If it were that easy, most people would have done it long ago. They need a broader conceptual framework that provides them with a structure to help them adopt behaviors that will lead to improved performance and productivity.

Competencies are of limited use unless they are broken down into smaller units that can be understood and analyzed. In our methodology we call these components *key behaviors*, the behaviors that, when demonstrated, result in proficiency in the competency. In Chapter 2 we listed sample key behaviors for many of the competencies in our methodology. Key behaviors can themselves be categorized as basic or advanced, based on the degree of difficulty or complexity associated with their execution. This kind of approach provides employees with a developmental pathway to improve themselves on the competency, helping them focus on performing the behaviors that will improve their competence and their job success. In Table 8.2, we have provided some examples of basic and advanced key behaviors for several competencies.

How Is Competency Proficiency Measured?

Measurement is one of the most critical elements of a competency methodology, and is intrinsic to the structure of a competency. It is sufficiently important and complex enough to be covered in its own section in Chapter 9.

How Will Competencies Be Utilized for Each Potential Application?

An organization needs to take its competency methodology and create processes to apply it to the HR practices that it has determined will improve organizational effectiveness. If the organization is going to use it for succession planning, it will need to determine the process by which the

Table 8.2   Sample basic and advanced key behaviors for several competencies.

Competency	Basic Key Behavior	Advanced Key Behavior
Influence	Uncovers the concerns, wants, and needs of others.	Identifies key decision makers and key influencers of decision makers.
Service orientation	Acts to resolve customers' complaints and keep them satisfied.	Elicits feedback from customers to identify their needs and monitor their satisfaction.
Developing others	Makes helpful suggestions and gives compliments for good performance.	Gives people a quality and depth of feedback and encouragement that empowers them to develop and grow.
Strategic thinking	Understands organizational strengths and weaknesses.	Utilizes knowledge of industry and market trends to develop long-term strategies.
Integrity and truth	Admits minor mistakes when encouraged to when there is no risk.	Takes stands on behalf of one's values that put oneself at considerable personal or professional risk.

methodology will be used. We will demonstrate how this is done in selection and performance appraisal and development in later chapters.

THE ORDER OF IMPLEMENTATION

Few organizations decide to implement a number of competency-based applications simultaneously. The kind of fundamental shift in approach represented by competency-based selection or a performance development system requires concentrated effort on the part of both HR and line management, and most organizations want to take on only one initiative like this at a time (for good reason).

Often companies will install a competency-based selection system as the first step in the transformation to a competency-based corporate culture. Selection does not get at the heart of the corporate culture like a performance development system does. You can easily sell a competency-based selection system without managers and employees feeling threatened by the idea of an organizational transformation. Almost everyone will agree that hiring strong performers is a good idea, and most will be willing to help in the effort. The only change that is required on their part is a change in interview style and practice, which is not central to their day-to-day functioning.

Of course, as interviewers utilize the rating system to evaluate candidates, they will invariably begin to evaluate themselves, their managers, and others in their own minds. For those involved in the hiring process, this introduction to competencies can serve as both an introduction and a persuasive tool that shows them the benefits of assessing people on their ability to succeed at the things that determine job success. The Chicago public school system provides an example of how this can happen.

Several years ago the school system adopted a principal evaluation process that focused mainly on measuring objective data—national test scores, pupil absentee rates, graduation rates, and so on. While this data is objective and certainly deserves to be an important component of the evaluation process, the process did not include much assessment of principals' behavior. Principals had no way of utilizing the evaluations to improve their performances or those of their schools. Furthermore, because they were judged mainly on the basis of data that they were only partially responsible for producing, it was not the best judge of their effectiveness as educational leaders.

In the Chicago public school system there has been a high level of distrust among principals, the central administration of the school system, and local school councils for years. (There are of course some exceptions to this generalization.) In most of the inner city the teaching conditions are extremely difficult, with high absenteeism, low average scores on standardized tests, considerable gang activity, relatively low literacy rates, and a degree of hopelessness that would make learning more difficult under the best of academic circumstances. The tendency for the different parties—central administrators, principals, teachers, parents, community groups, and staff—to blame each other for the problems runs rampant. Principals feel blamed for the problems, and feel vulnerable to losing their jobs as a result of that blame.

In this environment you might expect it to be difficult to install a meaningful performance appraisal system for principals. Principals have tended to view their appraisals as a means and an excuse for blaming them for their school's problems and as the justification for their termination at the end of their four-year contracts. Furthermore, neither the central administration nor the local school councils expressed much interest in developing a meaningful assessment vehicle for principals.

The drive to improve the quality of educational leadership came from outside the school system entirely, with the effort initiated by a subcommittee of the Civic Committee of Chicago, an organization whose members are the CEOs of the largest companies in the Chicago area. It was decided to begin the initiative by improving the quality of the new principals hired into the school system. Our company was chosen to develop a competency-based selection system for the local school councils to use to select and hire their principals. As a part of this process we developed a set of behaviorally anchored rating scales to assess principal candidates. The scales we developed proved to be a key factor in helping all parties agree that a meaningful principal evaluation process would serve the educational community, the principals, and most importantly the children. A sample scale is included in Figure 8.1.

When people in the school system saw the rating scales, almost all had a positive response. Principals, administrators, and local school council members agreed that principals who scored high on the competency scales would be strong principals, and they responded well to the suggestion of using similar scales for evaluating and developing principals. When the selection process was determined to be a success, the groundwork was laid for gaining the political support necessary to develop a competency-based evaluation and development process for principals. Without the positive attention resulting from the successful selection installation, it is highly unlikely that we could have gained alignment behind a competency-based development process for principals.

The other approach regarding the order of implementation is to focus first on the HR practice for which senior management has the most concern. If the CEO or the management team is concerned about the lack of innovation and initiative in the workforce, then performance management may be seen as the tool that will provide the best lever to improve organizational performance.

Installing a competency-based performance development system will change the corporate culture. It results in more direct feedback to managers and employees. Managers and employees will face truths about their weaknesses that they have never faced. They will also need to focus on their own development in ways that most of them never have before. Managers will need to become coaches and developers of people to fully succeed at their jobs. Perhaps the most threatening aspect of installing a competency-based performance development system is that it often exposes the weaknesses of senior-level managers. If they are not committed to leading and participating in a developmental culture, the organization may be in for considerable turmoil and upheaval.

Compensation is probably one of the last areas in which to involve competencies (if at all). Because of the emotionally charged nature of compensation, any direct relationship between competency evaluation and compensation will be likely to cause a reaction that could verge on organizational rebellion.

Definition: Promotes the success of all students by advocating, nurturing, and sustaining a school culture and instructional program conducive to student learning and professional development.

Develops Curriculum

Key Behaviors

- Applies theories of learning to curriculum design and development.
- Uses research, teacher expertise, and recommendations of learned societies to make curriculum decisions.

Develops Learning Programs

Key Behaviors

- Possesses and applies a broad base of knowledge about curricula, subject matter, technology, and new methods of teaching.
- Develops effective learning programs.
- Considers diversity in developing learning experiences.

Encourages Learning

Key Behaviors

- Makes students and staff feel valued and important.
- Fosters teacher development focusing on student learning.
- Makes available multiple opportunities for all students to learn.
- Models and encourages lifelong learning.
- Creates a culture of high expectations for self, student, and staff performance.

Assesses and Solves Problems Related to Student Learning

Key Behaviors

- Identifies and addresses barriers to learning.
- Assesses student learning using a variety of techniques and multiple sources of information.

Scale:

- **−2** Demonstrates few or none of the key behaviors and obstructs those behaviors in others.
- **0** Demonstrates few or none of the key behaviors.
- **2** Occasionally demonstrates some of the key behaviors and is seldom able to effectively promote a developmental school culture and instructional program.
- **4** Occasionally promotes a developmental school culture and instructional program, but is often ineffective due to weakness in a number of the key behaviors.
- **6** Often successfully promotes a developmental school culture and instructional program, but is weak in some of the key behaviors, or has not demonstrated them in difficult learning environments similar to urban educational settings.
- **8** Has a track record of promoting a developmental school culture within difficult learning environments similar to urban educational settings by consistently demonstrating the key behaviors.
- **10** Inspires, models, leads, trains, and motivates students, parents, teachers, administrators, and the community to promote a developmental school culture and instructional program.

Figure 8.1   The competency of educational/curriculum leadership.

MAINTAINING ORGANIZATIONAL CONSISTENCY

When planning installation of a competency-based methodology, remember the importance of maintaining consistency within and among HR applications. It is surprising how many organizations use one set of competencies for selection and another for appraisal and development. The confusion this creates will make it difficult to gain the maximum benefit from the applications.

With large organizations, another consistency problem occurs. A 50-hospital system operating in 10 regions, for example, uses many consultants throughout the system who have some familiarity with competencies. Many of these consultants use their own set of competencies, and with its decentralized structure the system now has different parts of the organization using different competencies and different approaches. Again, the confusion and lack of alignment can only decrease synergy and the benefits received from using the applications.

DEALING WITH THE ISSUE OF INCLUSION

One of the questions regarding installing competency-based systems is whom to include in the process of determining the system and the process. The argument for inclusion is that when people are involved in the decision-making process, they are likely to become advocates and supporters of the process. If they feel left out, they are likely to turn their resentment into resistance to the process. To implement a competency-based selection process for principals in the Chicago public school system, for example, it was vitally important to include all the relevant parties—leaders from the Chicago Principals and Administrators' Association, executives from the central administration, and representatives from the local school councils. Exclusion of any of these groups would probably have killed the project.

When many people are included in the process, there are several phenomena that often occur:

They frequently criticize and change things to make the process their own. If you have presented them with the perfect system that can only be made worse by changing it, they will still "improve" it. It is a fascinating process to observe, and the implementation process is much less stressful if you expect it to occur. You present a solution, they find fault with it, you change it to meet their objections, and they become satisfied and support it. The need to touch it and change it seems to be an almost essential part of the ownership process.

They believe that they are unique. Just as people want to be seen as unique and special, they want to think of their organizations as unique and special. While this is not a universal phenomenon like the previous point, it is common and should be expected and prepared for. Plan to spend time listening to them talk about how they are different from other organizations, and understand that there is often little point in showing them that they are not so unique. Often what they really want is to feel important and listened to.

Problems with Inclusion

Inclusion has its downside risks, and being aware of them will help you be prepared to deal with them. One of the risks falls under the general category "Too many cooks spoil the broth." If many people are included in the development process, and all of them change the application to make it their own, you may end up with a process that no longer solves the problem effectively.

This is more of a problem if less competent managers become included in the process. They can easily water the project down by suggesting changes that will lower standards or decrease the degree of accountability in the application. Many mediocre performers, for example, will not endorse an appraisal process that will result in their careers being damaged as a result of an accurate evaluation of their performance. They will talk about how subjective the evaluation is, and how they are not completely responsible for the results on which they are assessed. While they are technically correct, the real issue is quite different from that being discussed.

A third issue is that of territory or turf. If people feel that you are infringing upon their areas of responsibility and they feel insecure about their status or position, you are likely to encounter either active or passive resistance. Including them in the process is a mixed blessing; you may be able to avoid their resistance later, but they may sabotage the project at the beginning.

Developing Competency Models

The development of competency models can be a relatively simple process, or it can take years and cost millions of dollars. There is no one correct way to develop competency models, and how it is done should depend on the nature of the organization and some basic considerations:

- The practices for which they will be used.
- The financial and personnel resources available.
- Who needs to be included in the process of developing and endorsing the applications.
- Who is going to be included in the implementation process.

Sometimes it is politically important to have a prestigious consulting firm involved in the competency modeling process in order to establish credibility with a critical constituency. Sometimes one must get "down and dirty" and use the least expensive competency modeling process because there simply are not the resources available to do the best job. Sometimes it is necessary to implement an inferior process, just because it is the one advocated by a particular executive who happens to be the only person with the authority and interest to assure organizational support.

There are three different kinds of competencies that can be included in competency models:

1. *Differentiating competencies*—those competencies that most differentiate superior performers from mediocre performers. Common differentiating competencies include results orientation, influence, and initiative.

2. *Threshold competencies*—those competencies in which a minimum level of proficiency is required for job success, but a higher level of proficiency is not highly correlated with superior performance. In some positions, for example, concern for quality does not greatly differentiate superior performers, but a certain level of proficiency is required for even minimal acceptability.

3. *Transformational competencies*—those competencies at which managers and/or employees are generally weak, which if improved will most likely result in improved performance. The competency of developing others, for example, is one at which most managers are weak. There are other competencies that are greater differentiators than developing others, but including the competency in a job model could be important if competency models are to be used for the purposes of appraisal and development.

Competency models normally include differentiating competencies. There may be a reason for including threshold competencies, but including them may cause more confusion than anything else. It is important to avoid confusion between threshold competencies and differentiating competencies. It can cause people to shift their focus from the competencies whose improvement will most leverage their performance onto competencies whose improvement results in little behavioral benefit.

Transformational competencies are the ones most often missed in competency models. This is a variation on the theme of "Ignorance is bliss"—if no one is strong in a competency, no one will be aware of the pervasive weakness. Nevertheless, the inclusion of transformational competencies is key to organizational improvement and creating a culture of competence.

Alternative Ways of Choosing the Competencies in Your Job Models

Many organizations choose their competency models by following the advice and approach of their consultant. While there is nothing wrong with following a consultant's advice, it is worthwhile to be aware of the alternative approaches for choosing the competencies in competency models.

Traditional approaches to determining competencies involve studying superior performers, and identifying the traits, characteristics, and behaviors that differentiate them from average performers. One of the ways this can be done is to follow superior and average performers as they go about their workday and write down detailed observations about what they do. Behavioral differences between the two groups can then be identified.

A second common approach is to perform interviews and organize focus groups of managers and superior performers, and ask them a series of questions along the lines of the following:

- What does it take to be successful at this position?
- Why have people failed at the position?
- What characteristics distinguish excellent from average performers?

You can also provide them a list of competencies and have them rank these in order of perceived importance in the job. You can use the interviews and focus groups as opportunities to extract from the interviewees confirmation that behavioral competencies predict superior performance better than do technical skills. One way to do this is by taking a small number of employees in the position and having the interviewees rank them three times—first, in order of their performance; second, in order of their proficiency in some of the competencies that the interviewees think differentiate superior performers; and third, in order of their proficiency in some of the technical skills that they think are most important for the position. By comparing the relative rankings, you can determine whether technical skills or competencies correlate better with performance.

Another approach to identifying differentiating competencies is to perform behavioral event interviews with superior and average performers. Using this method, interviewers ask the employees to describe events that best exemplify what they do. The interviewers ask follow-up questions to draw out the stories and obtain more detail regarding their behavior, thoughts, feelings, and effectiveness. The interviews are taped, transcribed, and coded by another researcher according to the competencies that are demonstrated in the transcript. A statistical analysis is then carried out to determine the frequency and extent to which different competencies differentiate the group of superior performers from the group of average performers.

A quicker and more efficient approach is possible if you can use effective behaviorally anchored rating scales to measure competency proficiency. The process is as follows:

1. Rate samples of superior and average employees using the scales for a large number of competencies—20 or more.
2. Calculate the average ratings for each group for each competency.
3. Subtract the overall average rating for average employees from the overall average rating for superior employees to determine the average difference between the two groups.
4. Rank order the competencies based on the average difference between the two groups.
5. The competency at the top of the list is the greatest differentiator; the second competency is the second greatest differentiator; and so on.

Tables 9.1 and 9.2 provide one example of this process in action, with three employees shown in each employee category (average and superior). The data came from a group of private bankers at one of the largest banks in the United States who were responsible for getting high-net-worth individuals to become new customers for the bank. This process provides a simple means of validating the process of determining which competencies really differentiate superior performers.

All of these approaches to competency modeling require that the organization employ a significant number of superior performers in the position being evaluated, and that these performers are known. Unfortunately, this is often not the case. In some positions, such as those of senior management, there may be only one. In other positions there may be only a few employees, not providing a large enough sample to provide validated results.

Some companies simply do not have enough superior performers with whom to compare their average employees. One manufacturing company was able to identify only three high-potential employees out of an employee population totaling 3,500. In a situation in which a company has not been hiring superior employees, the comparative analysis of stronger and weaker employees is likely to be flawed. The competencies that differentiate strong from weak employees may not be the same as those that differentiate truly outstanding professionals from the specific company's employees. In these situations a company may need to rely on competency research to supplement the intuition of company managers and professionals regarding key competencies for the position.

Another problem related to choosing competencies for a competency model is that there are some competencies in which most managers are weak, such as developing others. Developing others may not differentiate superior performers from average performers as much as other competencies, but it may still be important to include it in your competency model for its importance to future organizational success.

Table 9.1   Comparing the average competency ratings for superior and average private bankers. The third column of numbers is the difference between the average ratings for superior and average bankers, and the last column ranks the competencies, where 1 is the competency that most differentiates superior from average employees and 20 is the one that differentiates the least.

| | Average Ratings | | | |
	Average Employees	Superior Employees	Difference	Rank
1. Managing performance	**6.0**	**8.3**	**2.3**	**7**
2. Results orientation	**5.3**	**8.3**	**3.0**	**4**
3. Influence	**4.7**	**7.3**	**2.6**	**6**
4. Initiative	6.3	7.3	1.0	16
5. Entrepreneurial orientation	5.0	6.3	1.3	15
6. Concern for quality	6.3	7.0	0.7	17
7. Persuasive communication	**4.0**	**6.0**	**2.0**	**8**
8. Oral communication	6.0	6.0	0.0	19
9. Written communication	5.3	6.7	1.4	13
10. Attention to communication	6.7	6.3	–0.4	20
11. Interpersonal awareness	**4.3**	**8.3**	**4.0**	**2**
12. Conceptual thinking	4.7	6.3	1.6	12
13. Analytical thinking	6.3	7.0	0.7	17
14. Decision quality	5.3	6.7	1.4	13
15. Strategic thinking	**4.3**	**6.3**	**2.0**	**8**
16. Integrity and truth	6.0	7.7	1.7	10
17. Flexibility	**4.3**	**8.7**	**4.4**	**1**
18. Service orientation	**5.3**	**8.7**	**3.4**	**3**
19. Teamwork	6.0	7.7	1.7	10
20. Decisiveness	**6.0**	**8.7**	**2.7**	**5**

As a result of the time and expense involved in these methods for creating competency models, it is not surprising that many organizations take a less rigorous approach to competency modeling. These companies look at the options and decide to have a consultant give them the models, based on the consultant's presumed expertise and experience. I know of no evidence

Table 9.2 Ranking of competencies for a sample group of private bankers based on the extent to which the competencies differentiated superior from average performers.

Competency	Rank
Flexibility	1
Interpersonal awareness	2
Service orientation	3
Results orientation	4
Decisiveness	5
Influence	6
Managing performance	7
Strategic thinking	8
Persuasive communication	8

that shows such an approach produces better or worse results than those produced by more rigorous analysis.

Competency Models by Position, Function, Level, or Company?

For performance review, development, selection, and succession planning, you need a competency model for each position, a set of competencies on which employees or candidates can be evaluated. How many competency models do you need? One common model for every employee? A different competency model for every position? There are several options.

ONE UNIVERSAL SET OF COMPETENCIES FOR ALL EMPLOYEES AND POSITIONS

Many organizations choose simplicity and workability at the expense of rigor by using the same competencies for every position. There is merit to this approach:

- It builds a common language and frame of reference for everyone.
- It makes it easier to compare employees to one another across position and job functions.
- It eases administration of selection and development practices.
- It helps align everyone toward a common culture and can support the culture change process.

There are some common mistakes companies make in implementing a universal competency set. One is that while trying to cover so much ground in a small number of competencies, they make the competencies too broad and general to be meaningfully measurable. Competencies such as "leadership" exemplify this. Often they add what they call "subordinate competencies" in the attempt to clarify their meaning, and in the process they create the unwieldy system they are trying to avoid by creating a universal competency set.

A second mistake is making the universal competency set too big. One hospital chain has a set containing 22 competencies for all leaders in the organization. Managers and employees simply do not have the time to do an effective job of analyzing and measuring behavior and performance on that many competencies. I usually suggest 8 to 12 competencies as an optimal number. (The smaller the better, but there are so many competency concepts that are important!)

A sample universal competency set might include results orientation, initiative, service orientation, innovation, concern for quality, teamwork, analytical thinking, continuous improvement, and integrity and truth.

These competencies cover most aspects of job performance with the exception of critical managerial and leadership competencies such as developing others, motivating others, and strategic thinking. This points to a third common problem with universal competency models: Some competencies are absolutely critical to leadership and management and relatively unimportant to nonmanagerial individual contributor positions. Including them in a universal model causes confusion for individual contributors, and leaving them out reduces the effectiveness of the model for leaders and managers.

COMPETENCY MODELS BY POSITION

The opposite end of the spectrum is to develop different competency models for every position. While this may provide a greater degree of rigor than other, more broad categories, it presents several difficulties. First, developing models for each position will take considerable time, effort, and expense if done well. Second, the lack of competency commonality from position to position will make it more difficult to compare and contrast candidates currently in different positions. Third, every time employees move from one position to another, they will have to learn new competencies and perhaps abandon those they have been focusing on improving.

Where there are many employees in a position with a high degree of significance and impact, the argument for position-specific competency models becomes more compelling. For example, there are over 550 principals in the Chicago public school system. The job of principal is so important and so different from other jobs in the school system that it is useful to develop a model solely for this position. We used the following set of competencies to develop a selection system for principals in the school system:

- *Educational/curriculum leadership.* Promotes the success of all students by advocating, nurturing, and sustaining a school culture and instructional program conducive to student learning and staff professional development.
- *School management.* Manages school resources effectively, uses knowledge of relevant policies and procedures to make decisions within given parameters, and ensures the safe and efficient operation of the school.
- *Community awareness/involvement.* Collaborates with families and community members, responding to diverse community interests and needs and mobilizing community resources.
- *Visionary leadership/change management.* Facilitates the development, articulation, implementation, and stewardship of a vision of learning that is shared and supported by the school community.
- *Prioritizing, planning, and organizing.* Manages one's own and others' time to most effectively accomplish the school vision and mission.
- *Communication.* Expresses ideas clearly both verbally and in writing, adapting communication style to meet the needs of the audience.
- *Influencing/motivating.* Influences others to adopt values and accept ownership of goals; empowers and motivates individuals and groups to improve performance.
- *Interpersonal sensitivity.* Interacts effectively with diverse constituencies by understanding and responding to their values, goals, needs, concerns, feelings, and agendas.
- *Results orientation.* Sets and acts to achieve challenging, concrete, measurable goals for school improvement.

Focusing on this set of competencies has helped the local school councils improve the quality of the hiring and selection process.

COMPETENCY MODELS BY JOB FUNCTION

One of the most common approaches to competency modeling is to base them on job functions or categories. Every position within the job function has the competencies. A typical set of job functions in a manufacturing company might include sales, marketing, manufacturing, information technology, human resources, senior management, engineering, administration, customer service, and operations.

One advantage of defining competency models by job function is that the number of competency models—generally in the range of 10 to 15—is manageable in terms of both their creation and their maintenance. Another advantage is that the same model applies to all of the positions within a job function, so that employees can continue to focus on the same competencies. It is also easy to compare different employees in the same job function for the purposes of succession planning and organization development.

One disadvantage of this approach is that, as with universal competency models, managers have the same competency models as individual contributors within a job function, unless the approach is modified to add models specifically for managers and leaders.

A typical competency model for sales might include analytical thinking, concern for quality, service orientation, teamwork, influence, initiative, innovation, interpersonal awareness, managing performance, attention to communication, and results orientation.

COMPETENCY MODELS BY LEVEL AND POSITION/JOB FUNCTION

Another approach is to differentiate various levels of mastery in positions or job functions, and then to establish levels of competency for each level. A major accounting firm, for example, uses one basic competency model for its accounting professionals, from entry-level staff accountant to partner. At each progressive level, however, a higher level of proficiency is expected for each competency. In addition, at each level one to three competencies are added that become important at that level. For example, partners must be effective business developers, and need to be strong in relationship building and influence, competencies less important in lower-level accounting positions.

Another example is a law firm for which we developed competency models. Through research we found that one set of competencies differentiated superior from average associates, and another set of competencies differentiated partners from superior associates (Table 9.3). The law firm used this research as the basis of its competency models.

Table 9.3 Results from a study examining the competencies that differentiate associates from partners in a small law firm.

Competencies That Differentiate Superior from Nonsuperior Associates
Influence
Developing others
Teamwork
Managing performance
Results orientation
Continuous improvement
Initiative
Establishing focus
Concern for quality

Competencies That Differentiate Partners from Superior Associates
Entrepreneurial orientation
Conceptual thinking
Innovation
Analytical thinking
Decision quality
Service orientation
Attention to communication

MODIFICATIONS TO TRADITIONAL APPROACHES

One way to improve universal competency models is to create three positional levels: individual contributor, managerial, and executive. One model is used for all individual contributors, a small set of managerial competencies is added for all managers, and another set of competencies is added for senior executives. This preserves most of the simplicity of the universal approach and includes the competencies critical to managerial and executive success when they become relevant.

The same solution can improve the workability of the job function approach. You can create a competency model for sales management by adding managerial competencies to those in the sales competency model. The same managerial competencies, when added to the engineering competencies, create the engineering management competency model. This approach allows for the differentiation of job functions and for differentiation among executives, managers, and individual contributors.

Another modification to competency modeling is to identify a set of company-wide competencies that must be included in every competency model. This approach helps ensure that the company-wide competencies will be included in every HR practice in which competency models are used. The company-wide competencies can be used to reinforce core company values or to reinforce cultural change efforts.

In one example, American National Can uses a system of competency models by job function, with the following set of core company-wide competencies:

- Fostering New Ways.
- Teamwork.
- Influence Skill.
- Managing Performance.
- Results Orientation.

This set of competencies was developed as a part of a change strategy that included helping the organization and its employees focus on the behaviors needed to create organizational success.

How to Measure Competency

No matter what method of competency modeling is utilized, the effectiveness of the model depends on how well the competencies are measured. In the following pages we will examine some of the advantages and disadvantages of the common methods used for rating competency proficiency.

THE 1 TO 5 "SCHOOL GRADING" SYSTEM

The most common system of measurement for competencies seems to be a legacy from the grading system used throughout the U.S. educational system, where "A" is outstanding, "B" is good, "C" is fair, "D" is poor, and "F" is failing. Migrated to the corporate world, "F" to "A" has become "1" to "5": "5" is "outstanding", "4" is "exceeds expectations," "3" is "meets expectations," "2" is "below expectations," and "1" is "far below expectations." This grading system is the most common rating method for both selection and performance appraisal.

One of the problems with this method is the subjectivity of the measurement. If expectations are not precisely defined, then one person's expectations can be quite different from another's. Furthermore, the weaker the competence of employees, the more likely they are to rate other employees higher than their actual proficiency. An "A" level performer will tend to rate "C" level performers with a "C"; but a "C" level performer will be much more likely to rate "C" level performers with an "A" or a "B," because to rate them lower would lower their own self-image.

The subjectivity inherent in a rating system based on meeting expectations decreases the effectiveness of competency assessment. To make it useful, you need to precisely define and align everyone's expectations so that they are rating the same behavior with the same rating. This typically requires more training than most companies are willing to invest in for this purpose.

Another problem with the 1 to 5 grading system for performance appraisal and development is that the feedback from the rating provides little useful information to help employees improve their behavior and performance. It is the same problem you would have in schools if all you received were your final grades and had received no grades on any tests or homework during the grading period. The grade itself does nothing to help students know what they need to learn or how they should act differently in the future. The same applies to employee appraisal.

BEHAVIORALLY ANCHORED RATING SCALES

Behaviorally anchored rating scales are scales in which each rating level is defined by specific, observable behaviors. An example of a behaviorally anchored rating scale we use appears in Table 9.4.

Behaviorally anchored rating scales offer several advantages over the traditional 1 to 5 rating system. They provide raters with guidance on how to rate people based on either the behavior that they have observed (in the case of employees) or behavior that was described in detail (in the case of candidates in the interview process). They also provide a common framework and set of reference points for different raters to use, making it quicker and easier for them to rate people.

Behaviorally anchored rating scales serve as a powerful tool for an organization to communicate both the meaning of competencies as well as the organizational expectations about how they will be operationalized. Every time employees evaluate themselves or others, using the scales reminds them of the behaviors that are desirable and recognized by the organization. The scale for initiative, for example, tells employees that the organization values employees who:

Table 9.4   Sample behaviorally anchored rating scale for the competency of initiative.

−2	Detrimental	Takes no initiative and acts to thwart the initiative of others.
0	Absent	Does almost nothing to identify and act on problems and opportunities.
2	Minimal	Gives some evidence of initiative; may avoid or miss opportunities to identify and act on problems and opportunites.
4	Moderately Effective	Sometimes shows initiative, exhibits some key behaviors; volunteers for tasks, persists in the face of difficulties, identifies what needs to be done, and takes action without being asked or required to do so.
6	Adept	Take initiative in most situations, sometimes displays advanced key behaviors: seizes opportunities and takes action to take advantage of them, initiates individual or group projects, and takes complete responsibility for their success.
8	Excellent	Takes initiative in even difficult or complex situations, displays many advanced key behaviors: freshly identifies what needs to be done in the face of obstacles, takes action until they are overcome, and takes responsibility to originate all steps of a project when the outcomes and circumstances are not well-defined.
10	Absent	Models, leads, trains, and motivates multiple levels of personnel to be excellent initiative.

- Seize opportunities and take action to take advantage of them.
- Initiate individual or group projects and take complete responsibility for their success.
- When faced with obstacles, freshly identify what needs to be done and take action until the obstacles are overcome.

Using behaviorally anchored rating scales can actually change the organizational vocabulary, as the concepts and behavioral descriptions become part of the language of the organization.

Behaviorally anchored rating scales can help managers and employees develop positive visions for themselves, their subordinates, and other employees. Instead of seeing themselves or others as permanently stuck at their current level of competency, the behavioral descriptions can help people create a picture of what the employee could be doing if he or she were more proficient in the competency. Using initiative as an example, employees who are currently rated a "4" volunteer for tasks and persist in the face of difficulties, but can see new behavioral choices for themselves: They can seize opportunities, initiate and take complete responsibility for projects, and aggressively overcome obstacles.

Using behaviorally anchored rating scales can also reduce training time for competency-based applications. Teaching people the difference between a "5" (meaning "outstanding") and a "4" (meaning "exceeds expectations") can be time-consuming if you really want consistency among raters. If the behavioral descriptions associated with each rating effectively and concisely describe a level of proficiency in the competency, the amount of time required for training people to rate themselves or others can be reduced.

One variant of behaviorally anchored rating scales occurs when a list of behaviors or traits is associated with each rating. An example of such an approach is provided in Table 9.5.

The main problem with this kind of scale occurs when employees exhibit some behaviors at one rating level and some behaviors at another. Sometimes their behavior and traits fall under three or even four different ratings. In Table 9.5, for example, how do you rate people who are strong at identifying long-range consequences of different options (rating a "5") but weak at identifying trends in the marketplace (rating a "2")? The confusion resulting from this situation can only increase employee frustration and resistance to the assessment process.

THE COMPETENCY MATRIX—
LEVEL AND PROFICIENCY

Another approach to competency measurement is to define levels of proficiency on competencies in terms of a set of behaviors expected for a grade level or rank at a particular position. Under this approach, the numbers in the rating system are replaced by job titles—in a publishing house the titles might be assistant editor, associate editor, editor, and senior editor, for example, or in an accounting firm they might be staff accountant, senior accountant, manager, senior manager, and partner.

The advantage of this approach is that the competency rating system helps employees understand the desired level of proficiency for each competency at each job level, thereby letting them know the behaviors they need to demonstrate to be promoted and to succeed at each level. The approach still causes difficulties when someone is strong at some of the behaviors and weak at others within a competency. What do you do when a partner is operating at only a senior accountant level of proficiency at a competency or in some of the behaviors described in the competency?

There are of course other variations on these themes of competency

Table 9.5   Example of a behaviorally anchored rating scale for decision quality, in which each rating level is defined by a set of behaviors.

1	2	3	4	5
Doesn't anticipate problems or consequences.	Thinks of short-term implications or consequences.	Identifies short-range consequences of different options in complex situations.	Identifies medium-range consequences of different options in complex situations.	Identifies long-range consequences of different options in complex situations.
Doesn't anticipate reactions to situations.	Anticipates reactions when they are fairly obvious.	Notices short-term trends in the market and determines impact on the organization.	Notices medium-range trends in the market and determines impact on the organization.	Notices long-range trends in the market and determines impact on the organization.
Doesn't think about the implications of different options.	Thinks about the implications of different options in simple situations.	Develops plans to prepare for opportunities or problems in relatively simple situations.	Develops plans to prepare for opportunities or problems in moderately complex situations.	Develops plans to prepare for opportunities or problems in complex situations.

measurement. The important point to remember is that *workability* and *leverage* are the most important criteria for evaluating a means of competency measurement. Is it easy to use? Is it enjoyable to use? Or does it cause anxiety or frustration? Is it easy to learn? Is the perceived gain greater than the implementation pain? Are you getting the greatest possible benefit for the time and resources expended? The answers to these questions should determine the rating approach you use.

Beware: Competency Implementation Raises Expectations or Despair

Introducing competencies is not a neutral act. It implies that you are raising the bar for employees, raising expectations of their performance. If you introduce the competency concept but do not use it to improve the HR practice to which it is applied, the consequence will be worse than if you did nothing. Credibility will be decreased, cynicism will rise, and it will be more difficult to change things in the future.

Several years ago I worked with a private bank in Switzerland. Switzerland is many years behind the United States in opportunities for professional advancement for women. Almost every private banker in Switzerland is male. The general manager of the bank had worked in the United States for many years, and was committed to removing the gender barrier in the bank. I met with some of the women in the bank whom the general manager thought to be the sharpest and most competent. (They were of course all in clerical jobs.) It was clear upon getting to know them that many of them were more capable than many of the male private bankers earning several times their compensation. When I expressed a vision to them in which all employees would be rewarded and given opportunities based on their talents and their contributions, I was met with skepticism and a sense of hopelessness. I saw the pain in their eyes and the frustration and bitterness in their voices as they told me how little they were respected and listened to, and how unwilling their male "superiors" were to give them more responsibility. I assured them that a new age was dawning, and that success in the bank in the future would be based on competency instead of gender.

Unfortunately, they were right. The introduction of competencies for assessment and the best intentions of the general manager were no match for the resistance of the Swiss culture to the idea of gender equality in the workplace. The men refused to consider treating the women as professionals. The HR manager reinforced and justified their behavior, patiently explaining to the general manager why he shouldn't expect so much change in their corporate culture so fast. As a result of the lack of change, the women in the organization became more bitter and cynical than they were before we started, and we made future progress more difficult because of our raising false hopes.

When you ask people to tell you their problems, they often expect that you intend to do something about them. Similarly, when you show people a vision of improved individual and organizational performance with an implied improvement in joy and satisfaction, they hope and expect that they will reap some of the benefits. If you introduce competencies into your HR applications, put in the thought, time, and effort to ensure their success. Take advantage of employees' raised expectations, and use them to fuel individual and organizational success.

10

Using Competency-Based Selection in the Ideal Hiring Process

In a recent meeting with the senior vice president of human resources of a packaging company with $200 million in sales, I heard the following lament:

> Last year we hired a new CFO, and it turned out to be a real nightmare. He interviewed great, and everyone liked him. He had just left one of our competitors, and knew our business inside and out. We spent $60,000 to relocate him and his family here. Inside of a month, though, we knew it was a mistake. He turned out to be a very different person from the guy we thought we had hired. He had said he was a team player, but within two weeks he had alienated the head of MIS [management information systems] and two of the business unit heads. He didn't listen well, and started disparaging people behind their backs. After about nine months we decided we had to admit that we made a mistake. That mistake has cost us a few hundred thousand dollars.

This company's selection system was typical of many companies. They used a search firm to generate a pool of interested candidates, interviewed several, and hired the one the CEO most liked. Their approach to interviewing was to hire the candidate with whom the CEO felt most comfortable. It didn't work. A better selection process could have prevented this mistake.

Is Your Hiring Process Much Better Than Random?

W. Edwards Deming, the father of the quality processes that brought Japanese carmakers to world dominance, used to make the point that before you reward or punish machine operators for errors, you should know the effect of random, noncontrollable factors on performance. He demonstrated this point by having seminar participants each grab (without looking) six marbles from a hat containing 80 percent green and 20 percent red marbles. Participants were then told that the green marbles met product specifications and the red marbles did not and were errors. Of course the red marbles were randomly distributed throughout the group, with some people having all green marbles and some having one, two, or even three red ones. His point was that before you can evaluate the effectiveness of a person or a process, you have to remove the random "noise" from the system. Let's apply this to the hiring process.

Imagine that you are hiring an accountant. (It could be any profession.) Those of us who took biology in school may remember that biological traits tend to distribute themselves in a normal or Gaussian distribution, also known as the bell curve. The bell curve is defined by the population's mean—the average value of the trait—and its standard deviation—the amount of variation from the mean. In the bell curve, most of the individuals cluster around the mean, and the farther you get from the mean, the fewer individuals manifest the value.

If you hypothetically graphed the distribution of accountants based on their overall competence, you might expect the distribution to look like that in Figure 10.1. Most accountants will be of average competence, falling near the mean. A small proportion will be superior performers, and an equally small proportion will be very weak performers.

In our hypothetical example, let's assume that you were hiring your accountant randomly from the population of accountants represented in Figure 10.1. Most of the time you would pick an average accountant—one near the mean—and might think that you did an average job of selection. Ten percent of the time you would pick a superior performer—a "top tenpercenter"—and you would be very happy with your selection process. And 10 percent of the time you would hire an accountant so weak that you might blame everyone involved in the process for doing such a terrible job

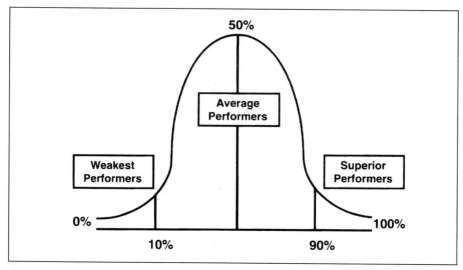

Figure 10.1   A hypothetical distribution of accountants based on their overall competency.

of selection. In reality, you did the same job of selection each time; the difference in candidate quality was purely the luck of the draw.

Now let's make the situation a little more realistic. Assuming the competence of accountants follows a normal distribution curve, which accountants are most likely to be reading the "Help Wanted" sections of the newspaper? Are they the outstanding performers at the top of the curve, the ones most likely to be appreciated and acknowledged for their performance? Or will they be the accountants at the bottom end of the distribution curve, whose poor performance has resulted in lackluster career success and greater job dissatisfaction? It is an accepted axiom in the field of executive search that if you want to hire superior performers you have to go after them aggressively. Newspaper ads seldom attract high-potential candidates or outstanding executives.

Is your hiring process much better than random? Perhaps not. Table 10.1 shows the result of research on the correlation between assessment methods and job performance.[1] Several studies revealed little correlation (less than .2) between the traditional job interview and performance. (The traditional job interview is one in which interviewers receive no training and ask the typical interview questions: Why are you interested in this job? Tell

---

[1]Spencer, Lyle M. & Spencer, Signe M. *Competence at Work*. New York: John Wiley & Sons, 1993.

Table 10.1   Research showing the correlation ("r") between different methods of assessment and job performance.

Assessment Method	r
Assessment centers	.65
Interviews (behavioral)	.48–.61
Work-sample tests	.54
Ability tests	.53
Modern personality tests	.39
Biodata	.38
References	.23
Interviews (nonbehavioral)	.05–.19

Source: Lyle M. Spencer & Signe M. Spencer, *Competence at Work*, New York: John Wiley & Sons, 1993, 242.

me about yourself. What are your strengths and weaknesses? And so on.) In these studies subjects interviewed several professionals who worked in the same organization and ranked them against one another, based solely on the interview. When the rankings from the interviews were compared with the professionals' actual rankings in their jobs, little relationship was found. These are sobering findings for the vast majority of organizations that rely on the traditional job interview for determining selection.

Problems with the Traditional Hiring Process

WE FAIL TO DEFINE THE POSITION ADEQUATELY

A common scenario for executive recruiters is that a search is underway for two months before the hiring manager has a clear picture of what the job is: its purposes and goals, how success will be measured, what the responsibilities are, and so on. It is not unusual for the job to be defined as hiring managers interview candidates and modify job descriptions as they expand their knowledge and understanding through the interview process.

WE HIRE ON THE BASIS OF EMOTIONAL ATTRACTION

The traditional selection process often doesn't do the job because it is based on emotional attraction—"Whom do I like best?"—rather than an assessment of the traits and characteristics that actually predict performance. Interviewers, using the typical "Tell me about yourself" interview style, tend to pick candidates who *interview well*, rather than those who will be successful at the job.

I believe that there is an unconscious mental and emotional process going on that determines to whom we are attracted in the interview process, defined by the following rules:

We are emotionally attracted to candidates who make us feel better about ourselves in one of two ways:

- They are strong in and reflect back to us the traits and qualities that we use to feel good about ourselves. Example: You interview someone who is a "get it done" kind of person; you have the same trait and are proud of that quality in yourself. You immediately like the candidate.
- They are strong in traits and qualities in which we perceive ourselves as weak and feel bad about. Example: You interview someone who is detail oriented and dedicated to high-quality customer service. You are great at creating customer solutions but lose interest once you know the solutions are going to work, and you feel bad about not being more concerned about service delivery. When you are with the candidate, you don't feel so bad about your own lack of interest in follow-through.

We are emotionally repelled by candidates who make us feel worse about ourselves in one of two ways:

- They are weak in the traits and qualities that we use to feel good about ourselves. Example: You are proud of being a "get it done" person, and have no respect for a candidate who takes little initiative and isn't a "get it done" person.
- They are weak in traits and qualities in which we perceive ourselves as weak and feel ashamed or embarrassed about. You feel bad about your lack of concern about service delivery, and you dislike candidates who show a similar lack of concern.

Most of the time the feelings and reactions just described operate at the unconscious level. What we feel is the liking and the excitement for some candidates, and a disliking or unhappiness with other candidates. However, if you ask yourself two questions, you can often get in touch with the deeper reactions. The first question is, "What is it I really like (or dislike) about the candidate?"; the second is, "In what ways do I exhibit that trait, and how do

I feel about myself in relation to the trait?" By tracking your own mental process, you can often bring to consciousness the mental and emotional connections that cause selection decisions to be made on emotional attraction.

WE BASE HIRING DECISIONS ON TECHNICAL ABILITY AND EXPERIENCE RATHER THAN COMPETENCY

People who are stronger technically are not necessarily the best performers. What makes a good CFO is not having the greatest knowledge of accounting theory and finance. Excellent CFOs are people who are strong influencers of others, who act as strategic partners to the CEO and the rest of the management team, who use their analytical and conceptual thinking to great benefit for the business, and who set and achieve challenging goals. The greatest knowledge of finance on the planet won't help much if the CFO does not apply it well through the exercise of these competencies.

One of the problems with the traditional hiring process is that while interviewing candidates, technical managers typically focus their questions and conversations on the areas in which they are most comfortable, which is technical expertise. So they focus on assessing technical skills, and if candidates are technically strong they will think that they are excellent candidates. Unfortunately, it isn't necessarily so.

There is a simple exercise that we use to demonstrate how poorly correlated technical skills are with performance (Table 10.2). Take five or six people in the same job in your company who can be ranked in order of overall job performance. Then rank those same five people in order of their proficiency in the competency of initiative, and then in their technical knowledge. When

Table 10.2   A sample exercise comparing rankings of overall performance, initiative, and technical knowledge of five engineers.

Employee Ranking of Overall Performance	Employee Name	Initiative	Technical Knowledge
#1	Morrie Williams	1	4
#2	Millie Rose	3	5
#3	Carrie Mustafa	2	3
#4	Mario Estrada	4	1
#5	Harry Jones	5	2

you compare which set of rankings is more similar to overall employee ranking, the competency ranking almost always is much closer.

It is important to assess technical skills in candidates. They need to have a sufficient level of technical skill, knowledge, and experience in order to perform the job. However, competency is much more predictive of overall performance.

WE FAIL TO DISTINGUISH BETWEEN NECESSARY AND DESIRED SKILL LEVELS AND EXPERIENCE

Another common problem with the selection process is that hiring managers often begin the hiring process saying that a particular technical skill, background, or work experience is a requirement for the job. They are steadfast in their insistence on the importance of the skill, background, or experience, and rule out candidates who do not have it. Then one of two things frequently happens: Either someone is hired who has the skill or background but lacks the competency to do the job well, or at some point the hiring managers hire someone they were referred to who fits *none* of the technical and experience criteria but who they believe is a "really good guy." In other words, they abandon the technical criteria and hire a seemingly competent person, dumbfounding all the HR resources that have been dedicated to finding a highly competent person in the first place.

WE FAIL TO TRAIN THE INTERVIEW TEAM

Organizations generally do a poor job of aligning or training the interview team. Few people receive training and know how to interview job candidates. In the absence of any training, interviewers do the best they can, using their common sense and any pieces of information or advice they have picked up over the years. "Tell me about yourself." "What do you want to be doing in five years?" "If you could be any kind of animal, what animal would you be?"

Some interviewers make the mistake of telling candidates exactly the answers they want to hear. Interviews like the following occur every day: In the absence of training, hiring managers often develop beliefs about hiring and selection criteria that not only have no relation to reality but that are outright discriminatory and prejudiced. Absurd statements I have heard are: "I won't hire anyone from New York." "I have found that women tend to get pregnant and quit." "I have had poor success with graduates of West Coast universities."

Providing managers with basic interview training is one of the best training investments an organization can make.

WE FAIL TO ALIGN THE INTERVIEW TEAM

Usually organizations do not take sufficient time to align their interview teams. Often different interviewers have different ideas about what is needed in the position. When performing searches, we frequently find some members of the interview team objecting to hiring someone for the position at all. Unless you obtain alignment regarding the purpose, goals, requirements, and needs for the position, interviewers may have different and sometimes conflicting agendas for the position, and they will evaluate candidates on criteria that may be quite different from those of the hiring manager.

WE DON'T OBTAIN IN-DEPTH REFERENCES

Through the typical interview process you do not have the opportunity to see candidates perform the job you are interviewing for. Instead you are estimating the probability of their success by talking to the them about performing the job. The opportunity to reference candidates with people who know them and in the course of performing their tasks is one that no hiring manager should turn down. Yet few managers know how to use the opportunity to further assess candidates or to get advice about how best to manage the successful candidate on the job.

The Ideal Selection Process

To hire the best person for each and every job in your organization, you need a comprehensive program to attract, select, hire, and retain top-quality employees. The remainder of this chapter will lay out a vision of a comprehensive hiring and selection process that maximizes the probability of your hiring the best available candidates to meet your organization's needs, fit your culture, and help you achieve organizational success.

SETTING UP THE HIRING PROCESS

Anyone who has developed software or managed any complex project knows the value of the initial planning process. Establishing the right process can facilitate every stage and help ensure that critical steps are not omitted. Everyone with extensive experience in hiring knows that Murphy's Law rules: Anything that can go wrong will.

Establishing the Steps and Time Lines for the Hiring and Selection Process

One of the first steps in hiring is to define the steps in the process and establish time lines, intended results, and accountability. Who will do what by when? How will we know that it is done? What needs to be accomplished by each milestone? How will we know how well it has been done? By answering these questions at the start, expectations and accountability are made clear, reducing later confusion and increasing the likelihood that the job will be accomplished. Table 10.3 shows an example of a time line for a hiring process.

Table 10.3   A sample time line for a hiring process for a midlevel professional position in an organization in which an HR staffing professional plays a lead facilitative role.

Step	Responsible Party	Other Involvement	Completion Date
Establish the hiring plan	Staffing manager	Hiring manager	May 1
Complete position specifications	Hiring manager	Staffing manager	May 8
Inform and align interview team	Hiring aanager	Staffing manager	May 8
Hire search firm	Staffing manager	Hiring manager	May 8
Manage candidate generation	Staffing aanager	Hiring manager	Ongoing
Meet with search firm	Staffing manager	Hiring manager	May 15
Screen candidate resumes	Staffing manager	Hiring manager	June 15
First-round candidate interviews	Staffing manager	Hiring manager	June 30
Train interview team	Staffing manager	Hiring manager	July 7
Second-round candidate interviews	Staffing manager	Interview team	July 14
Debriefing meetings	Staffing manager	Hiring manager	July 17
Referencing	Hiring manager	Staffing manager	July 24
Offer	Staffing manager	Hiring manager	July 31
Start date	Staffing manager	Hiring manager	August 31

Communicating to the Hiring Manager the Importance of Using Competencies in the Hiring Process

The job of orienting hiring managers is one that can require a significant amount of competency and skill on the part of hiring process facilitators, typically HR professionals. Managers need to be educated and influenced so that they understand the need for and the benefits of a rigorous selection process. They need to be educated and trained so that they understand the process and can use it to improve the quality of their hiring decisions. They need to become advocates for the process so that they will obtain the cooperation of their interview teams to put in the time and effort to contribute their talents to the assessment process.

Orienting hiring managers includes explaining the importance of behavioral competencies; the nature and benefits of competency-based selection; the proposed steps in the hiring process; the role of the interview team; and the options and choices available to hiring managers in each step of the process. Depending on your organization, managers will have varying degrees of latitude regarding use of the steps in the process. Some organizations establish hiring policies and procedures that hiring managers must follow, while others offer services that managers may use if they wish.

It is important for managers to feel that the purpose of the hiring process and the job of hiring process facilitator is to serve them and help them hire the best person to meet their needs. Without this communication, this effort will be perceived as just another bureaucratic procedure designed to make their lives more difficult.

Establishing the Interview Team

Determining who will be on the interview team can be an important part of the hiring process. There are many reasons why it might be important to include a variety of people on the team:

- They can assess particular technical skills well.
- Other perspectives on candidates improve assessment accuracy.
- They understand the job well.
- They are particularly good interviewers.
- Their participation in the assessment process is necessary or helpful in obtaining organizational approval to extend the candidate an offer.
- Their participation in the process will help ensure the successful orientation and integration of the new employee in the job.

Hiring managers should know the responsibilities and duties of members of the interview team: To attend an alignment meeting, to get trained in competency-based assessment, to interview candidates, to fill out a candidate assessment form, and to attend candidate debriefing meetings and give feedback on candidates.

Establishing the Business Context

Particularly for senior-level positions, it is important for both the hiring process facilitator and the hiring manager to understand the business context related to the position. This includes understanding the corporate culture, the key issues for the organization, and the organization's key value drivers and success factors. Examples of value drivers for different businesses are:

- The ability to control costs.
- Raw material prices.
- The ability to increase gross revenue.
- The ability to increase the number of inventory turns.
- Increasing the amount of revenue generated per production employee.

With senior management positions, the critical needs of the organization should be a key element in determining the specifications for the position and candidate requirements.

Creating Job Specifications for the Job Opening

There are several reasons for putting together a position description containing the specifications for the job. First, the act of thinking through each element of the position description will often help you work through important issues related to a successful hire. Second, the criteria on which candidates will be evaluated will be clearly defined in the process. Third, the document serves as a tool to focus, align, and orient the interview team toward a common vision of the position and its requirements.

The elements of a position description, elucidated in the next chapter, can include the following:

- The purpose of the position.
- Job goals, expectations, duties, and responsibilities.
- Critical technical skills and competencies.
- Key success factors.
- Reporting relationships.

- Accountability (how success will be measured).
- Job characteristics & preferences.
- Compensation (not shown to other interviewers).
- Potential career path.

Technical Skills and Experience

Too often managers don't decide what they really need until they have interviewed half a dozen candidates. A lot of time and expense can be saved by articulating position qualifications in the following areas:

- Critical technical skills and traits.
- Relationship and communication skills.
- Necessary and desired industry knowledge.
- Management and leadership skills and style.
- Teamwork skills and style.
- Ability to lead and manage change.
- Other traits and characteristics needed for success.

Be careful not to label too many of the technical skills as "absolutely must have" requirements. Someone who is weak in some of the technical skills but who is strong in competencies such as initiative and results orientation will often turn out to be the best employee or manager. Such a person will use initiative and goal orientation to quickly pick up the technical skills needed to succeed at the job.

Job Characteristics and Preferences

Job characteristics and preferences include elements of the job that affect whether people will enjoy doing it. These elements include:

- Amount of routine.
- Complexity.
- Detail orientation.
- Emotional warmth required.
- People contact.
- High-profile nature of the job duties.
- Independence.
- Intensity of emotion and activity.

- Amount of interaction with others.
- Job pace.
- Leadership role.
- Location.
- Overtime.
- Pay for performance.
- Physical environment.
- Promotion opportunities.
- Recognition.
- Team characteristics.
- Time in office.
- Travel requirements.
- Variety of duties.

It is important to identify these job characteristics because you will want to ensure that candidates for the job will find these characteristics acceptable to them.

Establishing Assessment Methods

We are strong proponents of behavioral interviewing as a method to assess both competence and technical proficiency. There are other approaches that can augment (or replace, though usually not as well) behavioral interviewing to expand the completeness of the assessment process:

Writing Samples

The approach has many variations, all based on the theme of having candidates demonstrate their ability to write and logically construct arguments and presentations in a manner similar to that required on the job. One trick is to ask candidates to write you a letter or send you an e-mail expressing why they are interested in the position. Here you kill two birds with one stone: You assess their writing skills and find out the extent and reasons for their interest in the opportunity. Using writing samples may have equal employment opportunity (EEO) implications, however.

Hypothetical Situations or Case Studies

Asking candidates how they would respond in hypothetical situations is a way to discover how their thought processes work, at least under hypothetical circumstances. When those hypothetical circumstances accurately mimic realistic job situations, they become more accurate predictors of performance. Handing a credit analyst a loan document to analyze, for example, can be a useful exercise to evaluate his or her analytical ability, knowledge of credit, and approach to credit analysis.

Testing for Technical Proficiency
For various positions there are tests that measure technical proficiency to a degree that provides useful input for candidate assessment. For example, typing tests that measure typing speed and accuracy are useful tools to help assess candidate qualification for jobs requiring extensive keyboard skills. Tests exist for various professional jobs such as software development, various forms of engineering, and so on.

Assessing and Matching Candidate Preferences with Job Characteristics
One of the reasons for listing the characteristics of the position—location, amount of travel, overtime, independence, and so on—is to compare those characteristics with the wants and needs of candidates to determine the closeness of the match. It doesn't matter how competent candidates are managing a manufacturing plant if they refuse to live where the plant is located. It is important to examine whether the candidate will *like* the job; will it satisfy his or her preferences sufficiently on the job? While this seems like stating the obvious, time and resources get wasted every day because hiring and staffing managers forget to ask basic questions regarding whether candidates actually *want* to do the job for which they are applying. Figures 10.2 and 10.3 show the results of the process we use to assess candidate preferences.

Choosing How to Generate Candidates
The options for candidate generation include generating internal candidates, obtaining employee referrals, Internet job postings, Internet job site canvassing, advertising, contingency search firms, retained search firms, and direct candidate recruitment. Your needs for the position in terms of quality and quantity should determine how you go about finding candidates. Given the distribution of talent as evidenced by the bell curve, you should not expect to find many superior performers by advertising.

There are advantages and disadvantages to each method of candidate generation. The success of the candidate generation effort probably depends more on the competence of the person responsible for the candidate generation than it does on the particular method chosen in a particular situation. This applies both to HR staffing managers and to search consultants, both retained and contingency. If you want to do the best job you can

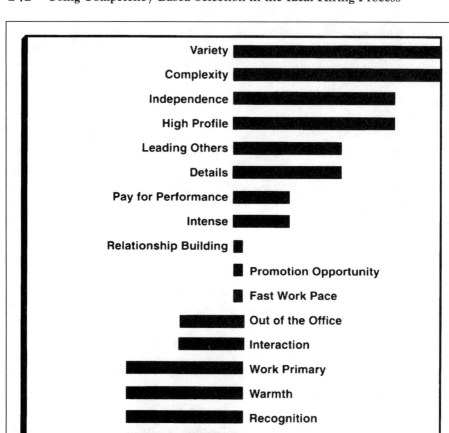

Figure 10.2   Candidate job preferences.

of choosing a recruiter, screen them on the competencies of service orientation, integrity and truth, concern for quality, innovation, flexibility, and managing performance. The good ones will stand out.

Whatever process you use, set specific, measurable, achievable, and time-bound objectives for candidate generation. How many candidates of what quality will be generated by when? Establishing specific objectives will

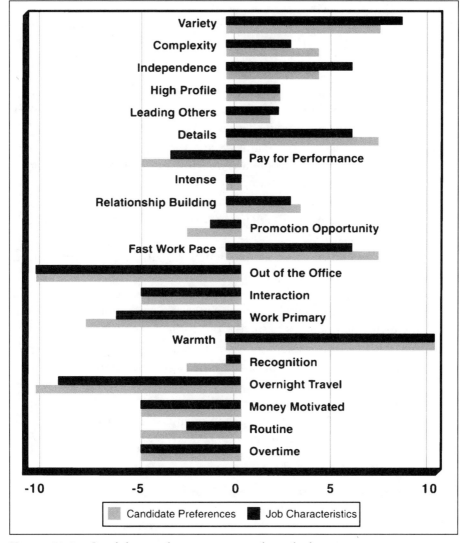

Figure 10.3 Candidate preferences compared to job characteristics.

result in quicker corrective action should the objectives not be met. This is equally true using search firms or through internally generated candidates.

FACILITATING THE SEARCH PROCESS

Once the hiring procedure has been established, active project management is usually required to ensure that the best candidate is hired in the shortest amount of time. This project management requires proficiency in many of the same competencies you are looking for in candidates. The following seven competencies are all critical to successful management of the hiring process:

1. *Service orientation.* You demonstrate an aggressive commitment to satisfy your organization's need and hiring managers by finding, selecting, and hiring outstanding candidates quickly.
2. *Concern for quality.* You facilitate an efficient process in which mistakes are minimized, people are well trained, and lessons are learned so that the process is better next time.
3. *Managing performance.* You track activity and results against expectations and time lines. Problems are responded to quickly, creatively, and decisively.
4. *Results orientation.* You set challenging goals and commit fully to achieving them.
5. *Flexibility.* You respond to changing circumstances with an open mind and a fresh perspective, adjust to the current situation, and utilize all the available resources to solve problems and move things forward.
6. *Interpersonal awareness.* You listen to and read people well, helping them feel heard and valued. You respond to their concerns and help get them met.
7. *Influence.* You get things done by understanding and responding to people's needs. You understand your organization and know where you need support to move the process forward and obtain closure. When obstacles emerge, you overcome them yourself or through others.

Managing Candidate Generation
The candidate generation process needs to be closely managed to ensure adequate quality and quantity of candidates. If you are using a recruiter whom you don't know well, obtain sample candidate resumes as soon as possible, and question the recruiter closely to determine how well candidates meet your qualifications. Literally months can be wasted by not ensuring that recruiters fully understand your qualifications.

Track candidate generation against predefined time lines and expectations regarding quantity and quality. When time lines are not met, communicate directly with the responsible party to determine causes and to seek remedies. Use the qualifications and standards from the position description or job specifications to measure candidates. Make sure that communication occurs regularly and as frequently as necessary.

Once candidates have been generated and are in process, make sure that they are communicated with in a timely manner. Good candidates are difficult to find; you don't want to lose them because they feel neglected or unappreciated.

Training the Hiring Manager
When we first developed our competency-based selection methodology for the executive search process, we trained the hiring manager along with the interview team after the hiring manager had completed the first round of interviews. However, we discovered a problem. We were losing competent candidates in the first round because they were not liked as much as other candidates. We revised our process so that competencies were assessed from the beginning of the candidate screening process. Our training of hiring managers includes the following:

- A brief introduction or a reminder of the theory and benefits of competency-based selection.
- Definition of the purposes of the first interview, including assessing chemistry, fit, technical qualification, and competence.
- Training in behavioral interviewing.
- Giving them the materials they need to conduct behavioral interviewing and assess technology skills and competencies.

Training the Interview Team
In executive search we typically train the interview team after candidates have passed through the first round of interviews, and deliver it as Just-in-Time training. If your organization has been training its managers in competency-based selection, then this step is not necessary except perhaps as a refresher for those interviewers who have not used the process recently or extensively. This training includes a more detailed description of how to gather the interview data necessary to assess competencies. We also cover the typical problems people encounter while conducting behavioral interviews. We describe the steps of the hiring process and make clear that the interview team's role is to gather information and not to vote on which candidate should be hired.

Aligning the Interview Team
It is critical to ensure that all interviewers have a common understanding of the job, including job purposes, goals, expectations, duties and responsibilities, and the technical skills, traits, and competencies important for job success.

This is also a good time to elicit from the interview team any particular issues they have regarding the job and to surface any relevent hidden agendas or concerns. For example, we have seen situations in which interviewers were adamant that the job should be filled by a current employee. If that issue is not addressed, those interviewers can subvert the interview process by aggressively finding fault with every external candidate.

Often we combine interview team alignment with training. While this has the advantage of reducing the number of meetings, it has the disadvantage of causing events to occur out of sequence. Ideally the alignment process should occur at the beginning of the hiring process, so that the hiring manager and hiring process facilitator have the benefit of the team's knowledge and wisdom from the beginning. If the interview team training occurs too far ahead of their interview of candidates, however, they will probably need refresher training more proximate to the interviews.

Managing the Interview and Assessment Process
Managing the interview process involves a series of administrative actions to organize the process. This includes the following steps:

- Coordinating and scheduling interviews with candidates and the interview team.
- Assigning responsibility to interviewers for particular technical skills and competencies on which candidates will be assessed.
- Distributing interview materials to interviewers.
- Gathering interviewer feedback.
- Convening and facilitating a debriefing meeting.
- Facilitating the decision-making process regarding next steps.
- Repeating the above steps as necessary.

Assigning Technical Skills and Competencies for Assessment
To obtain a sufficient depth of assessment on competencies and technical skills, it is necessary to divide them up among members of the interview team. Here are some basic guidelines for this process:

- Assign the assessment of technical skills and experience to the interviewers most knowledgeable in those areas.
- Assign no more than three or four competencies to an interviewer to assess, and allow a minimum of 15 minutes per competency.
- Give hiring managers first choice of competencies to assess.

- When feasible, allow interviewers to choose the competencies they will assess, or have hiring managers select competencies for members of their interview teams.
- Whenever possible have interviewers assess the same set of skills and competencies for every candidate for a position.

We have found that interviewers vastly prefer this interview process to the traditional one. Instead of being asked to decide whether candidates should be hired, a task for which they feel ill prepared, they are asked to assess particular traits and behaviors using tools they have been trained to use. They know what they're supposed to do and how they are supposed to do it. They are therefore more confident and less anxious about the interview process.

The most practical and efficient method for assessing competencies and technical skills is behavioral interviewing, which we will cover later in this chapter.

Compiling Interview Data

After members of the interview team complete their interviews, they need to transmit the results of their assessment back to the hiring manager. We have interviewers fill out assessment forms and return them to the hiring process facilitator. The hiring process facilitator has the assessment data compiled into a spreadsheet format showing both technical skills and competencies. Table 10.4 displays a sample compilation.

Facilitating the Debriefing Meeting

In the debriefing meeting, the interviewers meet and discuss the candidate (or candidates) recently interviewed. The meeting should be facilitated by the hiring process facilitator or the hiring manager to keep it focused on the agenda. The purpose of the debriefing meeting is to provide hiring managers with the information from the interview process to help them make the best decisions possible. The following process works well for the meeting:

- Ask interviewers to discuss the strengths and weaknesses of the candidates.
- Examine the ratings and discuss any ratings that are significantly lower than the other ratings.
- Discuss any mitigating factors in any of their scores. For example, if interviewers felt that the candidate had strong influence skills with clients, but was weak when trying to influence peers and superiors, they should clarify this disparity during the meeting.

Table 10.4   A sample compilation from a candidate interview process.

Candidate: Paul Hammer

Position: Chief financial officer

Technical Skills and Experience	LS	DR	DS	JP	Average Rating
Strategic planning and analysis experience	8			7	7.5
Budgeting, financial planning, and analysis experience		6			6
General accounting experience	7	7			7
Line-of-business accounting methodologies		7		7	
Cash management and forecasting experience			8	8	
Balance sheet management experience				8	8
Foreign exchange risk management experience	7				7
Understanding of tax issues	8				8
Treasury management experience		8			8
Understanding of inventory control	6				6
Ability to use financial performance measurements and financial analysis		7		6	6.5
Experience and ability managing people		6	8		7
Experience hiring and recruiting		8	9		8.5
Experience establishing processes to ensure proper financial management		7			7
Experience organizing an accounting area	8				8
Training experience				8	8
Experience communicating with a board of directors		8			8
Overall technical rating	**7.4**	**7.2**	**7.3**	**8.3**	**7.5**

Behavioral Competencies	LS	DR	DS	JP	Average Rating
Results orientation			8		8
Managing performance			7		7
Influence	5	7	6		
Attention to communication		6			6
Interpersonal awareness				9	9
Analytical thinking	7	6			6.5
Strategic thinking	6			7	6.5
Service orientation			7	6	6.5
Teamwork	7				7
Building organizational commitment			8		8
Establishing focus		8			8
Developing others				7	7
Overall behavioral competencies rating	**6.7**	**6.8**	**7.5**	**7.7**	**6.7**

- Discuss any questions they found the candidate unable or unwilling to answer.

- Discuss the candidate and the key success factors for the position, and how well the candidate meets the needs for the position.

- Gather opinions from the group about whether the candidate is potentially hirable—that is, if this candidate were the top candidate, would you hire him or her or go back to the well to get more candidates?

- Discuss their overall feelings about the candidate, any red flags that were raised, or any issues that interviewers feel should be addressed in future interviews or reference checks.

The debriefing meeting brings to focus the power of the competency-based selection process. Here is a place where you can gather a tremendous amount of information about candidates and how they operate in teams, how well they set goals and influence people, how well they motivate others, and so on. Use the opportunity to truly understand who candidates are and how they work and interact. Through this process you will discover that there are no perfect human beings and that every candidate is flawed. Instead of looking at candidates as potential saviors to solve all your problems, you can see them as people with strengths and weaknesses. You will also be better prepared to help them succeed on the job because you will have a better sense of who they are.

Psychometric Testing

Psychometric testing alone is a weak predictor of job performance. However, it can play a valuable role in the hiring process. Many of the better psychometric instruments are 80 to 85 percent accurate—that is, the reported personality characteristics fit the individuals tested 80 to 85 percent of the time. This rate of accuracy is high enough to warrant their usage for an important purpose: to confirm that your assessment of candidates is correct. I learned this lesson the hard way several years ago while conducting a search for a senior executive of a European bank. The job required a team-oriented executive who could work closely with others. I was surprised when the psychometric instruments showed that the finalist candidate was emotionally cold and insensitive, because he didn't come across that way in the interview process. When I showed the results to the general manager of the bank, he dismissed them immediately, saying that he had had dinner with the candidate the previous evening, and that the candidate had told him repeatedly that he was a team player. As you can guess, the tests were correct and the assessment from the interview process was wrong. After a year of conflict and frustration, the executive left the bank. Everyone involved suffered the consequences of ignoring a strong warning signal that the interview perceptions were incorrect.

If the results of psychometric testing differ from the interview assessment, explore the issue further. You may want to discuss the differences with the candidate to determine the degree of accuracy of the psychometric tool. That conversation should enlighten you on both the psychometric results and your interviewing assessment.

Competency-Based Reference Checking

The referencing process provides an ideal opportunity to validate the findings of the interview process and gather more information about areas of skill and competence in which candidates' proficiency is still uncertain. For senior-level positions we ask candidates for as many as 10 to 12 references, including superiors, subordinates, peers, and customers.

Before we begin referencing we identify the important areas to explore in the process, including particular competencies, technical skills, and any uncertainties regarding a candidate's career path and job history. We also ask questions to ascertain strength in the key success factors for the job. Here are the kinds of questions we ask:

- What has been the nature of your relationship with the candidate?
- What are her strengths?
- What are her weaknesses? (We try not to move on until we have at least three real weaknesses.)
- Why did she leave her job? What were the circumstances?
- On a scale of 1 to 10, where 10 is the highest, how would you rate her on results orientation, the ability to set and achieve challenging goals? (This question assumes that results orientation is one of the competencies we want to explore further.)
- Can you give me an example that demonstrates that rating?
- On a scale of 1 to 10, how would you rate her on her ability to develop others?
- Can you give me an example that demonstrates that rating?
- On the same 1 to 10 scale, how would you rate her on her knowledge and experience analyzing the creditworthiness of companies? (This is an example of a technical skill.)
- How would you compare her to her peers or to other people who have held that job—outstanding, above average, average, or below average?
- Would you hire her now?

- What advice do you have for us regarding managing her?
- What else should we know about her?

The answer to these questions will go a long way toward confirming your impressions through the interview process. Take the reference process seriously and use it to learn from the people who really know the candidate.

Feedback
Giving and receiving accurate, useful, and timely feedback regarding the interview process is an integral part of effective candidate management. Yet many hires don't happen because important feedback was not given or received and misunderstandings were not resolved.

The main reason feedback is not given or received is that people avoid asking or saying things that might upset others or embarrass themselves. So instead of asking what candidates' concerns are, hiring managers and hiring process facilitators avoid hearing what they don't want to hear. It is a classic problem among recruiters: The underlying belief (or rather fantasy) is that if they don't ask the question, they won't hear the answer they don't want to hear. It is by asking the difficult questions and hearing the truth that managers can effectively respond to real concerns and issues.

Facilitating the Selection Decision
Making selection decisions can be easy or difficult depending on a number of factors—the decisiveness of the hiring manager, the quality and fit of the candidates, the depth of the pool from which the candidates are drawn, and the importance of the position. Here are some guidelines for facilitating the decision.

Avoid the Tendency to Lower Your Competency Standards
Hiring is no different from manufacturing when it comes to maintaining standards. There are always reasons to make exceptions and accept candidates or products that do not meet the specifications called for in the plan. I have found that the long-term cost of sacrificing competency far exceeds the short-term gain of shortening the hiring process.

Research supports this supposition. Table 10.5 shows the results of research indicating the increase in productivity resulting from one standard deviation difference in capability for jobs with different levels of complexity.[2] It is clear that with complex jobs, the productivity gained

[2]Adapted from Hunter, J. E., Schmidt, F. L., & Judiesch, M. K. "Individual Differences in Output Variability as a Function of Job Complexity." *Journal of Applied Psychology*, 75(1990), 28–42.

Table 10.5   Results of research showing the percent increase in productivity resulting from one standard deviation difference in ability for positions with varying complexity and for sales positions.

Job Complexity	Percent Increase in Productivity
Low complexity	19%
Moderate complexity	32%
High complexity	48%
Sales	48–120%

by hiring a more competent employee is worth the extra time and effort put into the hiring process to ensure that the best available candidate is hired.

Gather Extensive Information, Then Make Your Own Decision
I believe that organizations work best when ultimate accountability is defined and localized, when individuals know that they are responsible for the success or failure of particular initiatives. The same applies to the hiring decision. Gathering information from other interviewers and managers does not mean that the hiring decision becomes a committee decision in which each interviewer has a vote—which would set up an unhealthy dynamic in which managers hire people without fully owning the decisions, reducing their sense of accountability and responsibility for the employees' success. We have found that it works well to frame the interview and selection process as one in which members of the interview team have the responsibility to gather the best information possible, so that the hiring manager can make the best informed decision possible.

Distinguish between "Hirable" and "Best Available" Candidates
Just because someone is the best candidate interviewed doesn't mean that the candidate should be hired. Figures 10.4 and 10.5 show the difference between situations in which candidates are hirable or not. There are actually two different questions to ask regarding any candidate:

1. Is the candidate hirable? That is, is the individual good enough to hire if he or she is the best candidate?
2. Is this the best hirable candidate? If so, this is the person who should be pursued.

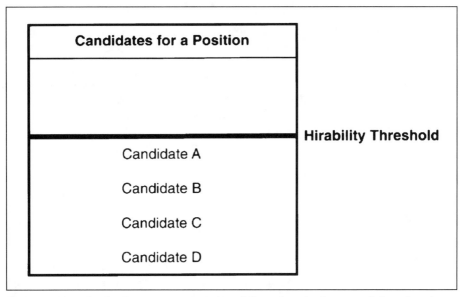

Figure 10.4   In this hiring situation, Candidate A is the best candidate, but does not meet the competency and quality requirements to be a hirable candidate. In this situation you should find more candidates.

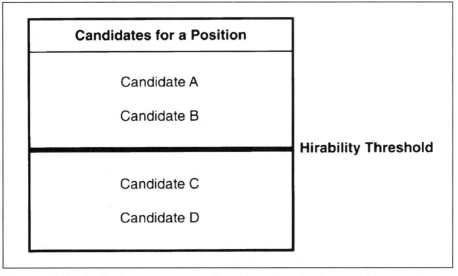

Figure 10.5   In this hiring situation, Candidate A is the best candidate, and both A and B meet the competency and quality requirements to be hirable candidates. In this situation, you pursue Candidate A, and proceed to try to hire Candidate B if Candidate A does not work out.

254 Using Competency-Based Selection in the Ideal Hiring Process

Invite Opinions Different from Your Own

Because of the tendency to evaluate people on the basis of how they make us feel about ourselves rather than their likelihood of success on the job, it is an excellent practice to seek out and draw out people who oppose the selection of the candidate of your choice. Why don't they think the candidate is a good choice? Write down all their reasons, and don't argue with them. See it from their perspective, and try it on as your own. It will help you make a better-informed decision.

Examine Your Darker Motivations

Instead of justifying your hiring decision in terms of the rational positives and negatives of the decision, take some time to examine your other, baser motivations:

- *How will the candidate make you feel good about yourself?* This may help you see how your perception of the candidate may be colored by the things you like and don't like about yourself, things that may have nothing to do with job success.
- *How will the candidate make you look good to others?* Sometimes hiring managers hire people whom their managers or others like, while they themselves have serious doubts about whether the candidates can do the job well.
- *What have you been afraid to ask the candidate?* Often managers avoid asking candidates questions when they don't want to hear the answers. Sometimes managers are so frustrated about not finding good candidates that they decide to hire a candidate below the hirability threshold and unconsciously decide not to find out why they shouldn't hire the person. Here are some sample questions that hiring managers might tend to avoid asking:

- Why have you had so many jobs? Why did you leave each of the jobs?
- What have been the barriers to greater success in your career?
- What were the biggest problems you had as a manager?

- *What doubts about the candidate have you not expressed? Why not?* Expressing these doubts openly may lead you to reconsider your decision, or at least help you improve a candidate's likelihood for success by addressing your concerns at the beginning of his or her employment.
- *What are you trying to avoid by hiring the candidate?* You may be avoiding the agony of interviewing more candidates, or avoiding hiring someone who will challenge you, or avoiding paying a search fee. By honestly answering this question, you will better be able to assess the viability of your hiring decision.

Using Behavioral Interviewing to Assess Competencies, Skills, and Traits

USING THE PAST TO PREDICT THE FUTURE

The most practical and efficient method to assess competencies, skills, and traits is to conduct historically based behavioral interviews. This interview approach is based on the same principle that financial professionals use to analyze and predict future financial success for companies: *The best predictor of future performance is past performance.* By determining the extent to which candidates evidenced these competencies in the past, you can help predict how well they will do so in the future.

To conduct behavioral interviews, simply ask candidates open-ended questions that lead them to tell you stories that demonstrate their ability and their mastery of the competency, skill, or trait. For example, the following questions will help you draw out information about teamwork for candidates for senior management positions.

- Can you give me an example of a time when you functioned well as a part of a management team?
- Give me an example of a time when the team worked well together. What was your role?
- Give me an example of a time when the team was not functioning well together. What happened and what was your role?
- What are your weaknesses as a team member? How do they affect team functioning?
- What strengths do you bring to a management team? Can you give me an example?
- Tell me about a time when you faced a business crisis that required a coordinated team effort to solve. What happened? What was your role? Was it solved to your satisfaction? What did you learn that will result in you doing it differently next time?

The answers to these questions will reveal behavioral information that you can use to assess the competency of teamwork.

These kinds of questions get beyond the superficiality of most interviews and will open a window through which you can see who candidates really are and how they are likely to act if they are working for you.

How do you determine the accuracy of the candidates' stories? By going for *detail*. When a candidate says, "*We* completed the project successfully," ask what the candidate's *personal* contribution to the project entailed. By getting into the details of the story, you can more clearly identify the specific actions and qualities of the candidate.

The interview process becomes very different from the traditional interview. Using behavioral interviewing, interviewers should talk 5 percent of the time. We ask follow-up questions to continue to draw out the story, to obtain more details, to clarify the candidate's role, and to focus the story on the behavioral areas the interviewer wants to address.

Here are examples of the kinds of questions that elicit the behavioral information we need:

- "What happened next?"
- "How did you handle that?"
- "Was it successful? Why (or why not)?"
- "What are some of the difficulties you faced? How did you deal with them?"
- "Where or how did you succeed? Tell me about it."
- "Where or how did you fail? Tell me about it."
- "What did you learn?"
- "How have you applied that learning?"

To make it easier for interviewers, put together sets of interview questions for each competency, so interviewers don't have to take the time to make them up themselves. They can do so, but it takes training and time that can be better spent in other ways. In our experience, interviewers are happier with the process when they are handed the tools instead of being asked to create them themselves.

One other aspect of the behavioral interviewing process that is different for many interviewers is the importance of writing down the details of the interview. Because candidates are telling their stories and revealing much information, most interviewers will not remember all the details helpful to assess competencies and explain to the hiring manager why they gave them the ratings they did. We tell interviewers that they should write down as much of what candidates say as possible. I used to take a quarter page of notes when I interviewed a candidate; now I usually write three single-spaced pages.

HANDLING COMMON INTERVIEWING PROBLEMS

When Candidates Speak in Generalities

If candidates speak in generalities ("always" and "never," for example), bring them back to specific details: "Can you tell me exactly what you did in the situation you are describing?" "Can you give me an example of that?"

When Candidates Use "We"
When candidates use the word "we" to describe events and behaviors in response to your questions, you don't know what exactly *they* did and what was done by others. People use "we" for different reasons:

- They think it shows that they are a team player.
- They use the word as a matter of habit.
- Due to their upbringing, they consider the use of "I" to be self-aggrandizing.
- They are trying to take credit for things that were done by others.

You don't know which reason is operating when they say "we," so you need to ask them to use "I" instead of "we," and explain why.

When Candidates Give Opinions Rather Than Facts
When candidates express their philosophies or opinions—"It is my belief that the customer always comes first," for example—ask them to provide specific examples that show their philosophy in action.

If they offer opinions as a way to demonstrate their abilities or competencies—"I don't think we handled the situation in the best way. I think we should have . . . "—ask them to describe a situation or experience in which they acted in accordance with their opinions.

When Candidates Talk about Their Future Plans
When candidates answer questions by saying that they plan to act in a certain way in the future or that they plan some course of action—for example, if a candidate says, "I plan to develop a better cost accounting system"—ask, "What steps have you taken in that regard?"

Hiring Senior Managers

The process we have described in this chapter works to hire employees at any level in an organization, from secretary to CEO. Because of the increased leverage and impact of senior-level management positions, it is worth the effort to focus time and attention on the hiring process commensurate with the organizational impact. When we perform CEO searches, we typically use 18 to 20 competencies in the assessment process. While the process takes too long and is too cumbersome for use in any large-scale hiring process, it is workable for senior-level hires.

Conclusion

One of the plant managers at a client said, "After we used this hiring process for a while, I looked back on the 20 hires we made at our plant prior to using it, and I realized six of those people would not have been hired had we been using this system." It works.

For even mid-level positions, over the first few years organizations invest hundreds of thousands of dollars in each employee, including compensation, employee benefits, training, and the ramping-up time required before the employee contributes significant value. Most companies would not consider making such an investment with as little rigor as is used in the typical hiring process. By using an effective process to assess competencies, skills, and traits, you can reduce hiring mistakes and better acquire the leaders you need to help take your organization where it wants to go.

CHAPTER

11

Using Competencies to Hire and Retain a High-Performance Workforce

It requires intention, commitment, and discipline to perform a rigorous selection process such as the one described in the previous chapter. To implement the practice throughout an organization, you need all the competencies and skills associated with effective change management. While the business case for improved selection practices is easy to justify, changing hiring practices is seldom simple. Your culture has many interrelated and interwoven elements that function together to maintain the selection and hiring process in its current state. To institute successful hiring practices you will need to change your corporate culture, and for that you need a comprehensive change strategy.

In conversations with HR executives across many industries, we hear the same story: Their organization is highly decentralized. They can't mandate that managers use *any* process for hiring. All they can do is to offer services for them to use if they want.

I am not arguing against decentralization. The principle of empowerment is founded on the premise that organizations function at their best and individuals develop faster when power and decision making reside at the lowest appropriate level in an organization. However, decentralization is not an effective strategy when choice about content and process reside with people who are not trained in either the content or the process. In this case the lack of standardization can severely damage the organization.

Imagine what would happen to a large insurance company if it completely decentralized its underwriting function, the function by which it decides whether to issue policies to customers. Imagine further that the company hired people for underwriting positions with no skill or experience, that there was no training, and that these new underwriters were invited to create their own criteria and methods for how they should measure risk. Individual underwriters would make their own decisions (perhaps as a part of a small team), and consistency would disappear. Without common standards, rules, and processes, many of the untrained underwriters would make judgments based on their emotions and gut feelings. In a short time the company would fold due to its mounting losses. The cost of poor underwriting decisions is so high that insurance companies *must* have standards and processes that are rigorously maintained and monitored throughout the organization. There is an equivalent cost associated with poor selection decisions.

The Cost of Poor Hiring Decisions

It is generally accepted that businesses expect employees to create economic value at the rate of three times their pay. If we combine this statistic with the percent increase in productivity that results from one standard deviation difference in competency, we can determine an approximate cost of hiring a weak performer. In Table 11.1, the annual cost in lost economic value to an organization *exceeds the annual salary of employees* for all but the most routine of positions, and, as you can see by the annual cost per weak

Table 11.1   The annual economic cost of a weak hire for five sample positions, based on the assumption that a weak performer differs in competence from a superior performer by one standard deviation.

Position	Job Complexity	Annual Pay	Expected Economic Contribution to Company	Percent Increase in Productivity	Annual Cost per Weak Hire
Janitor	Low	$20,000	$60,000	19%	$11,400
Machine operator	Medium	$24,000	$72,000	32%	$23,040
Engineer	High	$45,000	$135,000	48%	$64,800
Programmer	High	$60,000	$180,000	48%	$86,400
CFO	High	$150,000	$450,000	48%	$216,000

hire, even in medium-complexity positions the lost economic value almost equals the salary. Organization that refuse to standardize their hiring and selection processes based on best practices pay a big price.

Selection and hiring practices deserve the same respect as any other organizational process having significant economic impact. This chapter will help you implement company-wide standardized best practices for selection.

Utilizing Job Descriptions

The job description is a tool that can either form the foundation for the entire employment system in an organization, or it can be a colossal waste of time and resources. If it is utilized well, it can communicate to the organization the overall purpose of the job and how it relates to the greater objectives of the organization. It can identify and clarify job roles and activities, and communicate to employees and managers the performance standards for the job. By identifying the competencies the organization considers most important for job success, it can provide a framework for assessing and selecting internal and external job candidates. It can facilitate communication between the employee and the manager about the competency levels and technical skills required for superior performance in the job, and can facilitate the process of setting goals and objectives for the job. Finally, it can provide the framework for compensation decisions.

Figure 11.1 shows an example of a competency-based job description for a purchasing manager. The description includes key components that our experience has told us will help to clarify the job's role, define its overall contribution to the organization's success, and set expectations for job incumbents. The following pages will provide you an explanation for each component of a purchasing manager job description along with a brief explanation of its purpose, the rationale for including it in a model you might develop for your own selection system, and a representative example for the purchasing manager.

Components of a Competency-Based Job Description

Key components for an effective job description that can be used as a foundation for a competency-based hiring practice can include:

- Job purpose.
- Goals and objectives.

Title: Purchasing Manager

Job Purpose: To purchase the products and services the company needs at the best price and quality and in sufficient quantity, so that the company can achieve its sales, quality, and profitability objectives.

Goals and Objectives:
- To ensure that all products and services purchased meet the quality standards of the company.
- To ensure a sufficient flow of products and services so insufficient or inadequate materials or labor never slows production down.
- To ensure that the company pays as little as possible for material and labor without sacrificing quality or quantity.

Reporting Relationships:
- Reports to the general manager.
- No direct reports.

Duties and Responsibilities:
- Establishes and validates market pricing for materials and labor.
- Evaluates various types of materials.
- Considers alternative design approaches that optimize efficiency.
- Seeks methods of simplifying the construction process.
- Evaluates product costs to determine if the effective value of finished products contributes to profitability.
- Seeks out the needs of the production force to fill labor requirements in a cost-effective manner. Continually tests the status quo of current pricing.
- Consults with director of product development to determine design and material requirements. Evaluates various material types; considers alternative design approaches that optimize efficiency.
- Consults with chief estimator to understand database protocol for new resources.
- Consults with vendors on a daily basis to obtain and qualify bids. Vendors include manufacturers, contractors, and suppliers. All pricing will be obtained through competitive bidding and negotiated contracts.
- Consults with director of construction and product managers to obtain field requirements for labor and services. Seeks methods to simplify the construction process.
- Consults with customer service to determine performance levels of various products.

Figure 11.1   Sample job description: purchasing manager.

Duties and Responsibilities continued:
- Establishes performance requirements for vendors and endeavors to continually improve performance by informing vendors of these requirements and how well they are measured against them.
- Continuously seeks opportunities to purchase materials and services in a competitive manner.

Key Technical Skills and Knowledge:
- Validating market pricing for material and labor.
- Evaluating product designs to optimize efficiency and cost.
- Managing vendor relationships, including competitive bidding and negotiated contracts.
- Understanding the construction process.
- Establishing performance requirements for vendors.

Key Cultural Competency Factors:

High in:
- Teamwork
- Results Orientation
- Initiative
- Managing Performance

Low in:
- Motivating Others
- Developing Others
- Conflict Resolution
- Attention to Communication

Key Success Factors:
- Ability to work closely with other managers to ensure that product designs allow for cost-effective purchasing.
- Ability to minimize the cost of materials and services while maintaining adequate supplies through effective vendor management.

Performance Measures:
- The overall cost of materials and labor increases no more than the rate of inflation.
- There are no lost production days due to a shortage of either material or labor.
- Material quality is maintained.
- Labor quality is maintained or improved.
- Quarterly reports demonstrate the effective value of finished products in relation to cost and profitability.
- Product designs are improved to optimize efficiency as a result of consulting with the Director of Product Development.
- Performance requirements for vendors are written down and communicated to them quarterly.
- Pricing is validated quarterly.

Figure 11.1   *(Continued)*

Competency Model:
- Teamwork.
- Initiative.
- Innovation.
- Managing performance.
- Results orientation.
- Influence.
- Decisiveness.
- Analytical thinking.
- Decision quality.
- Service focus.

Preferences:
- Little overnight travel (less than 10 nights per year).
- Multitasking environment.
- High independence.
- Intense activity, high energy, fast pace.
- Extensive interpersonal interaction.
- Long hours (over 50 per week).
- No direct management of others but extensive leadership of others.

Career Pathways:
- Potential growth to director of operations.

Figure 11.1   (Continued)

- Reporting relationships.
- Duties and responsibilities.
- Key technical skills and knowledge.
- Key success factors.
- Performance measures.
- Competency model.
- Preferences.
- Career pathways.

This is a daunting list of items to include in a job description. While there is good reason to include each of these items, bear in mind that if the process of creating job descriptions is too distressing to managers, the resistance created may outweigh their benefit.

JOB PURPOSE

This section should be a one-sentence description of the overall purpose or mission of the job. The job purpose provides focus and rationale behind why the job exists and how it contributes to the overall organization. All remaining components included in the description should align with the purpose. For the employee, the job purpose can also reinforce the critical role played by incumbents in the organization's success and help them to align their own purpose and values to organization. The *job purpose* for the *purchasing manager* is:

> To purchase the products and services the company needs at the best price and quality and in sufficient quantity, so that the company can achieve its sales, quality, and profitability objectives.

GOALS AND OBJECTIVES

This section provides key criteria for setting performance objectives. It should include several bullet points indicating what the person should be accomplishing in the areas for which the person has responsibility. The goals and objectives should be broad and general and will change only if the scope of the job changes. The *goals and objectives* for the *purchasing manager* position are:

To ensure that all products and services purchased meet the quality standards of the company.

To ensure a sufficient flow of products and services so insufficient or inadequate materials or labor never slows production down.

To ensure that the company pays as little as possible for materials and labor without sacrificing quality or quantity.

REPORTING RELATIONSHIPS

This section describes the reporting relationships between the position and others: To whom does the person in the position report? Who reports to the position holder? What are the "dotted line" reporting relationships? The answers to these questions provide clarity and focus on leadership and support for those in the position. Often an organizational chart sufficiently describes reporting relationships. *Reporting relationships* for the *purchasing manager* are:

- Reports to the general manager.
- No direct reports.

DUTIES AND RESPONSIBILITIES

This section includes a list of duties and responsibilities for the position. It is also a good idea to include a general statement that explicitly states that the list is not meant to be exhaustive. This will help minimize the problem of employees claiming that a particular task was not included in their job descriptions. This list is also often used to assess the position's overall contribution to the organization, providing a primary link to compensation. Examples of the *duties and responsibilities* performed by the *purchasing manager* include:

- Establishes and validates market pricing for materials and labor.
- Evaluates various types of materials.
- Considers alternative design approaches that optimize efficiency.
- Seeks methods of simplifying the construction process.
- Evaluates product costs to determine if the effective value of finished products contributes to profitability.
- Seeks out the needs of the production force to fill labor requirements in a cost-effective manner.

KEY TECHNICAL SKILLS AND KNOWLEDGE

This section includes the important technical skills and knowledge needed to perform the position well. This list of skills and knowledge can be used in the selection process to qualify candidates, and will help employees and managers evaluate employees' technical capabilities for development purposes. Identifying the key skills and knowledge can also provide a basis for developing job-specific training and development. Some of the *key technical skills and knowledge* required for *purchasing managers* are:

- Validating market pricing for materials and labor.
- Evaluating product designs to optimize efficiency and cost.
- Managing vendor relationships, including competitive bidding and negotiated contracts.
- Understanding the construction process.

KEY SUCCESS FACTORS

While most positions have a variety of duties and require a number of technical skills and competencies, usually there are a few key factors that most relate to success on the job. We call these key success factors. In the job description these are brief descriptions of behaviors and abilities that are critical to achieving the position's mission and goals. This can be an essential component when there is a high degree of change or shifting priorities. The *key success factors* for the *purchasing manager* are:

- Ability to work closely with other managers to ensure product designs allow for cost-effective purchasing.
- Ability to minimize the cost of materials and services while maintaining adequate supplies through effective vendor management.

PERFORMANCE MEASURES: MEASURABLE ACTIVITIES AND RESULTS

Performance measures are the measures by which people in the position are held accountable, and are the means by which you know how well the job is being performed. This is a good reference for managers and employees when setting criteria for annual performance goals or objectives. Examples of *performance measures* for the *purchasing manager* are:

- The overall cost of materials and labor increases no more than the rate of inflation.
- There are no lost production days due to a shortage of either material or labor.
- Material quality is maintained.
- Labor quality is maintained or improved.
- Quarterly reports demonstrate the effective value of finished products in relation to cost and profitability.
- Pricing is validated quarterly.

COMPETENCY MODEL

The competency model includes those behavioral competencies that differentiate superior performers in the position. A sample *competency model* for the *purchasing manager* position includes:

Teamwork,

initiative,

innovation,

managing performance,

results orientation,

influence,

decisiveness,

analytical thinking,

decision quality, and

service orientation.

PREFERENCES

This section refers to features of the position that need to match the employee's personality characteristics, traits, and desires for the employee to be successful and enjoy the job. The degree to which the employee finds the job satisfying or dissatisfying can impact turnover and decisions to apply internally for a specific position. Examples of *preferences* highlighted in the *purchasing manager* job description are:

- Little overnight travel (less than 10 nights per year).
- Multitasking environment.

- High independence.
- Intense activity, high energy, fast pace.

Using Job Descriptions Well

If it is used well, the job description will be referenced every time candidates are assessed to fill an open position. The standards, needs, expectations, and performance measures should be utilized in selection, performance reviews, employee development, and succession planning. And it will serve as a guide to help employees understand their jobs and what they need to do to succeed at them.

It is worth taking the time to develop meaningful job descriptions only if they are going to be used effectively. Developing them takes time and thought. In many organizations managers resist taking the time to create them and see them as just another bureaucratic HR practice that keeps them from doing their jobs. My advice is twofold:

1. Make sure that the job description is going to be used as the foundation of several HR practices before you push managers to take the time to make them meaningful.

2. If you are going to use them well, create and execute a communications and marketing plan to sell job descriptions to the organization. Make sure that managers see the benefits that job descriptions offer them in hiring, succession planning, performance development, and ultimately their own professional success.

Installing and Managing a Company-Wide Competency-Based Selection System

There are many options and choices to consider in the process of designing and installing a competency-based selection system in your organization. The thing to remember is that *workability* and *leverage* are the most important considerations. The most scientifically valid concept in the world will have no value if you can't make it work in your organization. You want to optimize your practices by taking the best selection system and making it as practical as possible for your organization. Thoughtful consideration around the job description and its individual components will increase that possibility.

CUSTOMIZING THE SYSTEM

Whatever methodology you use for your selection system, it needs to be customized to work within your organizational culture. If your organization has district managers in remote locations who hire sales representatives without the involvement of other interviewers, you will likely need a different process than an organization whose employees all work in a central location. If your organization is used to extensive interview processes, you will be able to develop different procedures than an organization used to quick and simple hiring procedures.

Customizing Competency Models to Fit Your Organizational Process

Competency models need to be customized based on the nature of your organizational culture. Here are some important questions to ask about your organization and its culture. The answers can impact your modeling process:

To what extent can you set policy regarding hiring practices and require adherence to the policy?

How much must you rely on persuasion and influence?

What is your current hiring process?

How does your process vary with location, job level, and position?

How many interviewers are usually involved in hiring?

How much does senior management support the new selection process?

To what extent do line managers recognize the need for a better selection process?

The answers to these questions will determine how you customize your selection process and build the necessary support to ensure long-term success.

Will Using the Competency-Based Selection System Be Mandatory?

It is more efficient to mandate use of a process than it is to persuade people to use it. If your organization will easily accept a mandated change in hiring procedures and if you have the support of senior management, you can install the system by training first your HR staff and then your line managers. If you establish workable procedures for executing, managing, and monitoring the process, the installation can go smoothly.

If managers have the choice of whether to use the new system, you need a different kind of implementation strategy. You may carefully pick where first to apply the new selection practice, choosing high-profile, supportive managers with status and prestige who will influence others. You may need to make special efforts to gain the support of key influencers and culture leaders in the organization, so that they will use their authority to support the new system. Every organization is different, and the exact approach and strategy will vary based on your particular situation.

Modifying the Number of Competencies

Another key consideration is the number of competencies and amount of information you will need to collect in order to guarantee a successful hire. The amount of time, money, need for accuracy, legal defensibility, and buy-in will impact the decisions you make around the various selection components and strategies you use to gather information from prospective candidates. Go through the organization and map the process flow for hiring in different levels, job functions, and locations. Ask yourself:

Are candidates screened over the telephone?

How many interviewers are involved?

How long is the typical interview?

Do the same set of interviewers interview every candidate for a position?

How many rounds of interviews does a candidate experience?

Based on the answers to these questions, you will modify the number of competencies on which candidates will be assessed. We base our design on the assumption that time must be allotted for the following elements of the interview process:

- Establishing rapport.
- Presenting the position, the job, and the organization to the candidate.
- Determining candidate motivations, interests, and desires.
- Assessing the candidate's technical skills and knowledge.
- Assessing competencies.
- Answering the candidate's questions.
- Arranging next steps.

It generally takes 15 to 20 minutes for interviewers to assess candidates on a competency. By analyzing the interview process and examining how it can be modified, you can determine how many competencies can be assessed and used to make the selection decision. Let's look at an example.

In one company's current hiring practice, candidates for many positions above the level of first line supervisor are interviewed by the hiring manager and a staffing manager in the first round. If they remain potential candidates, they come back for a second interview round with the hiring manager and his or her manager. An offer can follow. First-round interviews generally take 30 to 45 minutes, and second-round interviews usually take 45 to 60 minutes. In the first round the staffing manager usually talks about the organization and does an initial assessment of the candidate's motivation and fit with the organization. The hiring manager usually assesses technical capability and knowledge as a part of the first interview.

This is how we analyzed the situation to determine our approach to the interview. There are two interviews in the first round. The hiring manager and staffing manager can each assess at least one competency in the first interview round in addition to the technical assessment for the hiring manager and the company orientation and assessment of motivational fit for the staffing manager. In the second interview round the hiring manager and his or her boss can each assess two or three competencies in their interviews, bringing the total to six to eight competencies. If the staffing manager and the hiring manager are willing to lengthen their first-round interviews to an hour if candidates seem strong, they can each assess an additional competency in the first round, bringing the number of competencies up to 8 to 10. If candidates are typically screened in a telephone interview, another competency can be assessed over the phone. Thus with little change in process flow, up to 11 competencies can be assessed in the interview process.

In our consulting practice, we discuss with the client how much flexibility exists within the culture regarding the interview process. By adding another interviewer, they can assess three additional competencies; by adding two interviewers, another six competencies. As we work through the issues, we arrive at a solution that balances organizational cultural dynamics and rigor in assessment. Through this process, we arrive at a maximum number of competencies that can be included in a competency model for the purpose of selection.

With more senior-level positions and their increased leverage and importance, you will often want to assess more competencies in the interview process. Since more people tend to be involved in the interview process at more senior levels, using this approach allows you to add more competencies to their competency models, assigning the additional competencies to the additional interviewers.

We take the principle of workability and apply it to optimize the hiring process in the context of the organizational culture in which we are applying competency methodology to selection. We have found this approach to be effective in organizations ranging from Fortune 100 companies to entrepreneurial start-ups to the Chicago public school system.

Telephone Screening

Many companies use some form of telephone screening as a part of the assessment process. The cost and time alone of interviewing candidates in person who should have been disqualified as candidates over the telephone should motivate both hiring managers and staffing managers to utilize the telephone as effectively as possible to evaluate potential candidates. For out-of-town candidates, the economic benefit of improved telephone screening is even more compelling.

Fortunately, behavioral interviewing over the telephone can be a very effective assessment tool. Detailed stories about candidates' work experiences can be conveyed over the telephone, and the telephone interviewer can probe for details and explore areas of question almost as well as in person. Effective use of competency-based telephone screening can literally save a large company millions of dollars per year in time and money.

Remote Locations with Solo Hiring Managers

It is difficult to raise hiring standards to optimal levels in situations in which only one manager is available to interview candidates face-to-face. This is a common occurrence in some companies that have regional sales and service managers in distant locations. The act of including competency-based behavioral interviewing in the selection process will improve the quality of sales representatives hired, but more can be done to improve it. For example, telephone interviewing can be expanded to include other managers at either headquarters or other remote locations. Written answers to behavioral interview questions can also be used to augment the live interview process.

INTRODUCING COMPETENCY-BASED SELECTION

The general guidelines and principles about introducing competency-based HR applications apply to selection and hiring. The implementation plan should be customized based on the corporate culture and how its elements relate to the selection process. If the culture is slow to respond to new ideas and new ways of doing things, determine how new ideas are best brought into the culture. Apply your learning to the introduction of competency-based selection.

TRAINING

Training is an important part of the implementation process, and the training for selection adheres to the same principles as any other HR application. The training should include the business case for using the application, a conceptual framework to help employees apply the material, practical examples to illustrate important points, visual materials to aid comprehension, and role playing to ground the learning. Our training sessions for competency-based selection typically include the following elements:

- *Explaining the theory and methodology.* This includes an introduction to competencies, their application to selection, and the benefits to hiring managers and the organization. It also includes how competency models are developed, how to assess and measure competency proficiency, and the role of technical skill assessment.

- *Training in behavioral interviewing.* This training includes techniques, examples, and opportunities to practice through role playing.

- *Presenting the new competency-based process.* The new process flow for selection and hiring is discussed, including how technical skills and competencies are established, how interviewers will be assigned skills and competencies to assess, how candidates will be rated and results compiled, and how the results can be used to improve hiring decisions.

Education is an important component of training. Part of the value of competency-based training is that it helps employees learn about the behaviors and traits that go into superior performance. Because competencies affect so many aspects of organizational behavior, the benefits from this training can extend far beyond the realm of hiring.

It is important to explain to trainees their role in the assessment and hiring process. They are there to gather the best information possible to help the hiring manager (or whoever the decision makers are) to make the most informed decision. Competency-based selection is supposed to communicate as much information as possible to the decision makers, not to turn the hiring decision into a democratic vote. Once this is made clear, interviewers are usually quite comfortable with their role.

We have found that with the use of behaviorally anchored rating scales to measure competency proficiency, employees can be trained to perform behavioral interviewing in four hours or less. At the end of the training they will not have mastered behavioral interviewing, but they will gain competence quickly as they use the scales to assess candidates.

MANAGING INTERVIEW INFORMATION

By using behavioral interviewing and behaviorally anchored rating scales, you can accumulate interview data that can be used to analyze and evaluate the candidates for a particular job opening. If you collect and aggregate the interview data you can also analyze the quality of your selection process across the organization, by location, by job function, and even by hiring manager. You will find that some interviewers consistently rate candidates higher than others, and can use the information to focus additional training and consultation in places where it is most needed.

We have found that some hiring managers, particularly those in technical professions, tend to want to base their hiring decisions entirely on the numbers generated by a competency-based rating process. The candidates with the highest average competency rating will be the ones they want to hire. These hiring managers need to be reminded that while behavioral interviewing is one of the best assessment methods available, it is not 100 percent correlated with performance, and is not meant to replace the best thinking of the hiring manager. It is still the hiring manager's job to make the final decision, which should be based on a compilation and integration of *all* relevant information, not just rating statistics.

QUALITY CONTROL AND STANDARDS

As with any other standardized process, it is important to set up standards to monitor and control the selection process. Stay informed as to where, when, and how well the competency-based assessment is being used for selection in the organization. You need a plan and a means to evaluate the extent and effectiveness of its usage. Depending on how well you keep track of the interview information, you can use it to monitor the effectiveness of the selection process.

To ensure a regular, unbiased assessment, some companies use external consultants to perform operational audits of their selection systems. The consultants come back each year and conduct focus groups of managers and employees in different locations, asking them detailed questions about their hiring procedures and the quality of their interviewing and selection practices. This information is compiled and delivered to corporate HR, allowing the human resources department to take the appropriate action to improve the application.

MAXIMIZING ORGANIZATIONAL SUPPORT FOR COMPETENCY-BASED SELECTION

To ensure the successful implementation of a competency-based selection system, it is important to align as many elements of the corporate culture as possible behind the practice. Without such alignment, the new process will quickly be rejected by the cultural mechanisms that cause most changes to be perceived and expelled as threats to the culture. For competency-based selection to take hold and become a part of the corporate culture, it must become ingrained in the culture, and its practice must become entwined with other cultural practices. Here are some examples of how it is integrated in some companies.

• *Senior managers use, support, and promote the usage of competency-based selection throughout the organization.* By using the selection system enthusiastically themselves, senior managers let the organization know that they consider it to be important and useful. Senior managers can also talk to the organization about the selection process, thereby emphasizing its importance. The more people who hold power, influence, and prestige in the organization promote competency-based selection, the more seriously the rest of the organization will take it.

• *Effective execution of competency-based selection is rewarded.* If you really want to get managers to use competency-based selection, tie a portion of their compensation to its usage. By "putting your money where your mouth is," you will be communicating a powerful and consistent message throughout the organization. There are other ways to reward and recognize managers for utilizing competency-based selection effectively. You can mention their efforts in newsletters, provide them public recognition in meetings, or distribute awards. Using reward and recognition systems will help establish and maintain the hiring practice, which otherwise will tend to weaken and disappear with time.

• *Policies and procedures are established to standardize the selection process.* Policies and procedures create customs that transcend individual and departmental idiosyncratic behaviors. They say, "This is how we hire and bring people into our organization." Or, "When we install competency-based selection systems in companies, we work with HR to create manuals, forms, training materials, policies, and procedures that define all the steps in the process that managers are to follow in the selection system."

• *Ongoing training is provided to new managers on a regular basis, so that hiring traditions are maintained and passed on from one generation of managers to another.* Part of the orientation process for every manager should include an introduction to your organization's hiring practices, including at least an overview of policies and procedures. In fact, the selection criteria for managers should include an assessment of their willingness to utilize your selection procedures to fulfill their hiring needs in the organization.

These points are only a few of the elements of a comprehensive plan to ensure that an organization hires the people it needs to accomplish its mission and goals. The time taken to put the plan together will pay off in the quality of the people hired as a result.

Attracting the Right Candidates

Competency-based selection is only one aspect of bringing the best people into an organization. You also need to find and attract them. If the best people don't want to work for your organization, the best assessment process in the world won't help you hire them. The process of attracting candidate pools of sufficient quality and quantity deserves to be well thought out and planned for.

ATTRACTING SUPERIOR PERFORMERS IS A SALES AND MARKETING JOB

Attracting the potential employees you need requires the same kind of thinking that goes into marketing any product to a group of consumers. In the case of hiring, the "product" includes the entire employment package— the industry, the company, the manager, the job itself, advancement opportunities, compensation, coworkers, and so on. All the elements of a classical marketing plan apply to attracting superior performers.

Who are your potential consumers? What is the target market of potential employees? What are their demographics? Who are your competitors for those potential candidates?

What employee needs does your opportunity satisfy? What is important to potential employees in their jobs? Some needs apply to all people in all jobs—to be treated with respect, to have good working conditions, and so on. Other needs depend on the nature of the workforce. Flextime is a desirable feature for a young workforce, while retirement benefits may be more important for an aging baby boomer work population. In high-tech fields today, the nature of the work itself is an important factor determining job attractiveness, while in a retail environment, the quality of social relationships can be the major factor.

How is your product currently viewed and positioned? Is your target market aware of your product? How do they perceive it? What are its strengths and weaknesses? How does it compare to its competitors? Since the product includes the industry, the company, the division, the manager, the job, and so on, the analysis of perception and positioning can be complex. Companies like Motorola have less trouble and less cost attracting people because they are perceived to be an attractive company in an attractive industry. Companies in less "sexy" industries may be known as great places to work, yet they attract far fewer unsolicited employment inquiries because their industries are perceived by the employment marketplace as being unexciting. Take the time to analyze the position and the organization from the candidate's perspective.

Why Should and Shouldn't Someone Want to Work for Your Organization?

Another piece of your marketing strategy should be an analysis of the features and benefits that job opportunities provide prospective candidates. The following questions can help guide you through this analysis:

What differentiates your organization from its competitors?

What is great about working there?

What makes people feel good about working there?

What are employees proud of about the organization?

In what ways do employees benefit from working there that they wouldn't if they worked for other companies?

The best way to answer these questions is to gather the data from employees (as opposed to answering them yourself). Senior managers are often surprised by the degree to which their own opinions differ from those of lower-level employees. To explore perceptions of features and benefits at a target position or level, ask the employees at that level.

Understanding the company's market weaknesses is almost as important as understanding its strengths, because the weaknesses often need to be overcome or worked around in order to hire the people you want. Some questions to ask that bring out this information include:

Why do employees quit?

Why do candidates not want to consider working for your company?

Why do candidates not accept job offers?

What do recruiters say is the rap on your company?

What are the common employee complaints?

What are your complaints?

What Are the Position's Strengths and Weaknesses?
A similar set of questions applies to open positions in the organization. For each opening, the aspects of the job that will likely attract and repel target candidates can be identified and analyzed. This analysis can be used to prepare interviewers for interacting with candidates, and prepare hiring and staffing managers for helping candidates become and remain interested in particular positions.

Developing an Attraction Strategy and Plan
The information gathered about the company and the position as it relates to the candidate marketplace can be put together to formulate a strategy to increase the organization's ability to attract the candidates it needs. Such a strategy should include:

- An analysis of what might attract or repel prospective candidates.
- Goals and action steps for increasing the attracters and diminishing the repellers.
- A plan for training managers and interviewers in the attraction strategy.
- A communications strategy for improving internal and external perceptions of the organization.
- A means of measurement and accountability around the strategy to attract prospective candidates.

There are a number of company initiatives that can help improve the attractiveness of an organization to potential candidates. One of the most important is in some ways the easiest: Simply publicize the things that the organization is doing well and that employees consider important to employee satisfaction. These can include employee benefits, training and advancement opportunities, employee development, compensation, and anything else that employees find attractive about the organization and its culture.

Anything that the organization does to improve employee competency will also increase its attractiveness to target candidates. For example, the more proficient employees are at continuous improvement, teamwork, communication, and innovation, the more strongly will competent employees want to work at the organization. This applies to almost every competency. Because most people want to improve themselves and because most superior performers want to work with other strong performers, improving your culture will help you attract the people you wish to attract.

Developing and communicating an inspiring corporate philosophy can be another key component of a strategy to attract candidates. Because few organizations can demonstrate a commitment to operating according to higher principles and values, any real effort in that regard will be viewed positively by most candidates.

ATTRACTING EMPLOYEES IS A SALES PROCESS

We have been focusing on developing a marketing strategy to attract candidates to the organization and the opportunities it offers. Hand in hand with that strategy are the sales skills necessary to obtain candidates' interest and commitment to join the organization. The process of selling in the hiring situation is similar to other large-ticket sales situations, and requires similar skills:

- *Identify candidate needs.* You need to get to know candidates and identify their needs. These include their career aspirations, what they like and dislike about their current jobs and employers, their reasons for considering leaving their organizations and joining yours, what they are looking for in their next job, their compensation expectations, the criteria upon which they will make their decision whether to join your organization, and other opportunities they are exploring. By knowing the needs of the candidates, you can (and should) use your knowledge to help both you and the candidate to decide whether there is a match.

- *Communicate the benefits and features that meet candidate needs.* One of the classic mistakes that salespeople make is to emphasize product features that are of no interest to the customer. Once candidates' wants and needs have been elicited, you can talk about the aspects of the company and the position that satisfy them.

- *Elicit objections.* Many hiring managers talk at length about the benefits of the job and the company, but don't ask candidates about their concerns, issues, and misgivings. They are then surprised when candidates decline offers or withdraw from consideration. By eliciting objections, managers can at least try to overcome them before candidates make a decision based on them.

- *Correct misunderstandings and work around drawbacks.* Having received partial and limited information solely from the interview process, candidates often draw inaccurate conclusions. One benefit of eliciting objections is that these misunderstandings can often be corrected and the hiring process put back on track. Drawbacks—objections that cannot be overcome (such as not liking the location of the job)—can be dealt with by emphasizing other benefits of the job that are important to the candidate.

• *Close for the next step in the hiring process.* Obtain candidate agreement to do whatever the next step in the process may be—coming in for an interview, providing reference names, or accepting a job offer.

By using competency-based selection to assess candidates and using sales skills effectively in the hiring process, your organization can improve the competency of its people and consequently overall organizational performance.

Retaining the Right Employees

Retaining the right employees is just as important as hiring them. As difficult as it is to hire superior performers, it is more painful to lose the ones you have. Developing a corporate retention strategy should be a critical component of an organization's overall strategic plan.

The main purpose of a retention strategy is to help employees develop what can be called *attitudinal commitment.* Our goal is to have employees identify their well-being with the well-being of the organization. With attitudinal commitment, employees invest more human capital in their organizations than is required for them to keep their jobs.

Our research has shown that employees with attitudinal commitment generally feel a high degree of job fulfillment, see themselves as having significant growth opportunities in their organizations, and feel well recognized and fairly compensated. They form emotional bonds with their companies, and feel aligned with the organization's management team. They also feel as though they understand the big picture and grasp and identify with the corporate culture of the organization. Employees with attitudinal commitment generally feel affirmed and proud to work for the company. They feel cared about by the organization, feel encouraged to contribute, and feel that they belong.

Our research has also demonstrated that employees who leave their organizations tend to feel a lack in at least some of these areas. We conducted a study a few years ago to investigate what motivated employees to leave their current employers. We asked employees of a number of companies to list the factors that might cause them to leave their jobs. The most significant factors mentioned were as follows:

• Lack of advancement opportunity.
• Dissatisfaction with important aspects of the corporate culture.

- Uncertain future for the company (significant for baby boomers but not for Generation Xers).
- Dissatisfaction with management (significant for baby boomers but not for Generation Xers).
- Stress and burnout (significant for Generations Xers but not for baby boomers).

We also asked them what company programs were important factors in retaining them. The following factors were highly rated:

- Innovative compensation and benefits.
- Effective rewards and recognition.
- Strategies for increasing employee satisfaction.
- Performance management system.
- Career planning.
- Coaching for career development.

The results of our study are consistent with other studies: If employees perceive that their organizations are doing good things for them, they see those things as contributing to their staying at their organizations. Key factors are career opportunities, career development, rewards and recognition, management, and compensation. The implications are clear: To retain your employees, build the kind of high-performance corporate culture this book is committed to develop.

DEVELOPING A RETENTION STRATEGY

To develop a retention strategy for your organization, first perform an analysis of your situation. Who is leaving and why they are leaving? Use exit interviews to identify and track the reasons employees decided to quit. You also want to determine the demographics of those voluntarily leaving the organization in terms of tenure, function, gender, race and ethnicity, and performance level. If your strong performers are leaving the organization, you will have a considerably different response than if the vast majority of those leaving are the organization's weak performers.

You also want to know how other employees are feeling about the organization and what might cause them to leave. Employee surveys and interviews can both be used to gather retention data. As with the analysis of employees who have left the organization, this data should be analyzed demographically. With current employees you can ask two sets of questions: What factors and circumstances might cause you to leave the organization of your own volition? What aspects and features of the organization most keep you here?

Based on the responses to these questions you can determine the organizational strengths and weaknesses that most affect the retention of the employees that are important to keep. The results will help you create a retention plan that develops your strengths and shores up your weaknesses in the areas that most directly impact retention.

A retention strategy can include the following elements:

- An inspiring corporate philosophy.
- An innovative compensation plan.
- Innovative benefits, such as flextime, day care, and telecommuting.
- An effective rewards and recognition program.
- An effective employee development program.
- Career planning.
- Training.
- Mentoring/coaching.

As you can see from this list, a retention plan should not only improve retention but also improve the organization's ability to attract the kind of employees you need to achieve the organization's objectives. Because the strategies highlighted are designed to improve employee satisfaction, productivity and profitability should also improve.

The Benefits of Competency-Based Best Practices

Competency-based selection practices have been implemented in thousands of organizations with results that have been replicated over and over again. Specific benefits include:

- Lower employee turnover.
- Less time and money spent on the hiring process.
- A reputation of excellence in selection and hiring.
- Improved morale due to the perceived fairness of the selection process.

- Reduced training time and increased productivity of new employees.
- Greater skill and confidence of the interview team.
- Lower legal risks associated with the selection process.
- Greater involvement of interviewers in the selection process.
- Greater commitment by the interviewing team to the success of the selected employee.

One of the main criteria for evaluating CEOs is the quality of the management teams they hire and develop. By extension, the same can be said for the quality of the overall hiring process. By implementing a workable competency-based selection process, senior managers can impact their organizations in ways that will unquestionably improve the business.

12

Developing Your Employees: Competency-Based Performance Development

Developing the competence of an organization's workforce and creating a culture of competence will affect almost every facet of the organization. In practical terms, it means that employees will take more initiative, solve problems sooner, and seize opportunities that would otherwise have been missed. Customer needs will be better satisfied as employees increase their personal commitment to meeting their needs. Product lines will improve and expand as employees become more innovative and creative and encourage each other's creativity and experimentation.

Individual performance will improve as people set and commit to achieving challenging goals. Customer service and quality will improve as employees improve in the relevant competencies—concern for quality, managing performance, service orientation, initiative, and production efficiency, to name a few. Productivity and profitability will improve because people are engaging their talents and abilities to do their work better and more efficiently.

Managers will coach subordinates better, and be better at holding them accountable. They will treat subordinates as individuals and inspire them to do their best and to improve themselves. Employee satisfaction will increase. It will be easier to attract excellent candidates. Retention rates will improve. The organization will transform.

With such a rosy vision, why doesn't every organization create a developmental culture of competence? There are many reasons—managerial resistance to change, cultural norms against truthful and direct communication, authority issues among employees and managers, and so on. One of the biggest problems is that most people have few (if any) models of organizations and individuals fully supporting the growth and development of others. In this chapter we will lay out a comprehensive competency-based development system that can serve as such an organizational model.

Components of a Competency-Based Development System

To be effective, a competency-based development system needs to have more components than just a performance review, or just performance reviews and goal setting. Without some kind of regular reinforcement, people are unlikely to reach their goals. Anyone who has ever committed to losing weight understands how this can happen. Without regular weigh-ins and specific goals and action steps, a person may very well have gained weight when he or she assesses progress in six months. An effective system will include processes for planning, monitoring progress, addressing problems, providing coaching, training and assistance, and evaluating results.

These processes can be grouped into three phases, graphically depicted in Figure 12.1:

1. The planning phase, in which goals and action steps are established to accomplish performance objectives and individual development goals.
2. The execution phase, in which progress is monitored, coaching and supervision are provided, performance problems are addressed, and adjustments to the plan are made.
3. The assessment and evaluation phase, in which results are evaluated and competencies are assessed.

The Foundation for Development

What are the conditions and circumstances under which people change their behavior? Which elements of corporate culture promote and encour-

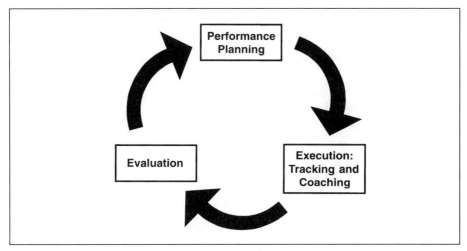

Figure 12.1   The cyclical developmental process.

age employees to put in extra time and effort and invest their own human capital in self-improvement?

Employees need to want to change the results they create. Change is usually accompanied by discomfort; if it weren't, it would have already been accomplished if we thought it would be at all beneficial. People will undergo the discomfort of change only if the resulting benefit outweighs the discomfort.

Training and developmental plans must correspond to what employees want for themselves. Otherwise they will view improvement plans as manipulative attempts to squeeze more productivity out of them rather than opportunities to help them increase their capabilities.

The assessment and development processes need to help employees accurately identify issues, diagnose problems, and come up with action plans to address them. Without accurate diagnosis and analysis, proposed solutions won't address the real problems.

Employees need to feel that their assessment and development plans are personal and customized. They must feel ownership of the plans and take personal responsibility for their execution.

The corporate culture needs to value and encourage interpersonal support and personal self-improvement. These values help motivate employees to focus on developing themselves.

The corporate culture needs to support personal risk taking and experimentation. When employees are recognized and acknowledged for taking risks to extend themselves, they will be more likely to try new behaviors and expand their competence.

Principles behind Performance Management

Several principles support an effective performance development system. Adherence to these principles will help ensure the success of the system, and failure to operate in accordance with them will contribute to its failure. These principles can be used to help design systems, implement them, train managers and employees, communicate with others, and solve implementation problems. These principles can also help set the tone and frame performance development in terms of higher purpose: We want you to be your best and be as successful as possible.

TRUTH

In relation to performance development, truth manifests itself in the communication of honest feedback to managers, employees, and coworkers. Truth includes the expression of opinions, facts, judgments, and feelings. Truth has many facets and levels, and those who use the assessment process to explore truth broadly and deeply will gain the most benefit.

In our firm I use the assessment process to expand my understanding of my subordinates by inviting them to truthfully express what motivates them, what they like and dislike about what they do, what they want, what they care about, and how I can help them. I also tell them my truths in relation to them: What I like and dislike about what they have done over the review period, what I appreciate about them, my vision for them, my perceptions and judgments about their barriers to success, and any suggestions I have.

SERVICE

Every aspect of the performance development process should serve every stakeholder in the organization—employees, managers, owners, and customers. In the performance assessment process, feedback and assessment should serve the employee and ultimately those the employee serves; so should the development of a performance plan. The principle of service is one of the most powerful checks in assessment, planning, and coaching. "Am I serving her in this communication?" "Does requiring him to give me a weekly report serve him?"

One of the confusing aspects of this principle in the context of performance development is that what serves employees may not feel good to them, and often will upset them. Telling people what they don't want to hear might make them unhappy, but it may be just the thing to help them change their course and get on the right track. In my experience, learning to serve others well is a lifelong learning process in which I try things to help others improve, and learn what works and what doesn't. I have made plenty of mistakes, but I have improved my skills, my competence, and my ability to help others.

RESPONSIBILITY

The key concept in this principle—that we each create our own experiences—is the foundational principle behind performance development. It is by understanding and taking responsibility for what they did and didn't do to achieve their goals that employees learn what they need to improve. The performance development system is based on the premise that employees can impact their results by improving their proficiency on behavioral competencies. They need no one's permission to improve their competence—their fate is in their own hands.

From the manager's perspective, it is the manager's responsibility to ensure the successes of the subordinates. Of course no one completely controls one's own fate, but by focusing on what they *do* control, people increase the probability of successful outcomes.

PLAY

Play is the principle by which people get satisfaction from what they do. It is the principle of choice and the principle of engagement. The opposite of play is burden, the sense that we *have to* work, that we have no choices, and that work is unrewarding. The principles of play and responsibility together lead to some corollaries that may contradict commonly held beliefs:

- Everyone is responsible for creating one's own satisfaction through doing one's work and achieving goals.
- It is always possible to go for satisfaction.
- Feelings of burden and obligation are signals that people aren't taking responsibility for their own satisfaction.

The implication for performance development is that employees should be encouraged to use the process as a vehicle for creating their own job satisfaction. Managers should use the process to increase their own satisfaction in relation to employees. It is through the interactions between people going for what they want that creative solutions are born, and dynamic, productive work environments are created.

COMPASSION

Compassion is the principle by which we understand and empathize with others. Most people who don't exhibit compassion for others feel little compassion for themselves. Compassion allows people to put their mistakes behind them and begin the new day afresh. With compassion comes confidence and encouragement, key elements of performance development.

It is important not to confuse being compassionate with accepting excuses. Good managers are compassionate and also allow their subordinates to experience the natural consequences of their actions so that they can learn and improve themselves.

Assumptions and Beliefs Underlying Performance Development

The procedures in this performance development system are based on some assumptions that apply to all of the management practices described in this book:

- People can and want to learn and grow. Underneath surface feelings and attitudes, people would rather be stimulated and challenged than bored and disengaged.
- Consciousness and awareness can lead people to make different choices. By making conscious previously unconscious attitudes, beliefs, motivations, and behaviors, people can use their wills and their conscious minds to change their behavior.
- Giving and contributing to others benefit oneself as well.
- People grow faster, learn more, and are more satisfied when they participate in constructive interactions as a part of a community.

In the course of introducing managers and employees to performance development, we are explicit about these assumptions and beliefs. Although they may seem inherently true, they challenge people's deeply held beliefs about themselves and others. Therefore, verbalizing and discussing them brings to light a number of the issues that result in ineffective coaching and supervisory behavior.

Let us now proceed to discussing the phases of the performance development process. We could logically start with either performance planning—the phase in which goals are set—or the assessment phase, in which results are evaluated and competency assessment determined. We will begin with assessment, because a baseline competency evaluation is key to the development of an effective performance plan.

The Assessment Phase

The assessment phase of the performance development process— the performance review—has several purposes:

- Employees, managers, and the organization mark the degree to which goals and objectives have been achieved.
- Managers, employees, and sometimes others assess the overall competence of employees.
- Employees receive feedback about how they are perceived by the organization.
- Overall merit ratings provide the basis for determining compensation, promotion, and other career events.

When introducing assessment in training sessions, we often use a financial analogy to explain the structure of assessment. Financial experts analyze companies using two instruments, an income statement and a balance sheet. The income statement presents the results and accomplishments the organization has achieved over the last time period. The balance sheet lists the assets and liabilities of the corporation, providing a snapshot of the organization's overall capability to achieve its mission. The assessment phase of performance development serves the same two functions. Goal assessment provides the opportunity to report the results achieved during the review period, equivalent to the income statement. Competency assessment evaluates the overall capability of people to be successful in their jobs, the assets they have available to help them accomplish their job objectives, and the liabilities that may hinder them from succeeding.

In many organizations, performance reviews are perceived by both employees and managers as offering little or no value. In some companies it is a common practice for managers to pull out last year's review and simply change its date. In many companies employees receive the required annual performance review only once every three or four years. People are missing an invaluable opportunity to use the assessment process as a tool to help them accomplish their goals, improve themselves in important areas, and get feedback from the organization about their career opportunities within the organization.

WHAT SHOULD BE ASSESSED?

To accomplish all its potential purposes, the assessment process should measure three areas: goal achievement, performance improvement, and competencies. Assessment of goal achievement can include performance objectives (job- and results-related goals) and competency development goals (goals to support employee improvement in a competency). Competency assessment should include rating the competencies most important for success on the job, and possibly those competencies important for career development.

We have a simple point of view regarding performance reviews: Before a review period begins, people should know the criteria on which they are going to be evaluated. The results expected of them should be the performance objectives. The improvements they are expected to make should be their competency development goals or skill building goals. Further, they should know how much importance the organization places on the achievement of those goals.

Some organizations wish to include skill assessment in the assessment process—for example, reevaluating an employee's certifications, technical ability in the job, and so on. While it is conceptually a good idea, it has two practical problems: First, skill assessment can cause employees and managers to deemphasize competency assessment, because skill assessment is usually more concrete and understandable and because many employees and managers are more comfortable working with skills than they are with competencies. Second, it will decrease the time and attention placed on competency assessment by virtue of the time it takes to conduct the skill assessment. Because competencies tend to predict performance much better than skills, directing attention away from competencies to skills will tend to decrease the value of the assessment process.

Another question regarding assessment is whether activity as well as results should be measured. If salespeople achieve a goal in their plan to sell $1 million worth of widgets, does it matter whether they performed the actions in their plan that they said they would do, such as making 100 calls a week? As a secondary activity in the review process, it is worth discussing the work activity that was intended to support goal accomplishment, but it sends the wrong message to value activity in the same way that results are valued. Otherwise people will tend to focus on performing activities rather than accomplishing goals. In some companies where activity was overemphasized, we have seen midlevel managers and employees satisfied with mediocre business, because they accomplished their action steps.

WHO ASSESSES WHOM?

In almost every organization that does performance reviews, managers evaluate their subordinates. If assessment is to be as effective as possible, employees should also assess themselves. While our research has shown that self-assessment is frequently inaccurate, especially for areas of competency weakness, there is much benefit to be gained by having employees analyze their degree of proficiency on the competencies most important for success in their jobs. Even if their self-perceptions are completely inaccurate, their thinking about it will help them understand and discuss their manager's assessment of their competencies and help them to think about improving the competencies.

Multi-rater assessment adds another dimension to the evaluation process that can be particularly helpful in preparing for a development process. When a manager gives an employee a lower competency rating, employees may become defensive and make up their own rationalization for their manager's rating: Their manager is being unfair to them, or doesn't like them, or simply is wrong about their assessment. It is more difficult to deny the combined assessment of a whole group of people. Multi-rater assessment helps employees get additional perspective on their assessment, and helps them face themselves more truthfully.

Although multi-rater assessment is beneficial, not all companies may be able to implement it right away. When the culture is not ready for multi-rater assessment, it may do more harm than good. One problem with multi-rater assessment can occur when employees either are not well trained in assessment or collude to rate each other higher than they deserve. This can make it more difficult for managers to get their employees to understand their point of view when there is a significant disparity between manager and employee ratings.

Another problem with multi-rater assessment occurs in culture change situations in which the leadership is trying to instill a rapid change in employee attitude and behavior. In this case multi-rater feedback by "old culture" employees will often add to employees' resistance to change rather than help them adjust to it.

SHOULD PERFORMANCE REVIEW AND ASSESSMENT PROCESSES BE SEPARATED?

Many companies separate their development process from the appraisal process they use for the purpose of determining raises, bonuses, and promotions. The advantage of separating the two processes is that the development process is not encumbered with the emotional pressure associated with compensation. If a lower competency rating results in a smaller raise, employees are more likely to argue and deny the truth of the rating.

On the other hand, combining the performance appraisal and development processes serves to reinforce the reality that competence and performance are unalterably and intrinsically connected to each other. To improve performance, improve the competencies that determine the performance.

There will always be some tension between the accountability required to accomplish organizational objectives and the supportive environment necessary to motivate positive change. Pretending that the tension doesn't exist won't help the situation. The best way we have found to deal with it is to tell the truth about it—organizations both need performance from their employees and want them to develop. In fact, telling the truth about the contrasting perspectives is the best way I know to gain the respect of employees.

ASSESS HOW OFTEN?

In an ideal world, assessment would be a daily activity. Every day employees would receive feedback about how they were doing and their particular strengths and weaknesses. In the real world, however, people need to set specific times to structure feedback and assessment to ensure that it occurs.

In our experience, six months is often an optimal time frame for a review period, particularly for competency development. It is long enough to allow meaningful change to occur, yet not so long that the improvement process becomes stale. The problem with an annual review process is that a year is generally too long a time period to remain engaged in a development process for a competency without at least a midyear assessment. The development process needs to remain fresh in the minds of employees for them to stay focused on it.

THE ASSESSMENT PROCESS

Here is an outline of a sample assessment process:

At the Beginning of the Review Period

- Performance objectives and competency development goals are established.

- A means of measurement is defined as a part of the goal setting process, including definitions of what it means to meet and to exceed the goals.
- A tactical plan is developed that includes the specific steps necessary to achieve the goals and objectives.

During the Review Period

- Informal meetings take place between managers and their subordinates to discuss progress on performance objectives and competency development goals.
- Employees keep track of their progress toward their goals and the execution of their plans.

At the End of the Review Period

- Employees rate themselves on how well they have achieved their performance objectives and competency development goals, based on the definitions of success established at the beginning of the review period. They also rate themselves on the set of competencies appropriate for their jobs. They provide examples and evidence to justify their ratings.
- Managers rate their subordinates on the same performance objectives, competency development goals, and competencies, providing examples and comments to explain and justify the ratings. In any areas in which managers don't have enough information to rate accurately, they gather that information.
- Managers and employees prepare for meetings to discuss the assessments, analyzing employee performance and capability.
- Employees and their managers meet to discuss their ratings. They discuss disparities between their ratings, and the most important areas for employees to develop in order to improve their performances and achieve the job success they desire. Where performance objectives were not met, they discuss why they weren't, examining the causes and the behaviors that affected the results.
- As a result of the meetings, managers change their competency ratings if they feel that their ratings were incorrect.
- The information from the assessment process is used to help create the next review period's performance objectives and competency development goals.

THE ASSESSMENT MEETING

The assessment meeting between managers and employees has a number of purposes. It is an opportunity for managers to give feedback to and receive it from employees regarding their performance and their development. Managers can use the occasion to develop and communicate their vision to employees of how they see them developing and growing, inspiring employees to develop higher visions for themselves, their careers, and their performance.

Here are some guidelines for managers to facilitate the discussion:

- Express appreciation for the employee's contribution to the organization.
- Communicate the purpose of the meeting: to discuss the evaluation of performance objectives, competency development goals, and the employee's skills and competencies in order to understand each other and lay the foundation for continued employee development and job success.
- Go over each performance objective, appreciating successes and discussing the causes of objectives not being met.
- Review each competency together, noting employee strengths, weaknesses, and suggestions for improvement. Where there is a significant disparity between the employee's self scores and your scores for the employee, discuss the reasons for the disparity. If as a result of the discussion you think you rated the employee incorrectly, change your rating.
- Communicate your vision for the employee, and ask for the employee's response. You may wish to elicit their own visions for themselves. Your goal is to help employees see a bigger picture of what is possible for them, and how satisfied and how successful they can be. Once they buy in to a larger vision, discuss the details of how they can achieve it.
- At the end of the meeting, decide together which competencies the employee should focus on for improvement this year. To decide this, first ask the employee what competencies he or she thinks are most important to improve during the next review period, and ask why the person chose those competencies. Suggest choices of your own if you have different ones, giving your reasons for your choices. Work together to choose two or three developmental competencies. There are clear advantages to going along with at least one or two of the employee's choices; the employee is more likely to make the changes to improve mastery of the competency if it is the employee's own choice.

Here are some other suggestions for the discussion:

- Do what you can to create a positive environment.

- Do not be surprised if the employee is upset—some of the feedback is likely to be uncomfortable. Remember that the discomfort is not necessarily a problem, and it may provide some of the motivation for making a change.

- If employees are upset, *stop and listen*. Hear their point of view, and let them know that you understand their point of view. After they feel understood, express your viewpoint.

- Be willing to change your competency rating if you are wrong.

- Go for mutual understanding, if not agreement, where there is a disparity, making sure that each person understands the other's point of view.

- Keep your employees' best interests in mind. Focus on serving them in the meeting.

- Take the risk to be honest and straightforward, and encourage the employee to do the same.

It is easy to say that managers need to have the best interests of their subordinates in mind, or to say that they need to listen to their subordinates and use what they hear to align employees' personal goals with company needs. It is more difficult for managers to change their behavior so that they interact with their subordinates in these ways. Most managers need considerable training to acquire the skills necessary to support competency development and performance improvement in their subordinates.

Ideally, at the end of the assessment process, both employees and their managers have a clear and common understanding of employees' performance over the previous review period, their proficiency on the competencies important for their position and their career, the ways they improved themselves over the review period, and any other elements that are important to employees' success in the job and the organization. In other words, the assessment process should define the present state of each employee in relation to the organization. Once the present state has been defined, they can proceed to setting goals and developing plans to achieve them—the performance planning process.

The Performance Planning Phase

Performance planning is based on concepts that almost everyone agrees with but that few people practice:

- To create a good plan, employees need to know where they are now—the current state—and where they want to go—the goal state.
- Employees must believe that they will obtain personal benefit from achieving the goals in the plan commensurate with the commitment of their time and effort.
- Employees will be dedicated to accomplishing goals to the extent that they expect to achieve benefits in areas that are personally important to them. These areas are different for different people.
- Goals should be measurable. Employees and managers need to be able to say as unequivocally as possible the degree to which goals were achieved.
- Goals should be perceived by employees as achievable.
- An effective plan should include, in addition to goals, the strategy and tactics that will most likely lead to their achievement.
- Strategy and tactics should be based on both an analysis of the current state and an understanding of the desired goal state (the intended results).
- The strategy and tactics in the plan should take advantage of employee and organizational strengths.
- Strategy and tactics should take into account employee and organizational weaknesses, and either compensate for those weaknesses, improve them, or in other ways prevent them from interfering with goal achievement.
- The plan should include milestones and other means by which progress can be measured on an interim basis.
- The plan should include process and support during the execution phase to help managers and employees do the things necessary to have the plan succeed. This includes monitoring progress, identifying and addressing problems, and helping employees stay on their edge to maximize their growth and their performance.
- The plan should be modifiable during the execution phase to respond to changing circumstances.

Most of the problems with the goal setting process in organizations are related to these issues. In a common scenario, for example, a salesperson receives his sales quota for his territory based on an increase in sales of 20 percent. His sales have increased at a rate of 5 percent over the prior two years, and he knows that he is in danger of losing one of his biggest accounts. He would be happy to maintain an increase of 5 percent. He believes the 20 percent goal to be unrealistic. To him it demonstrates the company's lack of knowledge, understanding, and concern for him and his territory. The aggressive goal had the effect of discouraging and demotivating him, the opposite of what the company intended.

In another common situation, organizational priorities change in the middle of the execution phase, affecting employee performance plans. Halfway through a project occupying most of her time, an employee finds that a major portion of her performance plan has become irrelevant. When her performance review occurs, she knows that her ratings will be lower than they would have been had her project not been canceled, even though its cancellation had nothing to do with her performance.

Often employees define goals in ways that create ambiguity when it becomes time to evaluate their performances. If an employee's goal is "to improve the efficiency of the order entry process," how do the employee and his or her manager know that the goal has been reached if there is no clear way to measure order entry efficiency? Without a means of measurement and without being declared in measurable terms, goal achievement can become a contentious issue that leaves either the employee or the manager feeling dissatisfied and mistreated by the other.

These and many other problems can be avoided if the performance planning process includes all the elements just listed. This kind of in-depth planning takes time, and many managers and employees may feel that they are too busy to devote the time necessary to do the job well. This is another example of a self-fulfilling prophecy: If I don't take enough time to plan well, I work less efficiently, leaving me no time to plan, so I work less efficiently, and so on.

Most people resist planning for several reasons:

- They don't like to commit themselves to outcomes for which they will be held accountable.
- They are uncomfortable looking at their weaknesses and shortcomings, and don't know how to develop steps to overcome or compensate for them.
- They don't know how to set goals and develop strategies and tactics to achieve them.
- They don't buy into the organization's expectations of them, and believe that they and their managers cannot develop a workable plan that includes realistic goals and expectations.

These obstacles must be overcome if a performance plan is to succeed.

EFFECTIVE PLANNING REQUIRES EFFECTIVE LEADERSHIP: A CAUTIONARY TALE

The head of national sales for a utility wanted to institute a performance planning process for his sales force. The sales group had been given new, aggressive sales goals for the year. He liked the idea of his salespeople setting goals, developing action steps to achieve them, and monitoring their performance during execution. However, he wasn't committed to providing the leadership required to deal with the issues that arose when the process was introduced to the sales force. Here are some of the reactions of salespeople to performance planning:

"How can you expect us to meet goals when we can't even deliver gas to the companies I sell it to?"

"It takes me three weeks to get a customer a price. If I can't get a price on time, you can't blame me for not meeting a time line for sales."

"If we had the products and the services that companies need, we could meet our goals."

"Why is the sales department held responsible for everything? Why isn't customer support or marketing doing the same thing?"

"This is just another tool the company is going to use to blame the salespeople for the company's problems."

"I'm sick and tired of all these programs that take my time away from doing my job."

The objections and complaints that came up in the employee orientation process had nothing to do with performance planning per se. They related to the organizational problems that affected their ability to meet the expectations they anticipated to be included in the plan. Management needs to be prepared to respond to these kinds of complaints with honesty, good faith, and credible answers. In this case, the manager was not sufficiently proficient at organizational savvy, influence, and integrity and truth to gain the confidence of his people. They simply did not believe that he or the organization cared at all about them and what they needed in order to do the job that they were expected to do.

There are several lessons from this true story. First, managers need to practice what they preach. If the manager had himself created a realistic, achievable plan, he would have been better able to explain how his subordinates would be able to do so, even with the current organization problems. Second, managers need proficiency at a number of competencies in order to facilitate a planning process for their subordinates. These competencies include:

- Interpersonal awareness, to understand and respond to the needs and concerns of employees.
- Results orientation, to help them set challenging yet realistic goals.
- Managing performance, to help track progress toward goal achievement and promptly address problems that affect performance.
- Influence, to help enroll employees in the processes of setting and achieving performance objectives and competency development goals.
- Motivating others, to help employees commit themselves to both the development and execution of a performance plan.
- Empowering others, to provide subordinates with opportunities to expand their capabilities.
- Developing others, to help employees improve their skills and competencies.
- Integrity and truth, to be able to be seen by subordinates as coaches and supervisors they can count on.

This list is not complete, but it illustrates the importance of competency assessment and development for performance planning.

THE GOAL SETTING PROCESS

What Kinds of Goals Should Employees Set?

To create a culture of competence, ideally employees should set both performance objectives and competency development goals. Performance objectives are the goals that relate to business results: Increase sales by 15 percent, complete a new employee manual by June 30, complete the strategic plan by April 30, reduce waste by 5 percent, and so on. Competency development goals are the goals that relate to improving the capability of employees to perform work and produce results: Set more challenging goals, become a better coach, improve influence skills, improve interpersonal awareness, and so on.

Setting Performance Objectives

Who Should Set Performance Objectives?

In most organizations, only managers above a certain level and salespeople set performance objectives. However, it is possible for every employee to set performance objectives—administrative personnel, janitors, schoolteachers, engineers, and so on. Every job exists to perform specific functions within the organization. Performance objectives can be set in relation to each of those functions. Ideally, all employees should have performance objectives related to performing those functions as well as they can.

What Makes a Good Performance Objective?

In the best case, performance objectives should relate to the job goals defined in the job description. For example, if one of the goals in the job description for purchasing managers is to ensure that manufacturing has the materials it needs when it needs them, purchasing managers should have a performance objective that relates to this goal. For example, a goal might be defined in terms of decreasing the number of times during the year when production of a product was delayed because a material was not available.

Since many companies may not have current, meaningful job descriptions, the first step for most companies is to provide training, oversight, and a set of criteria to ensure that performance objectives make sense for the business. The acronym SMART is often used as a mnemonic to remind employees of how goals should be defined. Goals should be:

- **S**pecific—Exactly what is to be achieved?
- **M**easurable—How can it be measured? How will we know if it was accomplished?
- **A**ligned with the business objectives, and **A**chievable—Will achieving it help the business achieve its objectives? Can the goal be accomplished?
- **R**esults oriented—What is the result the goal is intended to achieve?
- **T**ime-bound—By when is the goal to be achieved?

If every performance objective in the organization met the SMART criteria, the corporate culture itself will become more results oriented. At American National Can, for example, it took several years for the elements in SMART to become a part of the culture. Today, however, you can say just about any goal and several employees will immediately pick out the characteristic the goal is lacking: "When will it be accomplished?" "By how much?" "How will we know when you have done it?" The skill of setting goals is critical to a powerful performance planning process.

Who Sets the Performance Objectives?

Different organizations have different policies and viewpoints on this, and different circumstances require different responses. If employees participate in the creation of their goals, they are more likely to invest the time, effort, and emotional resources required to achieve them. There are some performance objectives that senior management would find more sensible to set than to leave employees to develop them for themselves. For example, if a company is in the third year of a strategic plan calling for a 15 percent reduction in waste, a plant manager who has reduced waste by 10 percent may be told to reduce waste another 5 percent this year. Obtaining the plant manager's buy-in to the goal is important; it is not necessary for him or her to be either the initiator or the final authority on the objective.

The final authority on performance objectives needs to be company management. Management must know that employees are focusing on achieving results that will help the company achieve its overall objectives. Organizations should have a process through which they can audit employee goals and objectives to ensure that employees are working at common purposes and that course corrections can be made as soon as possible.

How Are Performance Objectives Prioritized?

Many companies do not assign priorities to performance objectives in the planning process, which may suggest to employees that they are all of equal value. Because one goal of the performance planning process is to let employees know what is expected of them, it is usually better to assign priority weightings to each performance objective, which lets employees know how important they are. For example, salespeople might have one goal to increase sales by 10 percent and another goal to complete all paperwork on time; it is important for them to know the relative importance of each goal.

One way to set priorities is to assign a percentage weight to each performance objective, with the total required to equal 100 percent. Here is one example:

Performance Objective	*Percentage Weighting*
Increase sales 10%	50%
Add three new accounts	20%
Improve relations with manufacturing	10%
Complete all paperwork on time	10%
Contribute in other ways to business objectives	10%
	100%

Another way to set priorities is to weight them on a three- or four-point scale, from most to least important. We usually use a simple three point system in our software: Critical, important and useful. Whatever scale is used, it is important to let employees know the organization's priorities so they can adjust their behavior accordingly.

Priorities are particularly important to communicate if the organization creates an overall merit rating for each employee. Merit ratings should be at least partly tied to the achievement of performance objectives, and it is both fair and common business sense to inform employees about the relative importance of their different job functions and objectives.

How Can Performance Objectives Be Measured?

Some performance objectives are simple to measure: Increase revenue dollars, complete a project on time, hire a certain number of people. Others are more difficult: Improve the quality of the hiring process, make the environment a more enjoyable place to work, work more efficiently. One solution for measuring these softer goals is to create a scale (1 to 5 or 1 to 10, for example) and have others rate the employee on the achievement of the objective. For example, administrative assistants might be rated on a 1 to 10 scale on how well they helped prepare management reports. Making the environment a more enjoyable place to work could be measured using before-and-after surveys of employees.

By determining measurements for performance objectives, employees and managers are forced to examine what results they want to achieve and how they know if they have been successful. The time put in at the beginning of the performance planning will reduce ambiguity and uncertainty through the execution and assessment phases, and lead to focus and clarity of purpose.

Setting Competency Development Goals

Who Should Have Competency Development Goals?

Everyone, from the CEO to the mail clerk, should have competency development goals. Improving the competencies most important for one's job will improve the performance of every employee.

How Many Competencies Should an Employee Try to Improve at the Same Time?

Competency improvement is difficult. Because it takes effort and focus to change competency behavior, trying to improve behavior on many competencies at once can be both discouraging and unlikely to result in much improvement anywhere. We recommend that our clients focus on improving only two or three competencies at a time. The improvement of those competencies will have a ripple effect on performance and will usually improve other competencies as well.

How Many Competency Development Goals Should an Employee Set?
One to three development goals per competency is enough to improve behavior, but not so many that the employee becomes overwhelmed. The
number of development goals also depends on the number of competencies
the employee is working to improve.

How Should Employees' Developmental Competencies Be Chosen?
Employees need to want to improve themselves if they are to take the risks
and face the challenges necessary for them to improve their proficiency on
competencies. If all their developmental competencies are dictated to them by
their managers, they are less likely to take them on as their own. Based on the
purposes and circumstances, developmental competencies can be chosen in
different ways. Sometimes organizations will have every employee work on the
same developmental competency. This approach can result in rapid organizational change, as every employee is working to improve in the same direction.

We usually recommend a combination of manager-chosen and
employee-chosen developmental competencies, so that employees feel
some control over the development process and managers have their
subordinates working to improve the competencies they view as most
important for success in the job.

How Are Competency Development Goals Set?
Competency development goals should meet the same SMART criteria as
performance objectives. In addition to SMART criteria, competency development goals should significantly improve proficiency in the targeted developmental competency. Most competency development goals will fall
into one of four categories:

1. An increase in rating on a behaviorally anchored scale: "My goal is to
   go from a '4' to a '6' in initiative."
2. Improvement in a competency without an associated rating measurement: "My goal is to become better at taking initiative."
3. Development of key behaviors that go into the competency: "My goal
   is to take complete responsibility for a complex project from start to
   finish."
4. A defined work project that directly relates to the competency: "My
   goal is to take complete responsibility for reducing waste by 5 percent
   in our plant."

The form of competency development goals can be established by the organization or left up to the discretion of each manager or employee. They
all can work so long as SMART criteria are met.

*What Is the Relationship between Competency Development Goals
and Performance Objectives?*
Performance objectives can be seen as the "what" of an employee's job, and
competency development goals are the "how." Achieving competency development goals should help employees achieve their performance objectives. Any competency development goal that does not either improve
current performance or prepare employees for future performance is an in-
appropriate goal.

How Should Competency Development Goals Be Measured?
Competency development goals can be measured the same way performance objectives are measured, except where behaviorally anchored rating
scales are used as the means for measuring success. If the rating scale itself is
used as the means for measurement—as in "raise my rating in motivating
others from a '6' to an '8' "—the definition of the rating level becomes the
criterion for measuring behavioral improvement.

ACTION STEPS TO ACHIEVE GOALS
AND OBJECTIVES

Goals are just one part of an effective performance plan. Without the
strategy and tactics to accomplish them, goals will provide little more
benefit than New Year's resolutions. Without a plan to detail how the
goals will be attained, they are much less likely to be accomplished. The
term *action steps* describes the tactics that serve as the means to achieve
performance objectives and competency development goals. Using the
analogy of a journey, the assessment process establishes the current location, the goals and objectives define the destination, and action steps
specify the route to get from one to the other. While many different
routes can get people to the same destination, planning the route almost
always makes the trip quicker and more direct. The same applies to developing action steps. Action steps are important only as the means to
achieving goals. If employees never perform any of their action steps yet
achieve their goals, they have still accomplished their objective. Most
people, however, need the steps to help keep them on the path to goal
achievement.

Action steps are most effective when they meet the criteria for being
SMART. In fact, it is useful to say that a behavior or activity is *not* an action step unless it is SMART—specific, measurable, aligned with the goal
and achievable, results oriented, and time-bound. Here are some examples
of goals and objectives and associated action steps:

- **Performance objective:** To sell $1 million in the next six months.

  Action step: Make 10 face-to-face sales calls per week.

  This action step is specific: The activity is clearly defined. It is measurable: The employee can count the number of sales calls that were made. It is aligned with the goal and with business objectives: Making sales calls should lead to sales, which is aligned with the business purpose. For this example, let's assume that the employee and the manager have agreed that it is achievable to make 10 sales calls per week. Action steps are results oriented if their execution will significantly help the employee achieve the goal. If 10 sales calls per week is a sufficient number for a high probability of selling $1 million, then the action step is results oriented. It is also time-bound: The 10 sales calls are to be made every week.

  There are many benefits to defining action steps in terms of SMART criteria. Often employees set goals and have no idea how they are going to achieve them. They also often put together plans to achieve their goals that simply don't add up; if they did all the actions they said they were going to do, they *still* wouldn't achieve the objective. One of the functions of action steps is to ground employees in the reality of goal achievement—what are the things they really need to do in order to accomplish what they say they want to.

- **Performance objective:** To prepare all proposals within 48 hours of the request.

  Action step: Develop a proposal template for each kind of project in the next 30 days.

  This action step meets all the criteria. It is specific (there is a definite plan of action), measurable (the employee can determine whether he or she has completed it), achievable and aligned with the goal (it will help reach the goal), results oriented (it is focused on getting the job done), and time-bound (by a completion date).

- **Competency development goal:** To become a better coach to my subordinates, as measured by their evaluation of me as a coach. (To improve the competency of developing others.)

  Action step: Conduct at least one coaching session every week with a subordinate, to be set up at the Monday morning staff meeting.

  One of the checks for action steps is to step back and ask, will performing this action step really help accomplish the goal? Is it a key element of the means to achieve the end? In combination, all the action steps together should ensure the accomplishment of the goal if they are all executed.

- **Competency development goal:** To improve my rating in initiative from a "4" to a "6".

    Action step: Every Friday identify one problem in my department and plan one action to take in the following week. E-mail my manager every Friday about what action I performed this week to solve a problem and what I plan to do next week.

    It is clear that this kind of activity would demonstrate a higher level of initiative for the employee who carries it out. And what manager doesn't long for employees to take this kind of initiative and responsibility!

The problems that occur with creating action steps are usually because SMART criteria have not been met. Often they are not time-bound:

> *"I will survey my department to identify critical needs." (By when?)*
> *"I will conduct coaching sessions with my subordinates." (How often?)*

Or they are not measurable:

> *"I will be in better contact with the plant managers." (How much or how often?)*

Or they are not achievable:

> *"I will make 100 cold calls every day between 9 a.m. and 10 a.m. (This is unrealistic.)*

By bringing action step development into your organization, you can create a discipline that will foster a results-oriented culture.

How to Develop Action Steps for Competency Development Goals Using Key Behaviors

It is often difficult for employees to think of action steps that will help them accomplish their goals, particularly in the area of competency development. Key behaviors can be used to make action step development much easier. The process is as follows:

- First rate the employee on the key behaviors associated with the competency.
- Second, assess which key behaviors, if improved, would most improve the overall competency.
- Third, develop action steps that specifically relate to those key behaviors.

Let's use as an example the competency of influence. Here are some of the key behaviors for influence:

- Uncovering the concerns, wants, and needs of others.
- Demonstrating how one's position benefits the audience.
- Eliciting and responding effectively to objections.
- Identifying key decision makers and key influencers of decision makers.
- Anticipating reactions and objections, and planning how to overcome them.

Suppose an employee was weak in the first key behavior: uncovering the concerns, wants, and needs of others. An appropriate action step might be to ask questions of a coworker, boss, subordinate, or customer to uncover someone's concerns, wants, and needs once each day. If an employee were weak in the key behavior of anticipating objections and planning how to overcome them, the person might develop an action step of making a proposal or suggestion that might elicit objections, anticipating those objections, planning how to respond and overcome them, and recording the incident in a journal or electronic file at least once per week.

By using the key behaviors as guides for creating action steps, employees will focus their development on the components whose improvement will increase their overall competence proficiency.

OVERCOMING THE OBSTACLES TO COMPETENCY DEVELOPMENT

In an ideal world, competency development would be easy. We would identify the knowledge, skills, and processes we needed to learn and proceed to do so. Obviously it is not so simple, and a number of factors interfere with employees' ability to improve their proficiency on the competencies that impact their performance.

Admitting Incompetence
In the culture of the business world, acknowledging weakness or insufficiency is tantamount to admitting that one is a worthless human being deserving termination. This is an overstatement, but the message communicated throughout most companies is clear: Never show a weakness; pretend to know as much as you can possibly get away with. (Even the word "competence" is loaded with judgment.)

The "look good" culture in which we live is contradictory to the perspective from which people learn and grow. If I don't admit that I don't know, how likely am I to invest in learning what I don't know? Not very.

When training employees in competency development, we discuss the learning model that begins with *unconscious incompetence*. With unconscious incompetence, people lack capability but don't know it. Most people live in this state in some areas of their lives. Many people think they are good listeners, for example, but their self-perceptions are contradicted by those who are supposedly being listened to. So long as people are unconsciously incompetent, they will resist any attempt to change them. They think, if it isn't broken, why fix it?

The progressive state from unconscious incompetence is *conscious incompetence*—people become aware that they lack capability. Once people become aware of a gap between what they can do and what they want to do, they can apply their will and intention to increasing their knowledge and acquiring the skills they need to perform better. They work on improving themselves, and they move from conscious incompetence to *conscious competence*. With enough practice and experience, they then move from conscious competence to *unconscious competence*. At this state people perform tasks well without consciously thinking about them at all.

From the perspective of learning and development, the critical transition is from unconscious to conscious incompetence. This transition is worthy of celebration, and we continually emphasize its importance in training. Admitting weakness is good, not bad. It is only by recognizing and admitting our faults that we can begin improving them. This point cannot be emphasized too often, because it is key to competency development.

Raising Expectations

In Chapter 6 we discussed at length the role of vision in competency development. The job of manager and coach includes helping people expand their vision for their jobs, so that they can fully utilize their talents, abilities, and potential. The main job of the coach is to create and then continually hold the higher vision for the employees in their jobs—to keep in mind what is possible for them if they were fully utilizing all their capabilities and talents. The coach's job is also to help employees see a higher vision of possibility for themselves, and to help them personally buy into that vision as something they want for themselves. The coach then needs to continually remind employees of that vision, encourage them to strive toward that vision, help them notice the gaps between the vision and current behavior, and help them develop goals and action steps to close the gap.

One of the worst things managers can do is to stop expecting things of their subordinates. Expecting the best of others is one of the greatest gifts managers can give to their employees. Vision is one of many ways to offer this gift. The important thing is to infuse in employees the sense that they are capable of bigger things and have the freedom to take the risks necessary to learn and grow.

Identifying Barriers

When there are barriers to performance and goal achievement, it is important to identify the nature of those barriers, so that they can be overcome effectively. Most barriers can be categorized as:

- Knowledge barriers.
- Skill barriers.
- Process barriers.
- Emotional barriers.

Knowledge barriers occur when employees do not have mastery of the information necessary to do their jobs. For example, employees new to a company usually do not know who all the decision makers and key influencers are within an organization. Someone learning how to operate a new piece of equipment for the first time does not have the information to run it successfully.

Skill barriers occur when employees know how to do things but have not developed the skills to do so as well, quickly, or consistently as is required by the job. For example, employees may have learned how to operate that new piece of equipment, but they have not run it enough times yet to be able to operate it efficiently. Or, employees understand how to facilitate conflict resolution, but they have not practiced it enough to have mastered it.

Process barriers occur when employees are not effectively managing a sequence or series of tasks or events to accomplish a result. They may be skilled at each separate task, but they lack the ability to consistently put them together in the right order at the right time in the right way to cause success. Examples of these kinds of processes include project management, complex sales, construction, product development, and so on.

Emotional barriers refer to causes that have their roots in psychological factors. Some employees don't stick up for what they think is right, for example, because they are afraid of conflict. Others won't set challenging goals because they are afraid to fail. Some employees don't admit mistakes or take responsibility for their actions because they are afraid of being blamed or mistreated. In each of these examples, emotional reactions rather than information, skill, or process deficits are responsible for diminished performance.

It is important to know in which category a performance obstacle resides, for the solution to overcoming the barrier is dependent on this analysis. If the problem is caused by inadequate skills, skill acquisition is the appropriate solution. If the employee has the skills but is not using them because of emotional blocks, focusing on skill acquisition will have little benefit. The solution needs to fit the problem.

It is common for performance problems to be misdiagnosed, frequently because the employee involved was not invited to participate in the analysis of the problem. In one case an employee's performance had deteriorated over a number of months, and his supervisor was ready to terminate him for poor performance and a negative attitude. Just before termination the employee was taken out for a cup of coffee, where the supervisor found out that the employee's son was dying of leukemia. The employee's poor performance had nothing to do with having a bad attitude or any intentional disrespect or irresponsibility—it had to do with a life crisis. Once the organization understood the employee's situation, it responded by providing some services that helped the employee and his family cope with their difficult and painful situation. His performance improved, and a good employee was saved.

Putting together an effective performance plan requires an understanding of the current state of employees' skills and competencies, their obstacles to better performance, and their career goals and desires. Based on this input, employees can, with their managers' support, create goals and action steps to bring about the behavioral changes and the performance results they want.

Including Support Mechanisms in the Performance Plan

Any good plan will include procedures to monitor and measure the execution of action steps and the progress toward goals. If someone has a goal to improve physical fitness by exercising four times per week, the plan will be more likely to succeed if it includes keeping track of the exercise periods. It will be even more likely to succeed if the plan calls for showing the exercise record to another person once per week. It will be still more likely to succeed if the plan calls for the person to hand to a friend 52 postdated checks made out to a charity for $50 each, and to have the friend mail a check each week the person does not exercise four times. Other support mechanisms include exercising with a friend or establishing a reward system for exercising four times per week for 10 consecutive weeks.

Old habits will not be replaced with new behaviors unless the new behaviors are reinforced in some way. Paradoxically, if the old habits have been interfering with success and satisfaction, they will be *more difficult* to change. As a rule, the more reinforcement is given for performing action steps and focusing on goal achievement, the more likely the plan is to succeed.

In most corporate cultures, behavioral reinforcement is consciously used in two contexts: discipline programs to deal with problem employees, and compensation and promotion plans to reward strong contributors. By consciously using behavioral reinforcement more creatively and more broadly, organizations can help every employee improve performance and competence. Here are some support mechanisms organizations and employees can use to help ensure the success of employee performance plans:

Recording Goal Progress and Action Step Execution
Writing down developments—how often an action step is performed or how much progress has been made toward achieving goals—is one of the simplest and most powerful means of behavioral reinforcement. If an employee has a goal of completing a waste reduction plan in 90 days, keeping track of progress toward the goal on a weekly basis will help the employee stay conscious of the goal and take the steps necessary to achieve it. Recording progress on action steps similarly helps employees remember to do them.

Communicating Progress to Others
Our social nature—the natural desire that people have to be accepted and liked by others—can be used to reinforce performance plans in ways that employees find supportive. Here are four ways that communication can be used to support performance planning execution:

1. *Buddies.* Have employees pair off into "buddy teams." The job of each member is to support his or her buddy to accomplish action steps and goals. We have found that daily communication between buddies is most effective, and in that contact they talk about their daily goals, plans, problems, and concerns. It usually works best for each person to take a five-minute turn in which the buddy simply listens while the employee talks about his or her workday. Buddies can also support each other to overcome obstacles and address problems that would often otherwise not be attended to.

2. *Work team or staff meetings.* Have work teams meet weekly and take three to five minutes apiece having each team member report on progress on goals and action steps. The mere act of reporting to a group of peers is often sufficient motivation to increase the amount of activity that is generated toward goal completion.

3. *Weekly e-mails to team members or managers.* While not as effective as in-person meetings, e-mail (or memo) communication about progress on goals and action steps also serves to remind employees of the importance of their goals and action steps. Often the desire to avoid the embarrassment of reporting that they didn't do their action steps is enough to focus employees on accomplishing them.

4. *Meetings with managers.* Interactions between managers and employees can be used to report on and address the status of performance planning execution. This interchange should be a part of the natural supervisory process. In situations where managers have many direct reports, it is helpful to augment this interaction with the other reporting and communication methods listed.

Using Rewards, Contests, and Consequences
Performance plans are at their most powerful when employees personally empower their plans by creating individual, self-motivated rewards and consequences:

"If I don't make ten sales calls this week, I won't play golf next weekend."

"I won't leave on Friday until the proposal is finished."

"If we achieve our waste reduction goal for the quarter, I'm going to take my family on a weekend vacation."

While this may seem unusual, corporate cultures do exist in which employees are invested in their goals at this level. Whether or not this is the case, the organization can encourage its managers to use rewards and contests to support goal and action step accomplishment. Parties and celebrations, cash awards, public recognition, and other creative devices can be used to help motivate employees to commit themselves to doing the things necessary to help the organization achieve its objectives and the employees to improve their competence.

The Execution Phase

The execution phase of the performance cycle—the "doing"—is the period with which employees are most familiar and comfortable. It is therefore the period during which employees are most likely to fall into old habits and behaviors that have interfered with goal achievement in the past. This is why it is so important to include the development of support mechanisms in the performance plan. Without them, employees would tend to continue doing what they always have done, despite the intentions laid out in the plan.

The job of management during the execution phase is twofold: first, to ensure that support mechanisms are functioning and are sufficient to keep employees on track toward goal achievement; and second, to ensure that performance problems are addressed promptly so they do not obstruct performance plans.

One of the most exciting aspects of the performance development system is that employees are truly empowered to take responsibility for their own success in ways not found in traditional organizational cultures. Managers and supervisors take the role of developers and motivators rather than taskmasters whose job it is to make sure that employees are not slacking off on the job. In my experience, it makes management a much more satisfying experience. And, more work gets done and more goals and objectives are accomplished.

The Competency Coaching Model

The performance development system functions well when managers are able to motivate their employees and coach them to improve their performance. However, many managers are not strong in either of these abilities. In fact, many managers do not even know what behaviors go into being a good coach. Toward that end, here is a list of behaviors and steps that make a good coach:

- *Communicate your vision for employees using the competency framework.* Use the language and competencies and key behaviors to communicate expanded possibilities for employees.
- *Listen.* Suspend your desire to control employees and get the job done and just listen to them. Work to understand who they are, what matters to them, how they are feeling, and what their concerns are.
- *Empathize.* Allow yourself to identify with them and what they are feeling. Put yourself in their shoes and imagine how they feel. Then talk to them and convey your understanding of both their situation and their feelings. Make sure they feel heard and understood. Do not jump quickly to solutions or explanations.
- *Give feedback.* Let them know how you perceive them. Give straight, honest feedback about behavior you observe and the consequences of

that behavior. Avoid pejorative judgments and accusations such as "You're so lazy," "You can't do anything right," and so on. Remember that the purpose of the feedback is to give them information they can use to help change their behavior.

- *Plan for and deal constructively with employee resistance, defensiveness, and blame.* Develop your set of skills to respond to it. These skills include using listening, empathy, expressing confidence, providing options and choices, inspiring them to a higher vision, pointing out logical flaws or inaccuracies in their thinking or perspective, asking for their help, taking principled stands, and appealing to their self-interest. In every situation you will want to choose the skill that you think will help employees most easily work through their resistance and that will align with their and the organization's best interests. Avoid the use of blame, shame, threat, and disparagement. Any behavior change in employees resulting from such tactics will be short-lived and will ultimately lead to more resistance.

- *Obtain employee buy-in toward a higher vision.* Help employees express their own hopes and dreams and work with them to help them relate those dreams to a vision of them within the company. The more they see their role in the company as a vehicle for their personal aspirations, the more they will invest in their development.

- *Use competencies to diagnose problems.* Competencies and key behaviors are effective means by which current behavior can be compared to ideal behaviors, resulting in identifiable gaps and pathways for improvement.

- *Identify obstacles.* Determine what information, skills, processes, and emotional blocks contribute to barriers to performance and development, and use the analysis to shape solutions.

- *Establish goals.* Use all available information (organization objectives, personal aspirations, vision, problem analysis, developmental competencies, etc.) to establish goals and performance objectives.

- *Develop action steps.* Establish SMART action steps to achieve the goals. Include action steps that will support the accomplishment of goals and the other action steps.

- *Track and monitor progress toward goals and action steps.* Keep track of and communicate progress on goals and action steps to ensure employee success, and promptly handle problems.

- *Share your own goals and action steps with your employees.* Show them how their work fits into your objectives, and model goal and action step tracking for them. The more your employees see you using the same processes you are asking them to use, the more they will be willing to do so themselves.

Implementing a Performance Development System

Implementation of a performance development system follows all the guidelines that apply to installing any competency-based HR practice that involves both training and orientation. Because of the nature of performance management, however, there are some points that are important to emphasize. First, performance development is an emotionally vulnerable process. Employee weaknesses are brought to light, and employees are supposed to talk about and solve difficult behavioral problems that impact competence, some of which they have been trying to hide for years. Solving these problems makes employees feel proud and self-confident, but the process can bring up feelings of fear, hurt, and embarrassment. If not handled well, employees can be resistant and resentful.

One of the most important rules to follow is that senior management should model performance development for themselves as a part of the implementation. Nothing sends the message more powerfully than for employees to know that the CEO and the senior management team are working to develop themselves just like every other employee. The alternative message is demotivating to an equal extent: "If senior managers are *not* working to improve their competence, then they must want me to do it just to benefit themselves. (If they are saying that it will make me a better, more capable, and more satisfied person, why aren't they doing it themselves?)"

Implementing a performance development system requires careful planning and well-organized training and orientation. If competencies are new to the organization, you will probably want to keep the initial installation as simple as possible. One client with a relatively unsophisticated workforce began by using only the same three competencies for all employees, with a simplified rating scale to make rating as easy as possible. The implementation plan included expanding the number of competencies and the power of the rating system as employees became comfortable with the concepts and saw the value of competency development for themselves.

There is considerable cynicism and skepticism among employees today regarding the introduction of any HR practice whose purpose is to improve performance. The credibility of the system's internal sponsor will be key to employees' openness and willingness to engage in a real development effort. If management either does not truly support it or is not trusted by most employees, implementation will be difficult.

Competency and Compensation

A frequently asked question is whether and how compensation should be tied to competency assessment and development. We have seen many different answers to this question, and believe there are many right answers. Here are some of the choices organizations have made, along with their advantages and disadvantages.

NO COMPENSATION FOR COMPETENCY

Using this approach, competency assessment and development play no direct role in determining either fixed or variable compensation. The way to present this to employees is that they will be paid for their performance. Competency assessment and development can help employees improve themselves and improve their performance. Their improved performance will result in increased compensation.

Advantages

- Competency assessment is not adulterated by compensation issues.
- Employees won't be tempted to raise their ratings to increase their pay.
- Discussions between managers and employees about competency strengths and weaknesses can be solely about development, without direct consequence to pay.

Weaknesses

- Compensation cannot be used to reward either competency proficiency or competency development.
- Employees invest less in competency development because they perceive little direct benefit from the effort invested.

COMPENSATION FOR COMPETENCY DEVELOPMENT

In this system, a portion of compensation is based on the degree to which competency is improved during the review period. Improvement will typically be rewarded by variable compensation (i.e., bonus pay).

Advantages

- Employees are directly rewarded for increasing their proficiency on the competencies that most impact their performance.
- Employees will invest in their competency development because they will be directly compensated for it.

Disadvantages

- The process of competency assessment is adversely affected by its influence on compensation.
- Employees will tend to raise their competency ratings because they will increase compensation.
- Rating disputes will arise because of their effect on pay.

COMPENSATION FOR COMPETENCY PROFICIENCY

Here employees get compensation for receiving high competency ratings. In other words, being more proficient on competencies results in more compensation. Some organizations use competency assessment to determine where base salaries fall within pay bands. Others use it as a portion of discretionary bonus.

Advantages

- Employees are directly rewarded for increasing their proficiency on the competencies that most impact their performance.
- The value of competency proficiency is supported and emphasized by the compensation system.
- Employees will tend to focus on performing the behaviors that relate to competency assessment, which in turn correlate with superior performance.

Disadvantages

- The process of competency assessment is adversely affected by its influence on compensation.
- Employees will tend to raise their competency ratings because they will increase compensation.
- Rating disputes will arise due to their effect on pay.

Because each approach has its advantages and disadvantages, each organization will have to decide which one makes the most sense for it. The question for each organization to address is which approach will most encourage employees to commit themselves to becoming the best, most satisfied, most productive employees they can be.

CHAPTER

13

Using Technology to Change Corporate Culture

Competency-based HR practices involve a conceptual framework and procedures that require training and ongoing maintenance to sustain the quality needed to produce the desired results—the selection, placement, and development of superior performers who work together to accomplish the organization's mission.

Traditional HR administrative systems have generally not been sufficient to support smoothly operating competency-based practices. These systems are usually not integrated: A report by the Hackett Group[1] indicates that typical organizations have almost 10 HR systems per 1,000 employees and that these systems are both unintegrated and aging. Because of the age and lack of functionality of these systems, many companies are due to update and replace their HR systems infrastructure. In addition, HR professionals are spending more of their time solving administrative problems. As a result, only 32 percent of HR professionals' time is devoted to hiring the best people, training and development, fostering productivity, and motivating

[1]From AnswerThink in the News Archives, October 21, 1998. "Companies Missing Tremendous Opportunities for Cost Savings and Improved Efficiency in Procurement, According to Hackett Group Study." Web site: www.answerthink.com/news_items/nr102698.

employees to adapt to a continually changing environment—in other words, to creating a culture of competence.

One example of the time needed for HR tasks is the following list of administrative steps needed to conduct a competency-based selection process:

- Establish or locate the competency model.
- Develop or locate the list of desired and required technical skills and traits.
- Determine or find the other important job characteristics on which candidates need to be assessed.
- Determine the pool of interviewers.
- Develop and print the documents or forms with the customized position specifications.
- Assign competencies, skills, and job characteristics for interviewers to assess candidates.
- Inform interviewers of their interview assignments.
- Arrange candidate interviews.
- Inform interviewers of their scheduled interviews.
- Distribute documents to interviewers containing candidate information and rating forms.
- Arrange training for new interviewers and provide training documents.
- Receive and enter interview results from interviewers.
- Compile and review interview results.
- Compare candidates.
- Communicate with candidates.
- Archive interview data for analysis and operational audit purposes.
- Compile and analyze the selection data to look at quality by department, by location, and by hiring manager.

It can easily take *one hour* to process the forms for *one* interview round for *one* candidate. Multiply this by the number of candidates interviewed by an organization in a year, and the operational difficulties associated with the process become apparent. For an HR process to have a long-term impact on an organization, it must be workable and easy to use administratively as well as functionally.

The Internet has created an economy of scale that can turn what had been an administrative burden into a quick and easy process that performs most if not all the steps in a fraction of the time and cost. What the fax machine did to interoffice communication and e-mail did to office memos, the Internet does for competency-based HR practices. What took an hour can be accomplished in a few minutes. In addition, the previously complicated process of centralizing data across an entire organization is now simple, no matter where offices and employees are located. All an employee needs is access to a computer with a browser, a modem, and a telephone line or other Internet connection.

Figure 13.1 shows a screen shot from SelectPlus.net™, CompetencySuite's tool for managing the competency-based selection process. On this screen, hiring and staffing managers can simply point and click to assign particular competencies and technical skills to interviewers for assessing candidates. After they have been assigned, interviewers can print all the information and forms they need to conduct interviews: job specifications, candidate information, competency scales, interview questions, rating forms, and interviewing tips. The hiring process becomes more standardized, and everyone involved in the process is happier and more productive.

True web-based HR applications differ from the common retail Internet applications like America Online in that there is no software to load onto employees' computers—all the processing occurs on the Internet server. Unlike client-server applications, the responsibility for updating the software resides with the firm hosting the software, not with the company using it. It is possible to integrate all of the applications into *one* updated, easy-to-use system for virtually every HR application. Human resources professionals can now focus on the functions that create true value for the organization.

Internet applications can make it significantly easier to administer a selection process. The same is true for other HR practices.

Sourcing Candidates

Many applications exist to broadcast job openings to the many Internet posting sites such as monster.com. Vendors like Personic, SkillSet, and HireSystems have the ability to scan resumes into a candidate database and apply search criteria against it to narrow the list of candidates for further follow-up in the selection process. This narrowed list can then be processed via Internet applications like SelectPlus.net.

Companies are deluged with resumes—either over the Internet, by mail, or through other sources like employee referrals. None of this data is

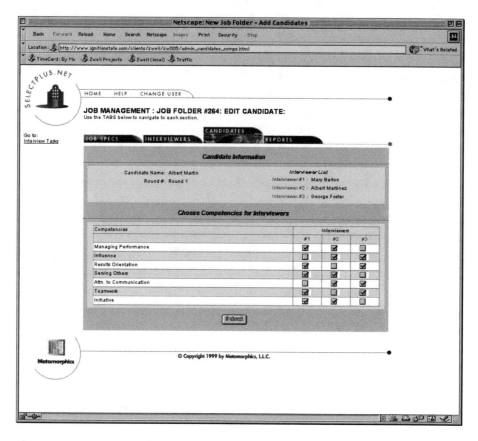

Figure 13.1 A screen shot showing how SelectPlus.net assigns competencies to interviewers for candidate assessment.

integrated, and managing this data is a major time consumer for HR departments. The applications just mentioned have the capability to automate the entire sourcing process, handle it completely on an outsourced basis, and provide companies with a limited, screened candidate pool from which to select candidates.

CREATING JOB DESCRIPTIONS

In Chapter 11, competency-based job descriptions were discussed in detail, showing how they can provide the foundation for the entire employment life cycle. Creating useful job descriptions is often a time-consuming and difficult task. It requires the ability to identify job purpose, overall job goals, duties and responsibilities, critical competencies and technical skills, job preferences, and key success factors. Because of the frequently changing nature of many jobs and the time and effort involved in writing and updating job descriptions, many companies either completely ignore the process or utilize it in a very ineffective manner.

With an automated Internet application, job descriptions can be created and utilized in ways that bring out their full power:

- A standardized process can be created that walks senior managers through the process of developing each component of the job description.

- The job description can be used to populate the position specifications for each job opening, establishing the requirements for competencies, technical skills, and job preferences. As a result, there will be greater consistency and standardization in the assessment process for hiring.

- The purpose and job goals in the job description can be viewed and utilized throughout the performance management process to help create performance objectives and action steps.

- Job descriptions can be used to focus the succession planning process. Competencies, technical skills, job preferences, and measures of accountability can all be used to help identify potential successors within the organization.

PERFORMANCE APPRAISAL

A competency-based appraisal process involving self-assessment, manager assessment, and possibly multi-rater (360°) feedback requires an even more complicated administrative process than selection. The process includes generating assessment forms for every employee and manager, customized for their particular competencies. If 360° feedback is utilized, multi-raters must be selected and forms generated, distributed, completed, and returned. The data then must be entered and compiled, and a report generated and distributed.

It is also difficult to administer and to maintain a high standard of quality for a comprehensive appraisal process. The more rigorous the process, the more time and effort are required on the part of managers and employees. Without sufficient support and reinforcement mechanisms to maintain momentum and encourage quality, development processes will usually regress to superficial and meaningless gestures that may cause more harm than good.

The Internet is a godsend to performance appraisal. Because a centralized server is accessible to all employees over the Internet, performance management can become a dynamic, fluid process in which employees and their managers (and multi-raters) enter their assessments, the data is compiled, and the results are available immediately with a few clicks of a mouse. The centralization of data allows management to view employee competency ratings by department, by location, and by manager with ease and simplicity. Job and development goals can be easily evaluated along with competency ratings.

Figure 13.2 shows a screen shot from PerformancePro.net™, Competency-Suite's tool for competency-based performance management. On this screen employees and managers rate the employee on a competency, also providing behavioral evidence to exemplify or justify the rating.

COMPETENCY DEVELOPMENT

Developing goals and action steps for self-development is seldom an easy task. The beauty of automation is that the development process can be guided by automated step-by-step procedures—"wizards"—that can take employees through the process and help them create the goals and action steps that will help them succeed at their jobs and achieve their professional and career objectives.

Because the development system is database-driven, goals and action steps can be recalled for the purposes of tracking progress and evaluating accomplishment. In PerformancePro.net, employees can not only create comprehensive performance plans, they can also track their progress on each goal and action step, choosing to update their progress daily, weekly, or monthly.

SUCCESSION PLANNING AND HIGH-POTENTIAL TRACKING

Succession planning across a large organization is another function that is facilitated by a web-based system. The ability to centralize and track the data gathering process helps unify the workforce and bring a broader pool of potential candidates to mind when looking for successors for position incumbents. By bringing organization-wide competency assessment into the succession planning process, the organization will be more likely to place strong performers into important and challenging positions. By bringing the whole organization together, the Internet increases the exposure and visibility of superior performers at all levels.

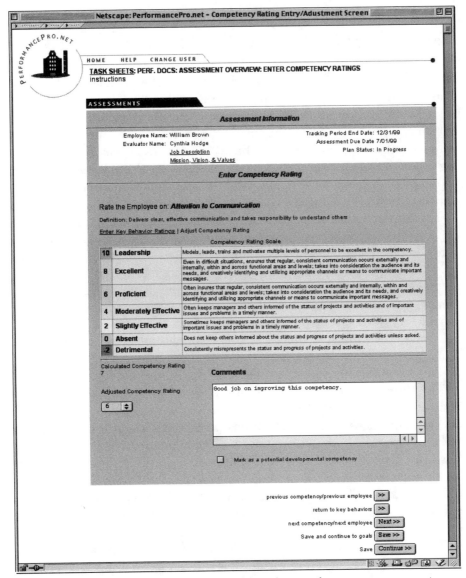

Figure 13.2 PerformancePro.net screen shot showing how competency ratings can be automated on the Internet.

Opportunities and Potential Problems Using Internet Applications

Human resources departments and processes are often the last to be automated: Automation priorities center on financial, sales, manufacturing, and related applications. Some HR departments have attempted to reduce the implementation cycle by creating internal human resources information systems departments. However, since the applications usually involve networking issues, they need to coordinate with the corporate MIS department. Turf battles often develop between HR and MIS, and implementation times have not been drastically reduced.

The Internet offers an opportunity to solve this problem. Although MIS departments may still be involved in setting corporate philosophy and standards, implementation using the Internet requires little effort or resources by either corporate MIS or HRIS. The problem remains that HR directors are being deluged with possible Internet solutions. They don't understand which applications work, which do not, and how they can be integrated to provide one workable system and solution. Because of the plethora of services and applications available, HR professionals are often confused and, as a result, often are not adopting these applications on an integrated, unified basis—if they are adopting them at all.

The Internet is not a perfect solution for managing and administering competency-based HR applications. Internet applications run more slowly than client-server applications, and connections are more likely to be dropped. Fear of security breaches is a commonly stated concern of less-informed potential users, but these concerns are rapidly dissipating as Internet usage grows, new technology is developed, and breaches remain minimal. (The success of Internet retailing today demonstrates the willingness of people to put their credit card information on the web, for example.)

The main problem with using the Internet has to do not so much with the Internet per se but rather with people's resistance to using computers in general. The resistance can be categorized as follows:

• *Learning difficulties.* A significant proportion of the employee population has difficulty learning, due to a variety of factors ranging from learning disabilities to level of intelligence. Because of the embarrassment and shame associated with learning problems for many people, the difficulty is compounded when employees do not acknowledge it and instead focus on some other reason to avoid using the new application.

• *Emotional resistance to change and doing things differently.* One of our clients is a bank in which all the calling officers have computer and e-mail access, yet 20 percent of the officers do not regularly read their e-mail. They do not resist using the computer for other things; e-mail is simply a new way of communicating that they are not in the habit of using and that they aren't eager to change. When asked, most of the calling officers agree that e-mail is a good idea and that they *ought* to check it. At the moment, however, there is more pleasure and less pain associated with avoiding e-mail than there is paying attention to it for those 20 percent of the bankers.

• *Emotional resistance to electronic processes.* Some people have a particular resistance to computers. Many senior executives never learned how to use a keyboard, having had their secretaries type documents and their analysts prepare and manipulate spreadsheets. Starting from scratch and learning a complex system is upsetting for many people, and excuses abound for not doing so.

However, even individuals who resist using computers on the job *do* use the Internet at home. Because of the increasing universality of the Internet, employees are more likely to accept Internet systems that appear to have the functionality and ease of use that they are likely to find on their home applications.

Whatever the cause of the resistance, organizations need to develop training programs that take into account these issues. They also need to analyze all of their HR processes and implement easy-to-use technologies. If individuals are trained in their use and if the systems are *actually* easy to use and *really* save time and improve organizational process and productivity, these new systems *will* be used.

14

Putting It All Together

Every element of a culture of competence described in this book exists in organizations today. The logic behind building organizations that exercise the full potential of their human capital is compelling: Who wouldn't want their employees to be contributing more to the bottom line? There is a catch, however. A culture of competence ultimately will thrive only if it is in the service of a higher purpose. Employees will respond to the calling to become their best to the degree that the calling is genuine and inspiring.

To create your culture of competence, utilize the tools in this book to walk you through each step.

Step One: Analyze Your Corporate Culture in Terms of Competencies

First, analyze and rank the competencies from strongest to weakest in your organization, both for general employee competencies and for leadership competencies. Perform this analysis for the organization in its current state and for the organization in its ideal state—the state the organization should be in to flourish in the future.

Second, examine the gaps between the competencies in the current and ideal states, and determine which ones are the most important to improve. Be sure to include senior management in this analysis, because their buy-in and commitment is crucial to the success of the entire journey. In fact, the greater the inclusion, the higher the likelihood of successful culture change.

Step Two: Develop a Competency-Based Vision for Your Organization

Use your competency analysis of your ideal culture as the beginning of the process of building your corporate philosophy—your mission, vision, and value statements. Bring as much of the organization into the process as feasible. Make sure that these statements reflect the important competencies for the organization, and that the competencies can be used to reinforce the vision and values.

Step Three: Analyze Your Organization's Leadership

Examine your leadership team regarding its strengths and weaknesses on both general and leadership competencies. Evaluate leaders individually, identifying competencies that contribute to their success and those that inhibit it. Establish levels of minimum proficiency for those leaders on the key leadership competencies, and replace the ones that you think will not reach that level quickly enough.

Determine the proficiency you think you need on leadership competencies in your ideal culture, and analyze the gap between the current state and the ideal. Use these competencies to develop a vision for leadership in the organization, based on the organization's mission, vision, and values.

Step Four: Analyze the Cultural Elements That Support and Resist Change

Identify the elements of the corporate culture that operate to support the status quo and resist change, and those that can be used to reinforce and reward change efforts. These elements include hiring practices, compensation, policies and procedures, customs, norms, and performance management practices. Determine how the cultural change resisters can be neutralized and the cultural change reinforcers best utilized.

Identify your allies in the organization, those managers and employees who will support the change effort. Notice who resists your efforts openly and who resists them surreptitiously. Analyze who will gain and who will lose as the culture of competence takes shape.

Step Five: Develop a Cultural Change Strategy

Based on the analysis of your current and ideal cultures, craft your strategy to create your desired culture of competence. Determine which aspect of the current culture you want to attack first. Rather than choosing the most entrenched element of the culture to change, go after easy victories, creating change that most employees will see as beneficial.

Build alliances within the organization with key influencers and opinion makers. Put allies in positions of control and influence. Create reward and recognition programs to reinforce the behaviors and values that represent your culture of competence.

Use competency-based selection to bring people into the organization who will help move the organization toward your ideal culture. Use competency-based performance development to encourage all employees to change the habits that keep the current culture in place. Use every means of public relations at your disposal to publicly recognize employees who act in accordance with the new culture. Revise your compensation plan to reward the behavior and performance you need in order to have a culture of competence.

Plot the steps in the culture change process. Celebrate victories, expect defeats, and tend to wounds. Remember the worthiness of the goal and the importance of the job. Appreciate and be generous with yourself as you engage in the battle. Changing the hearts and minds of a workforce is not easy.

Step Six: Perform Ongoing Assessment

Schedule regular evaluations to assess where you are on the path toward your ideal culture. Take the time to analyze your current state, appreciate how far you have come, and determine how far you have yet to go. Notice what you have learned about the organization, yourself, and the change process. Take a fresh look at the biggest issues and barriers you face, and develop tactics to address them.

The Journey Is As Important As the Destination

Creating a culture of competence is a journey that is engaging, challenging, rewarding—and one that is likely never to fully succeed. There will always be further to go and another step to take on the path. The challenges leaders face dealing with complex organizations never end. The organizational vision that looks beautiful from a distance has its own set of warts once you view it up close.

The pursuit of a culture of competence will feel thrilling at some times and painful at others. It is important to remember to get nourished by the journey, rather than waiting until the end to obtain satisfaction and fulfillment. As anyone who has engineered a culture change process knows, the journey is full of both pleasure and pain. The following quote from *The Pilgrimage* by Paulo Coelho aptly describes the importance of valuing the journey for its own sake.

FIGHTING THE GOOD FIGHT

The journey, which prior to this was torture because all you wanted to do was get there, is now beginning to become a pleasure. It is the pleasure of searching and the pleasure of an adventure. You are nourishing something that's very important—your dreams. . . .

We must never stop dreaming. Dreams provide nourishment for the soul, just as a meal does for the body. Many times in our lives we see our dreams shattered and our desires frustrated, but we have to continue dreaming. If we don't, our soul dies and agape (love) cannot reach it (because we have ceased fighting the good fight).

The good fight is the one we fight because our heart asks it of us. . . . The good fight is the one that's fought in the name of our dreams. When we're young and our dreams first explode inside us with all of their force, we are very courageous, but we haven't yet learned how to fight. With great effort, we learn how to fight, but then we no longer have the courage to go into combat. So we turn against ourselves and do the battle within. We become our own worst enemy. We say that our dreams are too childish, or too difficult to realize, or the result of our not having known enough about life. We kill our dreams because we are afraid to fight the good fight.

The first symptom of the process of our killing our dreams is the lack of time. The busiest people I have known in my life always have time enough to do everything. Those who do nothing are always tired and pay no attention to the little

*amount of work they are required to do. They complain constantly that their day is
too short. The truth is, they are afraid to fight the good fight.*

*The second symptom of the death of our dreams lies in our certainties. Because
we don't want to see life as a grand adventure, we begin to think of ourselves as
wise and fair and correct in asking so little of life. We look beyond the walls of our
day-to-day existence, and we hear the sound of lances breaking, we smell the dust
and the sweat, and we see the great defeats and the fire in the eyes of the warriors.
But we never see the delight, the immense delight in the hearts of those who are engaged in the battle.* For them, neither victory nor defeat is important; what's
important is only that they are fighting the good fight [my emphasis].[1]

A Few Final Words of Advice

The world of business and complex organizations is a wonderful vehicle for
improving the quality of life for vast numbers of people, including customers, employees, and shareholders. Goods and services are produced that
directly improve the quality of life for customers. Employees earn a living
and support families through the use of their talents and abilities. Employees can learn and grow through the challenges they face at work.

Building a culture of competence is a win for everyone. It is giving at its
best, creating a legacy that will continue to provide employees, their families, customers, and shareholders with the benefits from a work environment in which employees are expected to become their best selves. Here
are some final words about how to create this kind of culture:

- *Tell and trust the truth.* It provides the solid foundation upon which organizations and individuals can grow.

- *Feel your feelings and act on your best thinking.* Feelings are not necessarily a trustworthy guide for action, but they do provide important information that should be processed and analyzed, and that information
  should play a role in the decision-making process.

- *Expect a lot from people.* If you communicate to people that you expect
  them to operate from higher values and principles, they are more
  likely to do so.

- *Plan to deal with authority issues.* Everyone carries emotional and behavioral baggage from their childhoods, their schooling, and their previous
  work experiences. Be prepared to deal with feelings and behaviors that
  have little or nothing to do with you except for the role you fill. To

[1]Coelho, Paulo. *The Pilgrimage.* San Francisco: Harper, 1995, 50–51.

many employees you are "the boss" or "the parent," and part of your job is to help them relate to you, one human being to another.

- *Focus on higher principles.* People relate to higher principles and values, and want to be inspired to live according to them. Use principles to reorient yourself and others, and to help yourself and others choose the high road that earns oneself self-respect and true pride.

- *Invite others to join you, and join others.* This is not a solo venture. To create organizations that really operate to achieve their missions, people will need to work together. Use the synergy of common purpose to achieve common objectives.

- *Take risks to learn and grow.* Keep experimenting, trying things, observing results, noticing what works and what doesn't, learning all the time.

PLAY FOR KEEPS

Building a culture of competence is a grand adventure, one that requires all the skills, competencies, and resources one can bring to bear. It is fighting a war against complacency, bad habits, cynical attitudes, and limiting beliefs that sabotage organizational effectiveness and cause emotional deadness and dissatisfaction.

The greater your commitment to the adventure, the more likely your success. The greater your commitment to give, the more you get.

There is a story about two groups of warriors rowing to an island to battle each other. One group, upon reaching the island, burns their own boat, saying to each other, "If we leave the island, we leave in *their* boat." This is the kind of commitment that brings the victories and that stirs our souls and inspires us to be our best.

> *Until one is committed there is hesitancy, the chance to draw back, always ineffectiveness. Concerning all acts of initiative (and creation) there is one elementary truth, the ignorance of which kills countless ideas and splendid plans: the moment that one definitely commits one's self then Providence moves too. All sorts of things occur to help one that would otherwise never have occurred. A whole stream of events issues from the decision, raising in one's favor all manner of unforeseen incidents and meetings and material assistance, which no man or woman would have dreamt would have come his [or her] way. Whatever you can do or dream you can—begin it. Boldness has genius, power, and magic in it.*[2]

Use your competency and your leadership to create your organization to be its best.

[2]Goethe, Johann Wolfgang von, quoted in *Break-Point and Beyond*, ed. George Land and Beth Jarman, New York: HarperBusiness, 1992.

Bibliography

Collins, James C. & Porras, Jerry I. *Built to Last*. New York: HarperBusiness, 1994.

Davis, Brian L., Hellervik, Lowell W., Sheard, James L., Gebelein, Susan M., Skube, Carol J., *Successful Manager's Handbook*. Minneapolis: Personnel Decisions International, 1996.

Goffee, R. & Jones, G. *The Character of a Corporation: How Your Company's Culture Can Make or Break Your Business*. New York: HarperBusiness, 1998.

Goleman, Daniel. *Working with Emotional Intelligence*. New York: Bantam Books, 1998.

Hamel, G. & Prahalad, C. K. *Competing for the Future*. Harvard Business School Press, 1994.

Hunter, J. E., Schmidt, F. L., & Judiesch, M. K. "Individual Differences in Output Variability as a Function of Job Complexity." *Journal of Applied Psychology*, 75, 1990, 28–42.

Jackins, Harvey. *The Human Situation*. Seattle: Rational Island Publishers, 1973.

Kanter, R. M., Stein, B. A., & Jick, T. D. *The Challenge of Organizational Change*. New York: Free Press, 1992.

Kotter, John P. & Heskett, James L. *Corporate Culture and Performance*. New York: Free Press, 1992.

Levering, R., Moskowitz, M., & Katz, M. *The 100 Best Companies to Work for in America*. New York: New American Library, 1985.

Lombardo, Michael. Presentation at the Fourth Annual International Conference on Using Competency-Based Tools and Applications to Drive Organizational Performance, Boston, Massachusetts, September 1997.

Norretranders, Tor. *The User Illusion*. New York: Viking Press, 1998.

McClelland, D. C. Testing for competence rather than intelligence. *American Psychologist*, 28:1–14, 1973.

Schein, Edgar H. *Organizational Culture and Leadership*. San Francisco: Jossey-Bass Publishers, 1992.

Schisgall, Oscar. *Eyes on Tomorrow: The Evolution of Procter & Gamble*. New York: Doubleday, 1981.

Smart, Bradford D. *Topgrading: How Leading Companies Win by Hiring, Coaching, and Keeping the Best People*. Paramus, NJ: Prentice Hall, 1999.

Spencer, L. & Morrow, C. *The Economic Value of Competencies: Measuring the ROI*. Speech presented at the Third International Conference on Using Competency-Based Tools and Applications to Drive Organizational Performance, Chicago, Illinois, September 1996.

Spencer, Lyle M. & Spencer, Signe M. *Competence at Work*. New York: John Wiley & Sons, 1993.

Stack, Jack. *The Great Game of Business*. New York: Doubleday, 1992.

Swasy, Alecia. *Soap Opera: The Inside Story of Procter & Gamble*. New York: Times Books, 1993.

Treacy, Michael & Wiersema, Fred. *The Discipline of Market Leaders*. Reading, MA: Addison-Wesley, 1997.

Wright, Robert J. *Beyond Time Management: Business with Purpose*. Newton, MA: Butterworth-Heinemann, 1993.

Index